Mark,

Thank you for your
help, support and
encouragement over the
years. You continue
to be an inspiration
for me.

Stephane
10/25/01

Buckeye Women

Ohio Bicentennial Series

Editor: Clarence E. Wunderlin, Jr.

STEPHANE ELISE BOOTH

Buckeye
Women

The History of Ohio's Daughters

Ohio University Press | Athens

Ohio University Press, Athens, Ohio 45701
Printed in the United States of America

Ohio University Press books are printed on acid-free paper ∞ ™

09 08 07 06 05 04 03 02 01   5 4 3 2 1

The publication of this book was made possible in part
by the generous support of the Ohio Bicentennial
Commission.

Frontispiece photo of Annie Oakley courtesy Ohio
Historical Society.

Library of Congress Cataloging-in-Publication Data
Booth, Stephane Elise.
    Buckeye women : the history of Ohio's daughters /
Stephane Elise Booth.
            p. cm. — (Ohio bicentennial series)
    Includes bibliographical references (p.) and index.
    ISBN 0-8214-1390-2 (cloth : alk. paper) —
    ISBN 0-8214-1391-0 (pbk. : alk. paper)
    1. Women—Ohio—History.   2. Women—Ohio—
Social conditions.   3. Women—Employment—Ohio
—History.   4. Women's rights—Ohio—History.
5. Ohio—History.   6. Ohio—Social life and customs.
I. Title.   II. Series.

HQ1438.O3 B66 2001
977.1'0082—dc21

    00-069545

In honor of my grandmother,
Mamie Pianfetti Sandretto

Contents

Illustrations

Series Editor's Preface

THE APPROACH OF Ohio's bicentennial, with the attendant publicity and commitment of resources, affords scholars a unique opportunity to reevaluate the state's history in a systematic way. The Ohio Bicentennial Commission, supported by state funding, has underwritten academically based scholarship on a wide variety of historical topics. Numerous local and county projects have also been initiated around the state with the goal of advancing the study of local history.

In an effort to promote a more systematic assessment of the state's history, Ohio University Press has embarked on the publication of a series of monographs and special projects. When he first envisioned the Ohio Bicentennial Series, David Sanders, director of the press, had in mind the generation of a body of scholarship that would commemorate the state's anniversary by offering specialists, students, and knowledgeable generalists a comprehensive picture of Ohio's development. The first special project, *The Documentary Heritage of Ohio*, makes the textual record of the state's past more accessible for the student in the classroom and the general reader outside the academic setting. Other special projects include an illustrated history of the state and a biographical dictionary of Ohio governors.

The series also includes monographs that provide fresh assessments of important aspects of Ohio history. These monographs take a topical approach or focus on key societal groups, charting the history of specific categories of Ohioans over time. For these works, I have asked specialists in the relevant fields of history and related disciplines to provide readers with a fresh synthesis of the old and the new. Authors of these works will synthesize "old knowledge" already existing in a multitude of sources and, whenever possible, present the findings of their most recent research, adding a pinch of "new knowledge." Stephane Booth's study of Ohio women, the third volume in our series, accomplishes both of these tasks. It is a concise synthesis of existing knowledge with insights gained from new research and will surely serve as both a handy reference for scholars and interested readers and a springboard for more specialized research on the topic.

This new book chronicles the contributions of women to the settlement of Ohio and the history of the state. The author has arranged this story in six chapters. The first provides readers with an overview of Ohio's settlement period and particularly the role women played in that frontier settlement. Each of chapters 2 through 6 establishes a discrete category of analysis within which Professor Booth offers readers distinct but overlapping narratives of Ohio women, acting individually or in groups, across that long sweep of time from the pre–Civil War era to the postindustrial age. While we can see the contributions of women to Ohio politics, business, education, religion, and the arts, the full extent of the activities of Ohio's women can be determined only by looking across the separate categories, across the sweep of Booth's book, as it moves from frontier to modern society.

Booth's blend of old and new teaches us several lessons about the women of Ohio. First, they performed vital economic, social, and educational roles during the frontier period from 1788 to 1815. The early settlement succeeded because of the actions of women like Ann Newcomb Stoneman, Liwwat Boke, and Betsey Cowles. Second, women performed essential economic roles throughout the history of the state—not merely in the labor force, but as owners and managers of businesses. Such innovators and entrepreneurs as Zaide Palmer, Florence Hannaford, and Louise Miller were architects of the state's socioeconomic progress in the nineteenth century. Finally, it is clear that middle- and upper-class women were essential to the transplantation of East Coast social and cultural norms in the state. Middle-class women performed vital roles in the education of the state's future citizenry. Wealthy women, such as Cincinnati's Annie Sinton Taft, labored to establish what historian James Livingston has identified as a "cultural infrastructure" of museums, art galleries, and symphony orchestras in the urban centers of the state. The picture Booth paints indicates that these pioneers of Ohio gradually extended the acceptable sphere of women's activities and contributions, encountering and surmounting barriers across the sweep of time, even as they helped to reconstruct and reaffirm patriarchal society in the state. The cumulative record of individual accomplishments, related so well by Professor Booth, did little, however, to alter fundamentally the traditional values transplanted and nurtured by groups of women organized into formal social and civic associations beginning in the mid-nineteenth century. Associational activity seems to have upheld and restored hierarchies of class and gender. This dichotomy between individual and associational activity, with its inherent disagreements over the role of women and the definition of progress, continues to this day.

Ohioans have long needed a concise history of the women of the state. I am very pleased that Professor Booth agreed to author this third volume in the Ohio Bicentennial Series of Ohio University Press.

Clarence E. Wunderlin, Jr.

Preface

AS THE CITIZENS of Ohio celebrate the accomplishments that have had a significant impact on the development of the state, it is an appropriate time to reflect on the contribution that women have made during the past two hundred years. This book is a general history of the women of Ohio and is intended to reflect the myriad of challenges that Ohio's women have encountered over the past two hundred years—and their responses to those challenges.

The history of a people cannot reflect only the accomplishments of the famous or infamous. It is through the hard work and determination of countless women, in all walks of life, that Ohio has moved from a wilderness to a leading political and industrial state. It was the unknown women, who faced the wilderness and helped to subdue it during the state's first one hundred years, who set the tone for Ohio's place as a leader in political and social issues. It was the unheralded women who led in the establishment of educational, cultural, and medical institutions that now attract people from around the world.

The stories of many Ohio women have been lost to history. A few are famous. However, those of us with roots in Ohio need only look back within our own families to find the heart of Ohio—its women. I encourage readers to look through their attics for the diaries, letters, and mementos of women family members. It is only through their words and memories that their stories, and our history, will be kept alive.

I advise anyone interested in a more in-depth study of a specific region of the state to visit the local historical society or regional archives. A significant amount of information on women in Ohio is available at research facilities throughout the state, including the Ohio Historical Society, the Western Reserve Historical Society, the Cincinnati Historical Society, Wright State University Special Collections, Oberlin College Archives, the Cleveland Public Library, the Center for Archival Collections at Bowling Green State University, and the Ward M. Canady Center at the University of Toledo.

I would like to thank the numerous members of the Ohio Library Association who were helpful in suggesting collections that would be useful to me while doing research for this project. Lilith Kunkel and Cindy Rotterborn, the professional staff at the Kent State University Salem Campus Library, were very helpful in finding citations and sources. I greatly appreciate the efforts of Nancy Birk, Kent State University archivist, who indexed the manuscript and helped me obtain illustrations. Thanks also to Duryea Kemp of the Archives-Library Division at the Ohio Historical Library in helping me obtain the illustrations for the manuscript. I wish to thank Dr. Clarence Wunderlin, series editor, and Nancy Basmajian, Ohio University Press manuscript editor, for their useful and informative feedback on the manuscript. I would particularly like to thank my husband, David E. Booth, for his loving support and understanding throughout this project and for his help in reading countless pages of text numerous times. This work was undertaken through a research grant and a faculty professional development grant from Kent State University, both of which proved most useful in providing me with the time to visit various archives around the state.

CHAPTER ONE

Women and the Ohio Frontier

AUTHORIZED SETTLEMENT OF the Ohio Valley, and in particular the area that would become the state of Ohio, began soon after the passage of the Northwest Ordinance in 1787. However, missionaries had worked among the Native Americans much earlier. The birth of the first white child, Johanna Maria Heckewelder, the daughter of Moravian missionaries, was recorded as April 16, 1781, in the village of Salem near the Muskingum River.[1] The missionaries, and the soldiers and their wives who occupied forts in the area, were considered transients. The first permanent settlers, a group including men, women, and children who came with the Ohio Company in 1788–89, established the first authorized settlement at Marietta.

Settlers from all parts of the early colonies immigrated to Ohio. New Englanders settled in the Marietta area on lands owned by the Ohio Company; emigrés from Virginia settled between the Little Miami and the Scioto Rivers; people from New Jersey took up residence on the Symmes tract; Pennsylvanians made their home on the "Seven Ranges"; and farmers with their wives and families poured into the Western Reserve from Connecticut and New York.[2]

Ethnic settlements also developed during the frontier period. Travelers along Zane's Trace commented on the dominance of Germans in the Lancaster area. Store owners printed signs in both German and English, and in 1817 the General Assembly authorized the printing of the state's Constitution and laws in German. The Welsh settled in Licking, Butler, Delaware, Allen, Jackson, and

Gallia Counties. The French established a settlement in Gallipolis, and descendants of French trappers lived along the western shore of Lake Erie.[3]

As women encountered the frontier, they brought with them the values and expectations of their previous communities. Their encounters with the frontier would modify these values, resulting in changed behaviors. But just as these women were altered by their frontier experiences, the frontier was likewise transformed as the women built new lives for themselves and their families.

The hardships women endured on the journey to the Ohio Valley served as an indicator of the trials they would encounter on the frontier. Settlers traveled six hundred to eight hundred miles to reach the Ohio frontier, many walking the majority of the way over poorly kept or nonexistent roads through all types of weather. On her trip from Connecticut to Warren, Ohio, over the Forbes Road in 1810, Margaret Dwight wrote: "We found the roads past description, —worse than you can possibly imagine—Large stones and deep mud holes every step of the way—We were obliged to walk as much as we possibly could, as the horses could scarcely stir the waggon [sic] the mud was so deep & the stones so large—It has grown so cold that I feel we shall perish tomorrow."[4] Other women faced the perils of travel on Lake Erie. Rhoda Wills of Shelby, New York, came to Cleveland by boat with her four young children, while her husband made the trip on horseback. A storm came upon them while on Lake Erie, and she believed they would all be drowned. Upon landing in Cleveland, she and the children stayed the night at a log tavern. The next morning they began their walk to Brunswick. Similarly, Mrs. Wyatt Hartshorn, many years later, remembered her harrowing seven-and-a-half-week trip on a schooner from Buffalo to Sandusky as a young girl of thirteen.[5]

Many times the trip was made in small wagons, four feet by sixteen feet. Due to the lack of space, only necessities such as spinning wheels, beds, eating utensils, and iron pots could be brought to the settlers' new homes, forcing women to leave behind many of the articles that they associated with home, such as china, hope chests, and rocking chairs. Women also left behind the companionship of female kin and friends, something more valuable to them than any knickknack or piece of furniture. Those women who agreed to immigrate to the Ohio frontier only because they depended upon their husbands for livelihood and support felt the loss of this female communal society particularly keenly. Many of these women found themselves totally isolated from female companionship in their new homes. Most accepted the situation stoically and worked to establish the best possible home they could under the circumstances.[6]

One of the primary roles that women filled in their new communities, particularly as these communities changed in response to external circumstances, was keeper of culture. The women pouring into the Northwest Territory, later the state of Ohio, especially those from New England, were faced with the challenge of preserving the old way of life in a new and dramatically different environment. The two primary institutions women attempted to preserve were religion and education (churches and schools). According to Andrew Cayton in *The Frontier Republic*, the founders of Ohio wished to establish a society similar to the one they had left behind, but improved—their new society would be without the flaws of the old and elevated to an even higher level of development. The society would be "overseen by firm national authority and secured by institutions like churches and schools" that would keep frontier society from disintegrating into a barbaric state.[7]

The settlement of the Marietta area by the Ohio Company and the Western Reserve by the Connecticut Company produced two bulwarks of Puritanism and Congregationalism in the state. A strong Presbyterian faction was also introduced to the Mahoning Valley by settlers from western Pennsylvania. Women were instrumental in establishing the institutional presence of these groups as well as promulgating the moral values of each.

Women, in many communities, composed more than 50 percent of the charter members of early churches. When the early settlers formed the Congregational Church of Marietta on December 6, 1796, seventeen of the thirty-two charter members were women. Six charter members, of whom four were women, established the First Congregational Church in Warren. A twenty-member committee, including ten women, established the Presbyterian church in Harpersfield in 1809.[8] In areas where churches had not yet been established, women were noted for keeping people's attention on their previous religious affiliation. Mrs. Noble H. Merwin found no public form of worship when she arrived in Cleveland in 1815. She promptly invited her neighbors and "led them to the log courthouse and opened her Bible, leading the services until a missionary was sent to the people."[9] Others, with the same goal in mind, taught Sunday school in their homes. Mrs. Mary Lake taught Ohio's first Sunday school in Marietta in 1791. Others, such as Clarissa Rogers (Mrs. P. March) of Spencer, Medina County, followed in her footsteps. Mrs. March wrote Bible verses on scraps of paper for her charges to learn, since Bibles were not available. She organized the first church in Spencer in her kitchen, where the minister preached the first sermon.[10]

Women's religious participation was very public. They were active participants in the revivals and camp meetings held during this time. Mrs. Hannah Gillman participated in a revival in 1811 in Marietta. Others actually led services and preached. Rebekah Austin (Mrs. R. I. Coe) could be found preaching in Portage County after her arrival in 1824, and Ruth Boswell, a Quaker, preached the first sermon in Warren Township, Belmont County, in 1804.[11] Men attempted to make a mockery of women's public participation by accompanying them to the camp meetings, not to participate in the religious revival but to join in the gambling, fighting, and drinking that occurred on the periphery of the campgrounds.[12]

Religions outside the mainstream also found women participants. A Shaker society formed in Warrensville, Cuyahoga County, in 1821 attracted a substantial number of women, as did the Mormon community established in Kirtland. Several women signed the Oberlin Covenant when Congregationalists established the town in 1832. At its founding, the Covenant, which contained twelve ordinances, became the basis of the town's ideological foundation and operating system. Catherine Creswell Criswill and her family came to Greene County in 1802, some of the first Seceders to arrive in Ohio. She helped establish the United Congregation of Massies Creek and Sugar Creek and "exerted a dominant influence in the creation of proper social conditions hereabouts in the days of the very beginnings of the settlement."[13]

The reinstitutionalization of these churches on the frontier added a needed tie to what had been left back home, whether in New England, Pennsylvania, Virginia, or Europe. Religion added a familiarity to the constantly changing situations and environment. It also had, in the eyes of the settlers, a civilizing effect. No matter how savage or unrelenting the frontier could be, the familiar nature of religion—its practices, values, and expectations—was still a link to civilization. Women's participation in reestablishing formalized religious practices, along with their daily activities based on a "Christian" ethic, allowed society to flourish. As described by one pioneer, "they were, as a rule, pious women, diffusing about them an atmosphere of religious devotion and spirituality. . . . Such was the moral influence, not only on society then, but on later generations."[14]

Along with establishing churches and providing a moral tone for these new settlements, women were also instrumental in founding schools in these communities—many times starting by giving lessons in their homes and eventually moving to buildings specifically set aside for the purpose. Female teachers taught boys and girls basic subject matter along with deportment. Within one year of settlement in the Marietta area, formal classes had been established. These classes were taught by women and paid for by the Ohio Company and the students' parents. The first female teacher in the Ohio Territory was Bathsheba Rouse, who began teaching in Belpre during the summer of 1789 or 1790. Other communities soon followed suit. Mrs. Williams of Cincinnati opened a school for young ladies in 1802. Betsey Diver of Deerfield, Portage County, began teaching school in 1804. Miss Elizabeth Streator and Miss Rebecca Conant opened a school in a private houseboat in Windham, Portage County, one month after the first settlers arrived in 1811.[15]

Schools with the purpose of educating certain groups of students also opened in response to community expectations. During the late 1820s, Betsey M. Cowles opened infant schools throughout northeast Ohio. Still other communities saw the need for female academies. Professor and Mrs. Nutting opened such a school in Hudson in 1827. Community members in Kent established a similar female academy, where female teachers taught the basic academic subjects along with "embroidery and other fine needle work."[16]

The salary received by these women varied depending upon the community—some receiving cash payments, others receiving goods. Lucinda Walden in 1812 received a dollar's worth of flax and linen cloth per week, whereas Mentor hired Kate Smith for six schillings per week. In 1818, Mrs. Canfield in Wakeman, Huron County, received a dollar per week in produce and provided her own board. Similarly, Sarah Houghton was hired at seventy-five cents per week and rode on horseback to her school.[17]

Salary discrimination started immediately. A male teacher in Bedford, Cuyahoga County, received $20 per month for teaching sixteen male and six female students, while a female teacher received $4 per month for the same number of students. In Newbury, Geauga County, the directors denied teacher Martha Canfield (who in addition to teaching, also earned money by spinning) her salary of $1.25 per week because they "were afraid she would get rich too fast."[18]

Most of the women engaged as teachers were either unmarried or widowed, and they usually taught school for a relatively short time. Initially school terms for girls were held only in the summer, when the boys were working in the fields, so many women taught for a brief time prior to marriage. Many young women conducted schools in their parents' homes or the home of a local minister.

Few women continued to teach after marriage, but there were exceptions. In 1826, Abner Loveland Jr. brought his wife Amelia Dewolf to his log cabin, where she opened a school. Her students' fathers paid the tuition by chopping and logging on Mr. Loveland's clearing.[19]

Even though most women left the classroom upon marriage, they did not leave behind their role as educator. Community expectations were such that the primary responsibility for children's formal education fell upon their mothers. Although circumstances on the frontier changed the educational needs and behavioral expectations of their communities, women on the Ohio frontier continued to instill the beliefs and demand the behavior of those communities from which they came. This attempt to duplicate both the religious and educational experiences of a previous place and time provided a needed connection to something familiar when everything else in the environment seemed so different. Literary and singing societies and other forms of entertainment served this same purpose.

Women demonstrated their social value on the Ohio frontier through their ability to populate the area; offer hospitality to new settlers, neighbors, and strangers; establish and maintain a relationship with the natives; and provide their services as healers. Women generally married young on the frontier. With parental consent, a woman could marry at age fourteen. Life expectancy was thirty-four years in 1750 and increased only four years by the turn of the century. During her twenty years of married life, the number of pregnancies a woman could expect ran into double digits. Polly McDaniels married Henry Tucker on December 17, 1780. Upon her death she had ten surviving children who would produce seventy-three grandchildren.[20]

A woman's social value also rested on her ability to offer hospitality. Quaker Anna Briggs Bentley, newly arrived from Maryland, wrote to a friend about the helpfulness of her new neighbor, Friend Miller. Miller helped nurse Bentley's cow back to health and told her "now do send over for any vegetable and anything thee stands in need of."[21] It was also expected that when men came together to grub out underbrush, split rails, cut logs, or do any other work, women would provide the food and spirits. At the same time they would also be quilting, sewing, or spinning for some needy neighbor. Many women also opened their homes to total strangers. As settlers moved into the Ohio Territory, lodging was limited, and many travelers found themselves without shelter come nightfall. They would then ask for shelter at the next cabin, and it was expected that they would be taken in and provided with what they needed.

Women were also expected to interact with the Native Americans in the vicinity. Early settlers in the Northwest Territory were the Moravian missionaries. The first white child born in Ohio, Johanna Marie Heckewelder, was the daughter of missionaries who lived and worked among the natives at Salem, Gnadenhutten, and Schoenbrunn. This group of missionaries consisted of married couples, as well as single men and women.[22] Prior to 1812, recorded interactions between the settlers and Native Americans were generally cordial but cautious. Sarah Porter Elam, who lived in Greene County in 1802, recalled years later that "Sometimes it was her responsibility to deal with the Indians." When the men were working in the fields, "she would serve the Indians food and drink and treat them kindly, even though she would sometimes feel threatened with death if she were able to make a wrong move."[23] In 1803, Mr. and Mrs. Joel Owen found sixty natives living on their land in New Lyme, but the natives were peaceful and would often supply Mr. Owen with game in exchange for other goods. In another situation, Mrs. Oviatt of Hudson provided a lifesaving service for three Native Americans. She was able to speak Chippewa, Seneca, and Delaware, and because of this she acted as an interpreter and advocate for three natives who were on trial in Warren for their lives. Mrs. Samuel Ruple of East Cleveland hid a squaw from other members of her tribe who had condemned her as a witch. Mrs. Ruple fed the party looking for the young woman, in hopes of giving her time to escape. However, they captured the squaw the next day.[24]

After 1812, when the British were removed from the area, more white settlers began to move into the Ohio country, especially along Lake Erie. Women recorded a large number of hostile interactions with Native Americans during this time, but a hysteria seems to pervade these writings. However, even given the raids and kidnappings between 1812 and 1825, which led to the "Indian Wars," peaceable interaction was still possible. Mrs. Jane Holt Inscho in Hiram County reported that often the natives would stop at her cabin with venison and exchange it for wheat bread. They would fire their guns three times to signal their approach, and they would stack their guns in front of the cabin to denote peace and safety.[25] By the 1830s, almost all Native Americans had been removed from the state, leaving one less responsibility for women.

Perhaps one of the most vital services provided by frontier women was that of healer. Out of necessity, pioneer women were both nurse and physician. Virtually every woman gathered herbs each season and tied them to the rafters to dry. Their stock of herbs usually consisted of sage, peppermint, pennyroyal, hops, thoroughwart, smartweed, Solomon's seal, tansy, sassafras, ginseng, and a variety of roots and barks. It was reported that "Grandmother Chismark" of Euclid had a still where she distilled peppermint oil. As one local historian noted: "The process by which she procured opium was rather novel. . . . She grew large beds of poppies and as soon as the petals fell punctured the seed pods with a fine needle and after the milk dried, gathered them."[26]

Most women developed their medical expertise through trial and error and by sharing information with those around them. There were women on the frontier, however, who had received formal training. Liwwat Boke, who settled in Mercer County, received training as a midwife before emigrating from Germany. Mrs. John Stoneman (née Ann Newcomb) studied medicine with her father prior to her marriage. Mrs. Cox was the first traveling physician who made periodic visits to Brighton in Lorain County, and Mrs. Bartlett Leonard (Hannah Chapman) studied medicine in Massachusetts and was a "regular physician" in Williamsfield, Ashtabula

County. The community welcomed all these women for their expertise in dealing with medical conditions such as depression, childbirth, hernias, piles, sore throats, rheumatism, dropsy, bad eyes, and foot troubles. Mrs. Mary Lake, who served as a hospital matron at Fishhill and New Windsor during the American Revolution, aided her neighbors in Marietta when a smallpox epidemic swept through Campus Martius in 1790.[27]

Women's value to frontier society was not confined to the normal sphere of female influence. Women, who owned and operated businesses, managed farms, traveled the state alone, and involved themselves in politics, greatly expanded the boundaries of acceptable social behavior.

Many women found themselves running businesses in conjunction with their husbands, and in the event of a man's death, his wife might be called upon to take over the family business. In addition, women would often accept day-to-day duties of the business if their husbands were traveling or incapacitated. Mrs. Letitia Edwards in Mantua often ran gristmills in the absence of her husband, and Sally Randall in Kinsman tended the sawmill in her husband's absence.[28] Many couples ran inns together, with the wife assuming the role of hostess; upon the death of her husband, the wife might assume the running of the entire operation. Lydia Ford Hickox took over the Hickox Inn, "doing the managing herself, riding on horseback to Burton for supplies, mixing drinks at the bar for thirsty travelers openly and innocently."[29] Some women supported their husbands' businesses behind the scenes by doing the paperwork, as did Mrs. Sprague, who filled out all papers for her husband. In some cases, the husband received the compensation while his wife did the work. Rev. Elias Morse of Williamsfield was postmaster in that town for thirty years. However, because the post office was in his home, his wife Abiah Phelps Morse did the actual work.[30]

Most women found ways to supplement a family's income or, in time of hardship, provide the majority of income through home businesses. Some earned extra money by weaving. Mrs. Bartram was able to pay the taxes from her weaving earnings, while Lucetta Sage Crosby paid in weaving for the land upon which her first home was built. Elizabeth Woodruff Wittenbury earned thirty dollars per winter as an expert tailor. Other women raised poultry for "egg money" and produce to trade. Sugar making also provided supplemental income.

Many widows, upon the death of their spouses, had to run farms with the help of their children, while others had to devise other creative means to eke out a livelihood on the frontier. Mrs. Beckwith, whose husband died in 1803, remained in her cabin supporting herself and her children, in part by helping travelers cross the river with her canoe.[31]

Desertion of their families by husbands and fathers was not unknown during this time, and several women were left to raise families as best they could. Ruth Rising Harmon's husband left her with the care of their family and the management of a salt manufacturing business. Mrs. Hannah McUmber Sage became the first woman to keep the post office in Dorsct after her husband went west, leaving her with nine children to support.[32]

Women were also landowners on the frontier. Land companies often awarded land allotments to the wives of the first male settlers. The Connecticut Land Company gave Tabitha Stiles three parcels of land totaling 112 acres. In Burton, the company presented Mrs. Beard and Mrs. Umberfield each with sixty acres of land for being the first white women in the township. Other women purchased land in their own right. Sarah Pashall Adams, widowed before age forty, successfully bought a farm, built a house, and assisted in clearing the farm and building its fences —along with raising a family of six. The first settler in Fairfield, Huron County, was Mrs. Sample, a widow with a family who came from Newark, Ohio. As noted previously, Mrs. Lucetta Sage Crosby purchased her own land, to which she held the deed until her death.[33]

No matter the circumstances that brought these women to the Ohio frontier, most found themselves working in ways and under conditions that they had not experienced previously. The work was endless—indoors and outdoors, season after season. While trying to maintain a home, women kept kitchen gardens, raised chickens, pumped water, separated milk and cream, churned butter, dipped candles, preserved food, dried deer hides, made cloth, and sewed clothes. Forced to use the materials at hand, Mrs. Beardsly of Vermillion, Erie County, made caps for her sons from the skins of raccoons, and carded and spun the hair from opossums and raccoons for stockings.[34] However, even though they were faced with enormous responsibilities, women of all ages were still expanding their roles. Amelia Weeks Smith helped her husband make the rails to fence their land. Mrs. Harris drove the oxen for her husband to do his plowing.[35] Mrs. Jonathan Crum "helped to harvest their first wheat crop using the sickle like a man, doing the loading in the field and pitching into the mow, afterwards helping to thresh it with a flail." Mrs. Pettibone of Delaware laid all the bricks of the inside walls of her new home when her husband was unable to hire a mason.[36]

Some women were known for their abilities to excel at "men's work." Tabithy Phelps Alderman challenged her adult son, saying that she could chop down a tree quicker than he could—and won. Mrs. Smiley from Rochester was a champion sheep shearer and could shear sixty sheep per day. Mrs. Sample out-reaped a man in a race across a ten-acre grain field.[37]

Many women were left to do all this work with only their children for help. Rachel McElroy Marshall planted crops with the help of her children while her husband was in service during the War of 1812. Mrs. White was left to care for her family along with the cattle and farm, which meant she had to leave the children alone as she tended to the various chores.[38] Female children, as they became older, often helped clear the land by trimming the felled trees and burning the brush. Other young women helped to sow and harvest the wheat crop. But young males were very seldom required to do "women's work." Chopping and carrying wood was the closest most men got to "female" activity.

Women's ability to come and go on their own greatly expanded as they took on these new responsibilities. Women "healers" traveled the countryside on foot or horseback, most of the time unescorted. Those engaged in business had to travel great distances to reach Cleveland, Pittsburgh, or other trade centers. Mrs. Esther Sexton Dixon carried lace, cheese, and other products to Pittsburgh to exchange for calico, ribbons, tea, coffee, and other necessities. Mrs. John Durant walked to Cleveland and back in one day from Orange carrying "butter, eggs and chickens to the amount of 40 pounds." Other women made even longer trips alone. Mrs. Edwards crossed the Allegheny Mountains seven times on horseback, and Mrs. Williams Steel returned on foot to her old home in Maine upon the death of her husband and child.[39]

Women's expanded roles in the community led some to move into the area of political activity. By the mid-1800s Ohio would become a hotbed of women's activism in the areas of temperance, abolitionism, and woman's suffrage. But during the early frontier period, the women activists were not officially organized. There were women such as Liwwat Boke, who spoke about women's equality and their rights—"We women are equals," she insisted. Mrs. Nancy Card Hall, a businesswoman who had felt the unjust effects of the laws against women, encouraged agitation because she believed that women deserved to be fully equal under the law. "Let them agitate," she stated; "they will never get anything too good for women."[40]

Other women channeled their political activities toward specific projects in their own communities. Mrs. Caroline Gibbs, described as the first suffragist of Sharon Township, a Democrat, and one who was exceptionally well informed on current events, "personally helped clear the square; attired in suitable garments she grappled with logs and stumps of the new clearing." Another civic-minded woman, Mrs. Kent of Bainbridge, galvanized the community to make the roads passable by appointing a day when every man, woman, and child would gather to work on the road. She then provided dinner for everyone.[41] Most women engaged in these activities with little realization of their political value. They became involved in these activities to improve the quality of life in their communities, not to make a political statement.

More politically astute women were making their presence felt in other ways. Mrs. Tappan cajoled her husband to push for the clearing of ground in Ravenna in order to obtain the Portage county seat before Franklin Mills, now Kent, did. Many women were interested in political affairs and quite capable of carrying on an intelligent conversation about current issues. Jesse Lindsley Rice "was as well informed as a majority of men and was I think, as capable of voting," said one who knew her.[42]

A few Ohio women did hold positions of political power in a community setting. In York, citizens appointed Mrs. Leonard Bates postmistress, the first political official in town. Upon the death of Colonel John Garrett, the founder of Garrettsville, his widow Eleanor was left ownership and use of the lots for the village, and in the 1830s she became Garrettsville's first postmaster.[43] For the most part, however, women's influence was felt behind the scenes.

The activities, homes, and lifestyles of women on the frontier depended upon many factors—among these the regions they migrated from, ethnic and religious background, class, and the frontier environment itself. The buildings and communities of early Ohio are particularly revealing of their residents' backgrounds. We can examine factors such as town layout and building architecture to find clues about the inhabitants. Emigrants usually duplicated the style and building materials of the homes they had recently left. Clapboard homes in Granville, Worthington, Marietta, and the Western Reserve reflected the influences of New England architecture. Settlers coming from Pennsylvania built homes of stone and brick with Dutch doors and decorated woodwork. Brick residences dotted the landscape of southern Ohio, reflecting the tastes of settlers from Virginia and Maryland. Directors of the Ohio Company laid settlements out along the pattern of a New England town, including a commons, house lots, agricultural lots, and out lots for grazing. Each settlement was divided into sixty squares, which were then divided by streets one hundred feet wide. They reserved four squares for public use, and the remainder were divided into house lots.[44]

Wealthy or well-to-do settlers, particularly those who arrived after the War of 1812, had less of a need to adapt to their new environment. These individuals were able to bring more goods with them and could hire laborers to help with the clearing of the land and the building of homes. However, even these settlers had to deal with environmental factors that were totally alien to them. Each group attempted to deal with its situation by introducing as much of its previous lifestyle as possible into this foreign environment, including literary societies, singing societies, dances, civic dinners, church services, and schools. The attempt to introduce previous activities and institutions resulted in something new, not a duplication of the previous experience. As one historian noted about the early cultural life of Chillicothe: "With the old it mixed the new; there was the characteristic rowdyism of the frontier and the prevalence of revivalism in place of the serene ritualism of the Anglican Church."[45]

The first settlers coming into the Ohio country near Marietta were from New England. Many men had served as officers in the Continental Army; several had been educated at Harvard or Yale, and their wives had been prepared for the comfortable life of a wife of a professional. This group (along with their counterparts from Connecticut, who settled the Western Reserve) tried to establish their previous lifestyles in their new frontier setting. Leaders of these settlements laid out the town as if they were in New England. Houses were built around a common area and the local church was the center of all activity. Meanwhile, the women worked ceaselessly to set up churches and schools in their new settlements based on the needs and expectations of their previous experiences. But these expectations had to be modified due to the needs of the current situation. For example, schools could run only during the summer months, and formal church services employing ordained ministers were rare. The social life of a community, which had previously revolved around church activities, now rested on the needs of establishing the settlement—activities such as log rolling, land clearing, and house raisings. These became the accepted activities through which social relationships were developed.

Many of these settlers from New England were also economically better off than others. This enabled them to transport more household goods such as china, linens, and furniture on the initial trip or to have them shipped at a later date. This availability provided an opportunity to reestablish a home similar to the one left behind. But even the most beautiful quilts and china looked out of place in most of the initial primitive dwellings in which these women lived. As one woman found out, even though she had a pan in which to bake bread, the oven was too small to hold the pan. Faced with this problem she took matters into her own hands and built a bigger oven, making and laying the bricks herself. In order to further adjust to changes in their lives, many women planted gardens and cleared walks soon after a dwelling was built.

Settlers moving into the Miami Valley and the Virginia Military Tract were generally poorer and unable to buy land directly from the government, but they were able to buy lots and small farms from speculators. These women settlers were forced by economic circumstances to live in lean-tos for a longer time and learned to live off the land rather quickly. One woman reported having slept in the treetops for several nights until a lean-to could be built, and then she had to wait until a clearing could be made in the forest before a one-room log cabin could be built. A log cabin such as hers "had a pitched roof covered with wooden shakes, a door, one or two windows commonly covered with greased parchment, a dirt floor or one covered with logs lengthwise with the smooth side up, a stone hearth and a chimney commonly made of sticks and covered with clay."[46]

These women had to learn quickly to be self-sufficient. Trading centers were far away, as were neighbors. Money was virtually nonexistent, so women had to be ingenious in acquiring products that they could trade for necessities such as coffee, tea, salt, sugar, and implements. They found themselves making whiskey, trapping game, making potash, and collecting honey and ginseng to barter. They became very well acquainted with their new environment—it was important to know its benefits as well as its dangers.

Settlers were at the mercy of nature, facing unpredictable floods, droughts, high winds, hail, and early frosts. Other environmental hazards and pests, such as squirrels wolves, bears, wildcats, deer, and raccoons, were easier to deal with but no less dangerous to their well-being. Women learned to use firearms or whatever was handy to scare off dangerous animals. Mrs. Samuel French (née Amelia Belden) scared off a wolf by brandishing her umbrella.[47] But for most, the need to become handy with a firearm proved life-saving. Women who needed to travel alone had to be able to protect themselves, and those left alone on isolated farms for long periods of time had to use a weapon either for protection or to provide food for their families.

The isolation of the frontier and its physical environment caused a myriad of other problems to which women had to respond. In her recollections, Liwwat Boke wrote: "Life is a long struggle. We must fell the trees, but also cope with droughts, deep snow, sudden flooding, cloudbursts, forest fire, swarms of deerflies and mosquitoes and midges, snakes, wolves, and twice the wolves were mad. . . . There are many wild hens. Pigeons sometimes filt [sic] the woods here like clouds so that the sun is hidden! And they break the branches down. Squirrels in swarms eat up all the cornfields. In time some people here go completely mad, change, commit suicide. Countless people do not talk with their spouses; many women have miscarriages, then pregnancy lost." Children and adults were constantly becoming lost in the forest. "In the spring the children play in the warm forest, scurrying around and looking about, and carelessly they get turned around, don't recognize the surroundings, are lost! . . . After them the parents, unthinking and so badly upset, also become lost in their urgent haste."[48] Mrs. Oliver Forward of Aurora, Portage County, gave birth to a son and soon after became so despondent that she wandered off in the snow. Concerned family and friends found her near Mantua and sent her to Connecticut to recuperate.[49]

Accounts of frontier life reported that depression was a common occurrence in response to this isolation and constant work and fatigue. As one woman reported, "The women are not often praised, so they feel themselves abandoned in the world, facing their inner troubles. Also, the loneliness brings on drinking and suicide here."[50] Domestic abuse was an all too common occurrence, and murder of a spouse was not unknown. Thomas Fishburn of Easton murdered his wife, Florence, and then cut his own throat.[51]

As more people moved into Ohio and technology developed, the settlers would indeed conquer their environment. But for the initial female settlers, the environment they encountered proved a life-changing experience—one that constantly provided them with new challenges. With these new challenges came new expectations based on necessity, and the roles of women changed somewhat to fulfill the needs of the new society. But as this frontier society moved away from survival mode, the previous expectations returned to limit the role of women. The frontier experiences, however, laid the foundation for some women to continue to fight the societal expectations imposed on them.

CHAPTER TWO

Paid Employment

WOMEN HAVE ALWAYS worked, whether in the home, outside, or both. The frontier period called upon them to help clear the land, plow, plant, build homes, spin, sew, and cook, in addition to raising children. Many helped husbands with their home businesses, and in time others ran their own businesses. As the country industrialized, women moved into factory work to supplement family incomes. No matter what the setting, women found themselves working long hours with minimal compensation, and at times they faced the condemnation of society for stepping outside their defined sphere of the home and into the public sphere of the workplace.

Some women found themselves either helping to run family businesses or, upon the death of a husband, being left to run the business on their own. Lois Bartholomew Palmer served as hostess when her husband, Ambrose Palmer Jr., built the first tavern in Vernon, Trumbull County, and Mrs. Laura Harrington Criffen was landlady of her husband's Exchange Hotel in Monroeville for many years.[1] Mrs. Letitia Windsor Edwards ran the hand gristmill in Mantua, and Sally Randall tended the sawmill in Canfield during her husband's absence while simultaneously "spinning at the little wheel while the logs moved through."[2] Ruth Rising Harmon ran a salt manufacturing business after her husband deserted her and their family. Mrs. Sibyl Hayes Blue, upon the death of her husband, ran a store in Perry, Lake County. A few women opened their own businesses, such as Jeannette R. Miller of Norwalk, who ran a millinery business. In 1856, Piqua listed three women owning such establishments. By 1852, five women in Ohio held the job of post-mistress, including Mrs. Leonard Bates, of York, Medina County.[3]

Women were also able to make a little extra money by taking in sewing, spinning, or weaving, and doing laundry for others. There is evidence that a few women, in order to earn money, went from house to house sewing clothes for each member of the family in return for room and board. The itinerant practice of a trade was known as "whipping the cat," perhaps after the slang term for shoe-making. Others did spinning under the same arrangement. Indentured servitude, a form of employment that persisted into the nineteenth century, was also a way of life for some women. On November 29, 1833, Aramintha Grist was indentured to Zadok Street in Salem. Under her contract, "She was to be instructed in the art, trade and mystery of housewifery; to be trained to habits of obedience, industry and morality; to be taught to read, write, and cipher as far as the single rule of three; to be provided for, and be allowed meat, drink, washing, loading and apparel for summer and winter. She was to live with him until she was eighteen years of age and at the expiration of such service, he should give her a new Bible and at least two suits of common wearing apparel." Mary Sheets was apprenticed to Alexander Burns, also of Salem.[4]

Many working women, prior to the availability of factory work, worked in domestic service, particularly in the cities. Some worked in laundries, while others ran boardinghouses. Early city directories listed very few of these working women, but by the late 1850s and early 1860s the increasing number of working women is noted. The 1860 census shows 9,853 women employed in Ohio, compared to 65,749 men. Women tailors numbered 1,602, seamstresses 7,160, and milliners 1,990. Native-born women could be found in the chewing gum, laundry, paper box, garment, and paint industries, while foreign-born women dominated rag picking and paper mills. Most work done by women in factories was unskilled, but occasionally women were given an opportunity to learn a trade. Ella Wentwork, the editor of *The Literary Journal*, started a school for training women in the printing trade in Cincinnati in 1854, and by 1860 4.9 percent of the women employed in Cincinnati were in this industry.[5]

Some women were able to break the gender barrier and move into professions during the first half of the nineteenth century. As we have seen, teaching was well on its way to being a feminized profession, with nursing soon to follow. Journalism and publishing were fields where women would get an early toehold. Mrs. Maria M. Herrick, between 1837 and 1840, edited the early magazines *Mothers* and *Young Ladies' Guide* in Cleveland. A few female physicians appear in 1852, even though medical training was still in its infancy. Dr. Hannah Chapman Leonard practiced in Williamsfield, Ashtabula County, and Dr. Myra K. Merrick, the first woman physician in Ohio, moved to Cleveland in August 1852. Catharine I. Church, the widow of Dr. Church from Pittsburgh, opened an office in Salem, where she sold "herb medicines and give [sic] prescriptions." Ann Newcomb Stoneman, who had studied medicine with her father, used her knowledge and skills to help her neighbors in Orange, Cuyahoga County.[6]

During the nineteenth century, legislation regulating salaries and working conditions of workers was nonexistent, leaving all workers at the mercy of employers. For those women who did find themselves in the workplace, even more difficulties existed. Salaries were lower than those of their male counterparts, and women encountered the open hostility of male workers. Seamstresses working in factories in Cleveland in 1850 could earn $104 per year, but because of their frequent inability to work due to pregnancy, child care issues, and layoffs, many received only two-thirds of this amount. Most of these working women were widows trying to support families on their meager salaries. In Cincinnati, a woman working in a boot and shoe factory could earn three dollars per week. And out of this money, many workers had to pay for the implements they needed to do the job, such as needles and thread.

Working conditions were no better than the salaries. Factories were dimly lit, poorly ventilated, and often filled with machine

fumes. In the garment industry, where most women were employed, lint filled the air and, in turn, their lungs. Hours were long,
—twelve to sixteen hours per day, six and sometimes seven days
per week. Little time was given for lunch, restroom facilities were
filthy, and few factories had fresh drinking water available for
workers. The frantic pace of work led to accidents that could ter-
minate a woman's employment, thereby removing her only source
of income. Some benevolent individuals did call for changes but,
as Edward D. Mansfield pointed out in 1857, "The conditions of
these women has frequently been the subject of earnest inquiry by
benevolent persons, but every attempt to increase their wages is
met by the stern fact that any considerable increase could drive the
business from Cincinnati, from the State, and perhaps the United
States."[7]

Not everyone was of the same mind. Ella Wentworth, publisher
of *The Literary Journal* in Cincinnati, held progressive ideas for her
time. All mechanical production for the publication of Wentworth's journal was done by women. She provided the workers
with a library and a carpeted room furnished with a piano for use
during their breaks. The women were paid a dollar per day for an
eight-hour day—an exceptional wage for the time.[8]

Ohio was the first state to pass protective labor legislation for
women. In 1852, the Ohio legislature passed a law affecting women
and children under the age of eighteen, limiting their workday to
ten hours. However, the law applied only in cases where the worker
was "compelled" to work more than ten hours per day and did not
apply to those who volunteered to work more than ten hours.
Abuse of the law was rampant.[9]

The Female Protective Union was organized in 1850 to improve
the wages and working conditions of the female pieceworkers
in the Cleveland garment industry. The goals of the organization
were to increase wages (they were receiving two dollars per week
for working six sixteen-hour days) and to have those wages paid in
cash, not company store orders or credit. The Female Protective
Union in 1851 opened a Female Protective Union Clothing Store

that was set up to pay its female workers a higher wage than the other stores in the area. However, it was forced out of business by the other storeowners, who had no intention of paying higher wages.[10] Other groups, such as the Women's Christian Associations of both Cleveland and Cincinnati, tried to help relieve the plight of the working woman by opening homes that provided room and board at reasonable prices. One side effect of the low salaries paid to female workers was the increase in the number of prostitutes in urban areas. Many young women needing to supplement their meager incomes turned to prostitution, particularly in the bustling cities of Cincinnati and Cleveland. Cleveland's police records show the frequent arrest and conviction of both madams and prostitutes, but the trade continued to flourish.[11]

After the Civil War, as the United States moved rapidly towards industrialization, the demand for factory labor increased, particularly in unskilled and semiskilled occupations. The result was an influx of immigrants, both male and female, to fill the demand. The increased supply of labor kept wages depressed, and more women than ever turned to employment outside the home to supplement their families' incomes. In 1860, the female labor force in Cincinnati made up 15 percent of the overall workforce, and by 1900 it had increased to 22.4 percent. In 1880 and 1890, men's clothing continued to employ the highest percentage of female workers, 46.7 percent and 42 percent respectively. However, the types of industries employing women had doubled since 1860. By 1900, the female workforce was more diversified, with 18.1 percent employed in men's clothing, 17.4 percent employed in boots and shoes, and 14.5 percent employed in tobacco.[12] By 1880 in Cleveland, 18 percent of all workers were female, with three-quarters of these workers employed as domestic servants, laundresses, dressmakers, or milliners. By 1900, 20 percent of all workers were women, with one-fourth to one-third employed in twenty-six different industries, including shipping, iron, steel, paint, and chewing-gum production. Forty percent were employed in paper box factories, bakeries, laundries, cigar and tobacco factories, men's and women's garment factories, and woolen mills.[13] From 1860 to 1890, there were very few factory jobs for women in Piqua, but by 1920, more than 40 percent of all working women in that city were employed in local factories. Many of these jobs were in hosiery, underwear, box mattress, cigar, and garment factories. In 1890, of the 214 women listed in the Piqua City Directory as having an occupation, fifty were factory operatives. Between 1870 and 1920, women owned or managed more than one hundred different Piqua businesses, including "groceries, hotels, saloons, dry goods stores, notion stores, variety stores and ice cream parlors" with at least ten of these businesses continuing for more than twenty years under female management.[14]

The garment industry employed the largest number of women. It is very difficult to determine the exact number, as many women did piecework in their homes or in sweatshops. In these circumstances, the pay was low and the hours long. In Cleveland in 1879, a widow with one child was able to make enough vests in her room to earn two dollars per week, from which she had to pay two dollars per month for rent and three dollars per month for her sewing machine. This left her with only three dollars per month to buy everything else that was needed for herself and her child. By 1908, little had changed. The garment industry in Cleveland employed 3,125 women, not counting those working in sweatshops or at home. The work was seasonal, and therefore salaries varied.[15]

Laundries also employed a significant number of women. In 1900, Cleveland's thirty-two steam laundries employed more than 1,600 women and girls. They worked long grueling hours, a seventy-hour week, for which they received $4.50. Women were also employed in the tobacco and cigar industry, where they spent long hours stripping tobacco. Joseph Bell began employing women in his boot and shoe factory in 1870, as did the Brainard and Wetmore Bookbinding plant in Cleveland. This plant became the largest employer of women in the trade. By 1880, the J. B. Savage Company had that distinction when they employed twenty women, one-half of their workforce. The women were involved

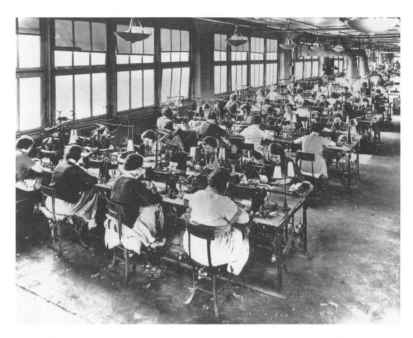

Williams Shoe Company, Portsmouth (Ohio Historical Society)

mainly in the preparation and finishing end of production—the lowest paid positions. Women also worked in the paint industry as can makers and labelers. One of the largest companies, Sherwin Williams, used women to fold price lists and sample pamphlets. Others worked in the color department, the tin shop, the storage department, and the varnish department. By 1888, Sherwin Williams had enough female employees to hire a female supervisor. This woman earned $576 per year, the highest salary of any employed woman in Cleveland. The paper box and candy factories employed the youngest girls, even though these industries were often the most dangerous. Coffin manufacturers hired women as coffin coverers, cutters, and robe makers, while the screw and bolt manufacturing companies hired them as packers.[16]

Even though more factories were employing women, wages were abysmally low and the hours long. According to a report of the

Ohio Bureau of Labor Statistics, women working as weavers, spinners, spoolers, and twisters in 1878 received an average wage of $4.33 per week for between fifty-four and sixty-six hours of work. Young women working in planing mills and as potters received fifty to seventy-eight cents per day, while men working the same jobs received from $1.50 to $2.00 per day. By 1890, the highest paid women were those who worked in the printing industry as composition and press feeders.[17]

The period of progressive reform at the turn of the century brought little relief for wage-earning women. By 1907, the average weekly wage for women workers in Cleveland, Columbus, and Cincinnati was $4.83, with an average workweek of fifty-seven hours. Weekly living expenses were estimated at $2.44 for food, $0.17 for rent, light, and heat; $1.25 for clothing; and $1.38 for other necessities. This left a deficit for most. In some industries the wages were even less. The *Cincinnati Enquirer* reported that women working in laundries and sewing shops made as little as $1.25 per week, and in Cleveland women in the garment industry earned even less than women in other industries in Cleveland.[18] One garment manufacturer, Joseph and Feiss, took a paternalistic attitude towards its workers, two-thirds of whom were female. The company "provided lunchrooms and inexpensive meals, showers, recreation facilities, a dispensary, a penny-savings bank, and classes in English."[19] In 1890, after an examination of the working conditions of women employed in tailoring, shoe fitting, laundries, housework, cloak and vest making, sewing, and restaurant work, the *Cincinnati Enquirer* concluded that "had the destitution uncovered in its investigations been caused by some sudden catastrophe, it 'would call for the sympathy of the world,' but, coming as it did, 'gradually, year by year, through the natural operation of business systems, it has been systematically ignored and its existence even denied.'"[20]

As in previous times, the attempt to address these problems through unionization did not meet with a great deal of success, but there were a few victories that inspired the emerging labor movement. Local 42 of the United Garment Workers in Cleveland celebrated its fifth anniversary in 1901. They had control of two factories, where they had gained the eight-hour day and "fair wages."[21] The waitress union had fifty-six members, and a woman served as vice president of the Central Labor Union. Another woman was on the board of the labor newspaper, the *Cleveland Citizen*.

Middle-class women, led by Mrs. Frederic C. Howe, who wished to promote women's unions, formed the Women's Trade Union League in 1903. The Cleveland branch of the WTUL, located at the Goodrich House, received the endorsement of the *Cleveland Citizen*. The Women's Industrial and Welfare League, formed in 1913 by members of the waitresses, housemaids, and garment workers unions, along with some professional women such as nurses and teachers, strived "to better the conditions of women in all lines of work . . . irrespective of religion or nationality."[22] Even though it was endorsed by the Central Labor Union, the group lasted only a few months. Even women's auxiliaries to male unions had a difficult time remaining viable. The Railroad Woman's Union was organized in 1878 to give aid socially, religiously, and charitably to all classes of railway workers. The Women's Federal Labor Union, formed to promote the use of the union label by manufacturers, was forced to disband in 1904 by male union members who believed women had no place in a union.

Women did go out on strike, but the results were usually negligible and in some cases detrimental. Three hundred women walked off the job at the Cleveland Paper Company in 1879 over a pay reduction. The company hired replacement workers, but the strikers prevented them from entering the factory. Eventually the police were called to escort the replacements into the mill, and the *Cleveland Plain Dealer* labeled the strikers "Amazons."[23]

The most celebrated women's strike during this time period in Ohio and throughout the country was the International Ladies' Garment Workers Union strike of 1911. The garment workers demanded a fifty-hour workweek, no more than two hours of overtime during the regular workweek, double pay for overtime, observance of legal holidays, elimination of shop agreements and inside contracting with individuals, and the elimination of charges for the use of machines, electricity, and thread. The owners refused to budge, and a call for a general strike was issued. On June 7, 1911, five thousand garment workers, a thousand of whom were women, walked off the job in Cleveland. The national union sent Pauline Newman to help organize the strike with the help of local leaders Josephine Casey and Becky Fisher. Fisher became a local hero for being arrested thirty-nine times, earning her an award from the American Federation of Labor for her devotion to the union cause. On June 14, the union held the first of several parades. Locals 27 and 29 led the parade in which six thousand demonstrators took part. However, many women did not support the strike, crossed the picket lines, and continued to work. The strike collapsed after nineteen weeks on October 15, with the demands unmet, due to the actions of the strikebreakers and the lack of support on the part of middle- and upper-class women who had previously supported the garment strikers in New York and Chicago.[24]

Little was done to place regulations on the industrial sector. Such regulations impinged on employers' rights to organize and operate their factories as they saw fit, and the government usually took a hands-off approach, adopting the attitude that what was good for business was good for Ohio. But state government gradually began to regulate the employment of women and teenagers. The minimum working age was raised to fifteen years for boys and sixteen years for girls in general industry, and higher for occupations considered dangerous or "morally deleterious." A graduated scale of maximum hours was set for females under the age of twenty-one. In 1911 the General Assembly did pass a nine-hour bill that applied to women working in mercantile establishments and factories. There was also an attempt to include women working in hotels, but this was defeated.[25] So once again, it was left to benevolent individuals and groups to try to provide better living and working conditions for women workers. The Women's Repository was established in Cleveland in December 1880 to provide an outlet for women to sell their handiwork and earn needed money. Also in 1880, the Women's Exchange, an organization providing a sales outlet for women's goods, opened. The Exchange was run by a committee that set prices. Both provided additional income to working women for a brief period of time. The Exchange soon became a social gathering spot for middle- and upper-class women. Another attempt to provide income was the Women's Employment Society, organized in November 1885, to employ "that class of working poor women of this city, who, otherwise, would suffer great destitution rather than be known as paupers." Only the most needy were accepted. During its first year of operation, the society obtained a government contract to supply clothing to the Bureau of Indian Affairs.[26]

Other groups also began to take note of the dire conditions of workers and make recommendations. The Ohio Consumers League was formed in 1900 at Goodrich House in Cleveland. Reformers soon organized branches in most major cities of Ohio. The League conducted studies of factories, published their findings, and promoted protective legislation. It also published a "white list" of those businesses that adhered to a set of standards, which were quite specific and included the following: "The minimum wage for sales women, eighteen years old and six months experience, is six dollars a week . . . [and] of cash girls . . . two dollars and a half. . . . [T]en hours constitutes a working day with an hour for lunch. . . . A general half-holiday is given on one day each week during at least two summer months. . . . Work, lunch and toilet rooms are apart from each other and conform to present sanitary laws. No boy under fifteen and no girl under sixteen years of age is employed [while school is in session] and no child under thirteen is employed at any." Few businesses made the initial lists.[27]

The Bureau of Labor Statistics in 1908 sent a special investigator to report on the conditions for women workers in Columbus. She visited twenty-five different types of industries, including awning and flag factories, bakeries, laundries, casket factories, paper bag and box plants, boot and shoe factories, and clothing factories. The investigator found that employers still paid by the piece, that women worked in unsanitary and dangerous conditions with few safeguards, that conditions were crowded and cluttered, that at times workplaces were either overheated or unheated, and that stairwells were filled, making it difficult to exit.[28] However, little notice was taken of the report, for any improvements in salaries or working conditions would have lowered profits. Low salaries still forced women into prostitution.

The number of factory jobs increased for women at the end of the nineteenth century, drawing many young women away from domestic service. Still, domestic service constituted one avenue of employment for recent immigrants and African American women. In the 1890 U.S. Census, the percentage of white women employed as housekeepers was 2.4 percent of the entire labor force in Cincinnati. Of this 2.4 percent, the majority of these women were foreign born. An additional 2.9 percent of the Cincinnati workforce consisted of "non white females" employed as housekeepers.[29] Outside the major cities, this shift in the demographic makeup of domestic servants did not occur until later. In Piqua in 1890, the majority of those in domestic service were young white girls from farm families. Only 19 percent were foreign born. However, by the end of World War I, black women had begun to dominate the number of domestic service workers.[30]

Some women kept boarders or ran boardinghouses to supplement their income. Piqua had twelve boardinghouses in 1890. After the turn of the century, households taking in boarders usually were headed by more recent immigrants. In 1911, the U.S. Immigration Commission reported that of the 617 Croatian households studied in Cleveland, 367 kept a total of 2,394 boarders, or 3.8 per household.[31]

Professions slowly and reluctantly opened their doors to women. Generally, these continued to be professions that allowed women to operate in a sphere that was an extension of the home. Teaching, nursing, and social work became the areas deemed most appropriate for single women; however, the number of women engaged in business, banking, journalism, and medicine continued to increase, albeit slowly. During this period, the position of librarian was added to the list of "acceptable" occupations for single women. In 1911, the ranks of Ohio professional women included 66 lawyers, 151 journalists, 62 commercial travelers (traveling companions), 15 bankers, 31 carpenters, 40 dentists, 203 ministers, and 451 physicians. These numbers were far above those found in 1875, when most city directories listed women as milliners, dressmakers, and an occasional saleslady, photographer, or compositor.[32]

The librarian as a professional evolved from the role of women in early literary societies. After the Civil War, and particularly with money from the Carnegie Endowment, more communities opened public libraries, with women as the driving force. Miss Nettie Wheeler was the first librarian of the Elyria Library. She assumed the post in 1870 and stayed there until her marriage in 1883. Frances D. Jermain served as librarian of the Toledo Public Library for twenty-four years, during which time she started a children's department. Mary Pauline Edgerton, who served as the Summit County Library's chief administrator for more than thirty years, developed a reference department, a catalog department, and expanded activities for children. Linda A. Eastman served as librarian for the Cleveland Public Library from 1893 to 1937, and Electra C. Doren worked in the Dayton Library (1879–1905; 1913–27), served as the first director of the Western Reserve Library School, and became the first woman to be elected to the American Library Association's publishing board. Some women even went an extra step to serve their communities. New London did not have a library in 1910, so Miss Elizabeth N. McConnell opened her home to the public for this purpose; in 1916 when the new Carnegie Library was opened, McConnell became its first librarian.[33]

Another literary endeavor that continued to draw women was journalism, both locally and nationally. Emily Bouton was the first editor of the "Women's Page" of the *Toledo Blade,* where she introduced health and beauty columns. Sophia McIlvaine Herrick, born in Knox County in 1837, went on to be the associate editor and

Ohio Newspaper Women's Association annual meeting, Dayton, 1919 (Ohio Historical Society)

business manager of the *Southern Review* from 1875 to 1878 in Baltimore, Maryland. She joined the editorial staff of *Scribner's Magazine* in 1878 and remained with the magazine and its successor, *The Century*, until 1907. In 1902, the Ohio Newspaper Women's Association organized in Toledo. Magazine and special writers were admitted in 1912 in hopes of strengthening the organization. Miss Louise Graham of the *Cleveland Leader* was president.[34]

Just as with the librarian positions, many of these women dedicated their entire life to the profession at a time when it was still expected that a woman would marry and have children. Mary Ann (Minnie) Ellet (1861–1945) served as a correspondent for the *Akron Beacon Journal* longer than any other staff member, working for a total of thirty-four editors. Anna Steese Richardson, who was born in Massillon, Stark County, in 1865, began as a reporter for the *Napariel*, a weekly in Council Bluffs, Iowa. She then worked as a freelance writer for the McClure Newspaper Syndicate and became editor of *Woman's Home Companion* in 1906, a position that she held for more than thirty years.[35]

Still other women took on the challenges of the publishing arena. Zell Hart Deming, a newspaper publisher born in Trumbull County, was the first female member of the Associated Press. Nellie Augusta Harter of Wadsworth began her career as a hand typesetter and became half owner of the *Banner Press* in 1929. By 1935, she was sole owner. The *Marion Star*, owned by Warren G. Harding, remained a small operation until his wife, Florence Kling Harding, became involved and helped make it a very profitable business.[36]

A few women owned their own businesses, usually millinery or dressmaking establishments. In Piqua in 1890, twelve women owned millinery businesses and twenty-three listed dressmaking as their occupation. Most of these women ran their businesses from their homes. Mrs. A. Layer built up a substantial millinery business, and in 1888 built her own business at 320 North Main Street. In Copley, Mrs. Eudora Trimble was the proprietor of a millinery establishment.[37]

A few women found themselves in very unusual businesses for the time. Miss Zaide Palmer opened a quarry outside of Van Wert during the summer of 1875. Realizing that a better mode of transportation was needed to haul the stone into town, she arranged for a tramway to be built. Soon after, she received the contract to improve the city's streets. Palmer was a hands-on owner and went every day to the quarry until 1877, when poor health forced her to give up her work and move to a better climate. However, she returned to Van Wert in the summer of 1890 and died there on August 12, 1891.[38]

Carolyn McCullough Everhard, born in Stark County in 1843, was the first woman in Ohio to hold the position of bank director. In 1912, Florence Heldmyer Hannaford was named trustee of her father's estate, and she assumed control of his business interests. She filled his place on the board of directors of the Elyria Savings

Victoria Claflin Woodhull
(Ohio Historical Society)

and Banking Company and, at that time, was the only woman in Ohio holding such a position.[39] Other unusual professional positions included owning and running an investment house. Victoria Woodhull, a former resident of Canton, started the investment company of Woodhull, Claflin and Company in New York, with the backing of Cornelius Vanderbilt. Victoria and her sister were the first women to hold seats on the New York Stock Exchange.[40] Louise Klein Miller (1854–1949) was the landscape architect who designed the Memorial Garden of Cleveland. Dolly Spencer from Milford was in 1914 the first woman to serve as chief of police, and Mary Green was the only female riverboat captain on the Ohio River. Green, captain of *The Argand,* developed a reputation for maintaining order on her boat. As a consequence, she established a huge passenger trade. After her husband's death, Green carried on the business, increasing the number of boats she owned to six. She continued to serve as captain, as did her two sons.[41]

The number of women physicians also continued to increase. Elizabeth Grissell set up practice in Salem in 1869. She moved to California around 1877, but returned to Salem and her practice in 1888. Other early Salem physicians included Della M. Walker, Mrs. Arter, and Mrs. Augusta Black. Lucy Hobbs of Cincinnati received her diploma from Ohio College of Dental Surgery in 1866 and became the first female dentist in the United States. The earliest woman physician known to have practiced in Piqua was Dr. Belle Buchanan. She was born in Piqua and opened her office there after receiving her degree in 1883. After one year she moved to Cincinnati. In the 1890s, Dr. J. D. Segley set up a practice in Piqua, where she practiced for several years. Osteopathy became popular at this time, and Emily Bronson Conger of Akron was one of the first women in the country to receive a degree in this field. She set up a practice in Akron but spent a great deal of her time fighting against legislation to ban the practice of osteopathy. She would later be elected vice president of the American Association of Osteopathy. Society increasingly accepted osteopathy as the decade progressed. Gertrude Crandell, after receiving her degree of Doctor of Osteopathy, came to Wooster in 1915, where she opened the Hill Sanitarium. She specialized in "mineral baths, electric light baths, colonic irrigation, violet ray and sunlight treatments." Irene Hardy was listed in the Massillon City Directories from 1903 to 1917 under the heading "Physicians and Surgeons." The first female physician listed in Stark County was Dr. Elizabeth L. Thomas, who practiced in Alliance with her husband. Dr. Jeannette Miller opened her practice in Massillon on May 19, 1908. She was one of the first physicians to urge women to have their babies at the Massillon City Hospital rather than at home. She later specialized in anesthesiology and retired after practicing medicine for fifty-one years.[42]

By the end of the nineteenth century, clerical and sales positions also began to open to women as men grew unwilling to do such work. Fewer than 2 percent of working women in Cleveland in 1870 were employed as clerks in stores and offices, but by 1910, 22.6 percent were employed in such positions. In 1890, 8.1 percent of the clerical and sales positions in Cincinnati were held by white females.[43] Local business "colleges" opened and began offering courses to women. People who possessed skills such as shorthand, typing, stenography, and bookkeeping were in great demand. Miss Rae Baily of Savannah began as a stenographer and bookkeeper in Elyria, moved to the "big city," and became a legal secretary from 1905 to 1915 in the law office of Griswold and White in Cleveland. She then became the confidential stenographer for Senator Attlee Pomerene, Democrat from Ohio, and also worked in his campaign office in Columbus. Retail work was considered socially acceptable for young single girls or older widows. The pay was generally less than some factory work, but the hours were usually more favorable, 9:00 A.M.–6:00 P.M. regularly and 9:00 A.M.–11:00 P.M. on market days. An ability to read, write, and do arithmetic was required. The job of telephone operator or "hello girl" was a new occupation at the latter part of the nineteenth century. The first telephone exchange in Piqua was installed in 1880, and by 1920 more than forty women were employed there as operators and supervisors in the local Ohio Bell Company.[44]

The entrance of the United States into World War I expanded the opportunities for women to work outside the home in industry, service-oriented businesses, and the professions. With a large segment of the male population in the military services, women found new prospects available to them. The Women's Division of the State-City Labor Exchange found that fifty-four iron and steel plants employed 4,165 women during the war, compared to 2,575 before the war. Goodyear Rubber hired women to make gas masks. Married women entered the teaching profession because of the shortage of male teachers. Some women, usually young and college-educated, worked for the federal government. Helen V. Shirey of Toledo accepted a position in the War Risk Insurance Office in Washington, D.C.[45]

The hiring of women by the Cleveland Street Railway Company prompted a strike during the war years. In August 1918, when the company hired approximately 190 women as streetcar conductors

Zanesville Telephone and Telegraph, 1905 (Ohio Historical Society)

due to the shortage of skilled workers, Local 268 of the Amalgamated Association of Street, Electric Railway, and Motor Coach Employees of America demanded that the women be fired and declared that, if they were not, a walkout would occur in December 1918. The women formed their own union, the Association of Women Street Railway Employees, led by Laura Prince. The women's union hired attorney Florence Allen and Rose Moriarty, a lawyer, a political activist, and a member of the Ohio Industrial Commission, to help them defend their right to these jobs. The initial ruling by the United States Department of Labor denied the right of women to their jobs, but Allen appealed the decision to Secretary William B. Wilson. The legality of their employment was finally upheld after the armistice, but the company no longer had to abide by the ruling.[46] In 1919, the Ohio General Assembly enacted House

Bill 362 which, while protecting many women on the job, specifically prohibited women from taking a wide variety of jobs and, in particular, prevented strenuous physical employment.

The number of women employed did increase after the war. In Piqua, the 1920 city directory listed 1,143 women having occupations, compared to 214 in 1890. Four hundred eighty of these were employed in factories, 231 were office clerks, and 131 were retail clerks. Overall, 40.2 percent of the female workforce was employed in clerical work. However, the numbers are deceiving, since this large percentage pertained only to white women. By 1920, less than 15 percent of all female workers were in domestic service, but 63 percent of all African American women were employed in this service industry. Only 3.7 percent of black women were clerks, and less than 20 percent worked in factories. The number employed in domestic service would continue to increase throughout the decade, and by 1930, 86.7 percent of the black women employed were working as domestics. Only 7.5 percent were employed in factories.[47]

A few professional positions continued to be occupied by women. Margaret Evelyn Baker became general manager of Champion Chemical Company in 1921. Elsie Katherine Laub became vice president and secretary of Jacob Laub Baking Company in 1910. Ruth Neely France, a reporter for the *Cincinnati Post, Times-Star,* and *Commercial Tribune,* became president of the Ohio Newspaper Women's Association in 1923.[48] A response to this growing number of professional and business women was the organization of the Ohio Federation of Business and Professional Women's Clubs. The first convention was held in Columbus on February 23, 1920, and Mrs. Mildred M. Hickman of Cleveland was elected president. The first year saw a membership of 2,625 women in seven clubs (Cincinnati, Clear Fork, Columbus, Springfield, Toledo, Warren, and Youngstown). By 1930, there were thirty-six clubs in Ohio.[49] This organization allowed members to address issues that faced women in the workplace and to act as advocates for benevolent civic activities.

Union activity had little success in women's industries in the 1920s, but there were some exceptions. The International Ladies Garment Workers Union continued to have some successes. The Ladies Union Label League was an independent women's organization that worked to promote the use of union labels in clothing and other manufactured items in Massillon. In some areas, women's auxiliaries such as the Ladies Auxiliary of the Brotherhood of Railway Trainmen continued to be popular.

Several private organizations, however, continued to monitor the conditions of women workers in Ohio, since the state government was doing little in that regard. In 1921 the state legislature passed the Bing Act, requiring students to remain in school until they received a diploma or until age eighteen, and barring people below the age of sixteen from employment in most industries.[50] This law was ignored not only by many businesses but also by parents who needed the added household income that young workers brought home. The Consumer League of Cincinnati issued a report, "Women Workers in Factories: A Study of Working Conditions in 275 Industrial Establishments in Cincinnati and Adjoining Towns," in 1918. The investigation covered thirteen months, April 1917 through May 1918, and found 16,924 women and girls employed out of 40,631 workers in the 275 sites visited. The investigation paid special attention to "location and construction, fire protection, condition of workrooms, halls and stairways; toilet accommodations; dressing rooms; washing facilities; lunch rooms; hours of labor; posture at work."[51] Investigators found that managers often violated the state law prohibiting the employment of women for more than fifty hours per week, as well as the child labor laws. Of the 275 businesses investigated, 22 employed women on an emergency basis during World War I. Eighteen of these had never employed women previously. The factories employing women included machine shops, foundries, electrical machinery plants, automobile part factories, electrical machinery plants, lumber mills, and packing houses. For the same work, women generally received two to nine cents per hour less than men, even though employers claimed they were more dependable and their output was greater.[52]

Conditions of women working at home in the clothing industry were also investigated. Investigators recommended the abolishment of all forms of home sewing work due to the bad sanitary conditions and health risks involved, as well as the very low wages received. The low wages paid to these women had a direct effect on the lower wages received by women working in clothing factories.[53]

Another study at the same time undertaken by Frances Ivins Rich and published by the Helen S. Trounstine Foundation and the Young Women's Christian Association of Cincinnati studied the wages of women employed in Cincinnati. The 1920 U.S. Census reported a total of 50,344 women "gainfully employed in Cincinnati, but between the ages of fifteen and twenty four years inclusive there were 15,956 white women and 1,309 colored (Negro) women or a total of 17,265." A sampling of this group showed that the average wage for the factory group was $19.26 per week, the wage for the store group was $15.81 per week, and the wage for the office group was $20.93 per week. The Ohio Minimum Wage Commission issued a report to the Ohio Legislature in winter 1924–25 stating their opinion that the wages of a woman living at home need not be as high as the wages of those living independently. And since only 25 percent of the women lived away from home, the conclusion was reached that higher wages were not necessary for the majority of women.[54]

The commission also reported that there was institutional housing available for 823 white women and 56 African American women in Cincinnati at this time. Rooming houses were available but more expensive and questionable in their "hygienic and moral conditions." It was also found that 70 percent of women factory workers had an eighth-grade education or less, while 58 percent of the office workers had completed high school or college.[55]

Another study, completed by the Consumers' League of Cincinnati in 1930, was based on one hundred personal interviews. Of the one hundred women interviewed, fifty-nine earned less than $17.50 per week (the amount needed to provide a minimum standard of living). State records showed that more than half of the women employed in Hamilton County in 1928 earned less than $15 per week. The report concluded that "If Cincinnati is to progress in industry and business as she has along other lines, employers must realize . . . that lessened need for organized relief; that increased consumer purchasing power, and that a city's reputation for enlightened business and industrial policies depend in large measure upon adequate earnings among her workers."[56]

In 1919, the Consumer League of Ohio inspected the factories in Cleveland that employed members of the Ladies Garment Manufacturers Association. The league rated these factories as "fair" but cited several concerns about sanitation. The Cleveland Hospital Council completed a survey of those women who had worked in war-related industries and found that most had returned to the textile and garment industry, candy factories, laundries, or stores. Working conditions had not improved in these businesses, and women were still ethnically and racially segregated in the workplace. More black women were employed in laundries, and they were paid less than white women.[57]

During the first quarter of the twentieth century, state and federal legislatures passed labor legislation designed to "protect" women workers. Some reformers based their argument for protective legislation on the grounds that women workers, much like children, needed protection. Still others pushed for protective legislation because most unions would not admit women workers and, in fact, worked to keep women out of the workplace. Legislation designed to protect women involved issues such as maximum number of hours women were permitted to work, minimum wages, regulations against night work, limitations on the weight women could lift, and where women could be employed. The Women's Trade Union League accepted protective legislation only as a last resort, because they realized the positive impact this legislation could have on the lives of working-class women. Many activists, however, viewed protective legislation as discriminatory towards women—just another excuse for employers not to hire women and to relegate them to low-paying jobs.[58]

The Depression slowed down and, in some cases, halted the gains women were making in the workplace. In Cleveland, for example, almost 12 percent of the female labor force in 1930 was employed in the professional sector, but by 1940 this number had dropped to 9.6 percent. About one-third of working women were employed in clerical jobs in 1940, down from 40.2 percent in 1920.[59] The profession in which women's numbers did increase was domestic service. In 1920 in Cleveland, 14.8 percent of all female workers were domestic servants; by 1930 it was 20.3 percent and by 1940, 26 percent. The majority of employed African American women (almost 70 percent) worked as domestic servants in 1930, with only 2.7 percent having professional jobs and 2.6 percent having clerical jobs. The same trends can be seen in Toledo. A 1930 survey of the wages of one hundred African American domestic workers in Columbus showed that sixty-two of the one hundred women made $9 or less per week, while only twenty-nine made more than $20 per week. By the end of the decade, eighty-six out of one hundred made $9 per week or less.[60] Due to the low wages in all areas, some women were forced to do piecework at home for four or five cents per hour, while others were driven into prostitution.

Some women were able to continue their professional careers during this time. Anne O'Hare McCormick, who made her home in Cleveland and Dayton, was the first woman to hold a place on the editorial council of the *New York Times.* She won a Pulitzer Prize in 1937 for her work as a foreign correspondent and was awarded the Medal for Eminent Achievement of the American Woman's Association in 1939. Nellie Becker Dorr from Massillon moved her photography studio to New York City in the 1930s, and Margaret Bourke-White, a photographer in Cleveland, began work for *Fortune* magazine after Henry Luce saw her photographs of the Otis Steel Works. Ruth Lyons was the program director at WKRC

Alice Von Sickle Cardington, honored at the annual Ohio Newspaper Women's Association Meeting in 1932 as the oldest living newspaperwoman in the United States (Ohio Historical Society)

radio in Cincinnati in 1933, and Olive Jane Brown was superintendent of Mansfield General Hospital. That was also the year that Mary Ann Campana of Youngstown broke the world light airplane endurance record by remaining airborne for twelve hours and twenty-seven minutes.[61]

Women were also able to continue in business. Lottie R. Olmutz from Norwalk managed her husband's insurance company upon his death in 1930. In 1939, Katherine Adams Lance Leslie was the owner and president of the S. & B. Millinery and Jewelry Wholesale Corporation in Toledo. Dorothea T. Rudd owned and managed Favorite Chemical and Supply Company from 1934 to 1942. She was the first black woman in Piqua to manage a local industrial firm.[62] The number of chapters of the Ohio Federation of Business and Professional Women's Clubs continued to grow during the Depression.

Union organizing efforts were very strong during the 1930s. New tactics such as the sit-down strike were introduced, and John L. Lewis, president of the United Mine Workers of America, spearheaded the organization of the Congress of Industrial Organizations (CIO), which organized workers by industry regardless of skill or ethnicity, or cultural background. That inclusiveness did not generally extend to women. Women were seen as a threat to a dwindling number of "men's" jobs and therefore were still not welcomed by many unions. The unions were taking their cue from the national and state governments that were working feverishly to limit the number of married women employed. In 1935, the following piece of legislation was introduced in Ohio: "No appointing officer of any of the various State departments and State educational institutions shall appoint or employ a person to a position in the classified or unclassified civil service, who occupies the legal status of marriage with another person in such service."[63] The governor supported the bill and it passed the House with only one negative vote. The Senate, however, referred it to the Judiciary Committee.

But the issue did not die. In January 1939, House Bill 26, known as the Dunn Bill, was introduced by Pat Dunn, a member of the Ohio House from Stark County. The Dunn Bill would have barred all married women from being state employees. The House Committee on State Government recommended its passage, and the bill was referred to the Committee on Commerce and Labor. At that point, the committee heard testimony from various groups who opposed the bill, such as the Ohio Federation of Business and Professional Women's Clubs, the League of Women Voters, and the Dayton Branch of the National Women's Party. Many of the cogent arguments that helped to defeat the bill were made by Marie Schaffler, a young attorney from Wooster. (Schaffler would go on to become the president of the Ohio Federation of Business and Professional Women's Clubs and vice president of the National Federation of Business and Professional Women's Clubs.)[64] But Representative Dunn did not give up. In the 1941 session, he and Senator Wayne Hays introduced bills to limit the employment of wives in state government. The measure failed again, this time because of the entrance of the United States into World War II. During this war, as earlier in the century, women were needed to fill the jobs left vacant while men left home to fight. Ohio was not the only state that attempted to limit women's ability to work. Between 1938 and 1939, twenty-two states tried to enact such measures.

The number of unemployed women in Cleveland rose from 5,224 in 1930 to 17,832 in 1931. But fewer women than men were homeless. In March 1933, 955 women and girls were living in shelters. This number doubled by 1935. Federal relief programs helped some women, but when funds were cut in these programs, women were usually the first to lose their jobs. Jobs in sewing rooms, offices, and schools were made available, and a few women worked in the artists' and theatre projects of the Works Progress Administration. Direct relief also increased in the 1930s. In January 1928, 435 women in Cleveland received mothers' pensions. That number increased to 1,010 in January 1935. By 1937, 1,116 women received Aid to Dependent Children.[65]

The entrance by the United States into World War II, along with the country's attempt to develop a total war industry, brought an end to the Depression. Hundreds of thousands of workers were needed, and as more men joined the military, this paved the way for women to enter the workforce in record numbers. However, it was not easy to reverse long-held attitudes. For years, both the American public and the United States government had urged women to stay in the home. Now these same women were needed in business and industry. The government spent thousands of dollars in ad campaigns, the most recognizable one being "Rosie the Riveter," to convince women it was their patriotic duty to work

Mrs. Elizabeth Green, forced from her home by an underground fire at the New Straitsville mine, Perry County (Ohio Historical Society)

outside the home. The safety of their loved ones depended on their ability to produce enough airplanes, ammunition, and all other wartime goods and supplies.

In Cleveland, several companies hired women, including American Steel and Wire, Cleveland Graphite Bronze, Cleveland Twist Drill, Cleveland Welding Company, General Electric, Reliance Electric, Warner and Swasey, Thompson Products, and Parker Appliances. By August 1943, the largest war materials manufacturers employed 28.7 percent women. Republic Steel employed 7,080 women in July 1943, up from 585 in October 1942.[66]

Some women were employed in munitions manufacture. Women's dexterity and smaller finger size made this a job at which they excelled, albeit a dangerous one. Mary Socash worked at the

Ravenna Arsenal, where she made bombs. The basic wage was sixty-five cents per hour, and men and women received equal pay, an unusual occurrence. The rubber industry also employed a significant number of women. One night shift at General Rubber, a group of women constructing life belts were noted as achieving the highest production rate of any shift at the plant. Mary Sande, a worker at Firestone in its tire building division, was the first woman to be an instructor and supervisor. She was chosen to represent the rubber industry at a ceremony in New York City in December 1943, honoring women who supported the war effort. Women's pay in this industry, however, was not equal to their male counterparts'. The 1941 Goodyear contract allowed men to be hired at seventy cents per hour and women at fifty-five cents. This disparity continued throughout the war.[67]

The attitude toward women workers manifested itself in more than salary disparities. Both men and women felt resentment in the workplace. Women resented the higher pay men received for the same work, while men resented the fact that women were present in the factory in any capacity. Some men held strong convictions against women working outside the home, while others begrudged the changes made in the workplace, such as restrooms and locker rooms that had to be altered for women's use. Others protested the "masculinization" of women that they believed was a result of women working in the factories. In the factory, women wore slacks, many for the first time — a shocking occurrence for some people. Women at Goodyear were able to buy special coveralls with an emblem reading "Remember Pearl Harbor." Other men resented taking orders from a woman. Helen Schrader worked as a federal inspector of gas masks in an Akron rubber company. One time, after discovering a shipment of defective masks, she ordered the men in charge to unload them. They refused. She immediately climbed to the top of the railroad car and began tossing the masks off the car.[68]

Women also had to deal with the issue of child care. The Cleveland Day Nursery Association, along with the Cleveland Associated

Charities, helped to establish and staff thirteen day-care centers in Cleveland by 1943. By the same time, the Akron Metropolitan Housing Authority established day-care facilities in four housing projects, and the local office of the Civil Defense helped find babysitters for the children of female rubber workers.[69]

Opportunities also opened up in industry for African American women. The Cleveland Urban League listed the number of black women in manufacturing jobs in 1945 at 6,000—a substantial increase from 400 in 1940. However, at the end of the war, 60 percent of the African American labor force in Cleveland was still in unskilled positions.[70]

With the end of the war came a push by companies, unions, the government, and the public for women to return to their homes. They had served in an exemplary way during the war, but their work was no longer needed. The war had been an extraordinary occurrence demanding extraordinary sacrifices from everyone, but most American felt it was now time for women to return to their homes and relinquish their jobs to returning veterans. Firestone released 2,700 employees from the aircraft division, 75 percent of whom were women.[71] This was the reality throughout the state and nation. However, many women did not wish to relinquish their jobs; they found them fulfilling and, in some cases, better paying than jobs they had held previously.

Women who wished or needed to continue to work found themselves once again relegated to "female" occupations with lower pay. One major effect of wartime employment was a shift in worker demographics. After the war, there was a continued increase in the number of married women who worked outside the home. In Cleveland in October 1950, 190,000 women worked in industry. By 1952 more than 30 percent of Cleveland's labor force was female: 200,000 of the 640,000 employed.[72] These numbers would continue to rise, and with this change in the demographics of working America, more discussions ensued over the role of women as wives and mothers and the role of women in the workplace.

Labor laws were once again resurrected to protect women in the

Mrs. Marian D. Clements, mail clerk, Kent State University Administration Building (Kent State University Archives)

workplace, and in time laws were put forth to address the inequities women found in the workplace. In 1951, an equal-pay bill was introduced in Ohio with the support of the Ohio Federation of the Business and Professional Women's Clubs, but it was defeated. The bill was introduced again in 1953, 1955, and 1957 with no more success. In 1959, the Ohio Federation of Business and Professional Women's Clubs wrote its own bill and set about trying to get it passed. Women met with their representatives, made phone calls, wrote letters, and appeared before both the Ohio House and Senate. The equal-pay law passed, but it applied only to employers with ten or more employees doing identical work and did not apply to domestic or farm laborers (section 4111.17 of the ORC). Protective labor legislation came under attack in Ohio in 1972. The Ohio Supreme Court's decision in the case *Jones Metal Productions v. Walker,* made most of Ohio's laws "restricting the hours and conditions under which private industry could employ women including the types of employment and laws affecting women" unenforceable.[73] Following federal law in 1973, Ohio HB 610 prohibited discrimination on the basis of sex in employment, public accommodations, and housing. The changes in the law, along with the new opportunities available to women in the area of education, allowed for more extensive job and career opportunities for women.

Business opportunities, though limited in scope, continued to attract qualified women. In 1964, Theresa Ferris, became Ohio's first woman president of a coal company, Ferris Coal Company. Two years later, Lois A. Reynolds became vice president of the First National Bank of Bowling Green. Also in 1966 Youngstown native Mary Georgene Wells established her own advertising agency, Wells, Rich, Green, Inc. Within six months the agency had over $30 million in billings and by 1972, Wells was the highest paid executive in the advertising industry. The number of Ohio professional women, though increasing over prewar levels, still was very small by the end of the 1960s. Women made up only 6.2 percent of the physicians and 2.5 percent of attorneys in Ohio. Fewer than 1 percent of engineers and architects in the state were women, and only 1 percent of certified public accountants and life underwriters were women. Female pharmacists made up 5 percent of the profession, while female anesthesiologists accounted for 10 percent of the total professionals in that field.[74]

The first *Ohio Women Entrepreneurs Directory* was not published until 1983. The 1984 directory listed 2,062 businesses owned by women, an increase of 30 percent over the previous year. The leading counties were Franklin (400), Cuyahoga (270), Montgomery (166), and Hamilton (164). The types of businesses varied widely, including Crowner Computing, Hattendorg-Bliss, Inc. (general construction contractor), Henry Tools, Inc., and O & P Oil and Gas Company.[75]

Journalism and publishing continued to attract women. Dorothy Fuldheim became a journalist for Scripps-Howard newspapers and then for the Scripps-Howard radio and television stations in Cleveland. She was one of the very first television correspondents and was known for asking tough questions. Fuldheim's career spanned almost forty years; her last interview was with President Ronald Reagan in 1984.[76] Bonnie Ranville d'Ettorre from North Fairfield became editor in chief of *Children's Playmate Magazine* in June 1961.

The antidiscrimination laws opened other opportunities to women. Jerrie Mock, who graduated from Ohio State University in 1964, was the first woman to fly solo around the world. She accomplished this feat in a Cessna 180, traveling 23,000 miles in 29.5 days. She also served on the Women's Advisory Committee on Aviation to the Federal Aviation Association, and she received more than one hundred awards and citations. In 1972, Susan L. Roley and Jennifer E. Pierce became the first two women to graduate as agents from the FBI Academy. And in 1973, Judith Gahm became the first woman in the Ohio State Highway Patrol; she served as a communications technician. Janice Cunningham became the first female weigh station attendant in 1973, and several communities, such as Germantown, hired their first female police officers in the 1970s.[77]

Interestingly, as more women entered the professions, the number of Business and Professional Women's Club chapters in Ohio began to decline. Similarly, as the numbers of women working in industry continued to grow, unions tended to ignore them, leaving many women to fend for themselves in hostile workplaces. Being the "token female" in a company could be a very lonely and demoralizing experience.

Increasingly larger numbers of African American women continued to be employed in domestic service. Geraldine Roberts of Cleveland decided to try to organize this particular segment of the workforce. She called the first meeting in September 1965 at St. James AME Church, and twenty women attended. The meetings continued, and in 1966 the group was chartered as the Domestic Workers of America. Word of the group traveled, and Roberts was contacted by women in neighboring communities, necessitating the establishment of a westside office on Lorain Avenue. With help from the Congress of Racial Equality (CORE), the group set up a phone bank to begin a registry of domestic workers. In 1968, Domestic Workers of America received $13,200 from the Office of Economic Opportunity to support a seven-month project. The support was extended for another eighteen months, enabling the Domestic Workers of America to staff a three-person office. The money helped to place domestics and to provide them with training and education. Josephine Hulett also helped organize domestics around the state.

A few unions tried to respond to women's needs, but in many instances it fell to private groups or individuals to work for change. The International Ladies Garment Workers Union continued to be active. Members picketed Higbee's Department Store in Cleveland in the late 1960s as part of a strike against Judy Bond Blouses. In Barberton, United Rubber Workers Local 58, based at Sun Rubber Company, was headed by Catherine "Kitty" Garlock. Cleveland Women Working, along with similar organizations across the nation, held a protest against women's low wages during National Secretaries' Week in 1979, and in 1980 they held another demonstration against low wages in the lobby of the National City Bank's headquarters in Cleveland. In 1983, they held another rally and named SOHIO "Scrooge of the Year" because of the low salaries paid to its women employees. Hard Hatted Women, an organization of women working in the construction trades, rallied at Cleveland's Public Square demanding that women be admitted to construction unions and hired on more jobs.[78]

As more women entered or attempted to enter the workforce in Ohio, it became apparent that there were definite obstacles to overcome and discriminatory practices to endure once employed. In 1965, the Ohio Legislative Services Committee did a partial study on labor laws affecting women, and the following year the Ohio Governor's Committee on the Status of Women conducted a study that resulted in the 1967 report "Women in the Wonderful

Cincinnati Women Working promote Raises, Not Roses during National Secretaries Week, April 1978 (Ohio Historical Society)

World of Ohio."[79] However, the world for Ohio's working women was not so wonderful in 1967.

The committee reported that 45 percent of the employers surveyed did not hire or promote women because of: (1) Ohio's female labor laws; (2) women's emotional instability; (3) women's physical limitations; (4) women's lack of technical skills and knowledge; (5) women's unwillingness to be re-educated; and (6) union regulations. Professions such as law, accounting, and engineering had no women associates and no female supervisors. When asked why women were not hired in professional positions, the reasons given included: (1) qualified women were not available; (2) clients would not accept women; (3) women have physical limitations; (4) women cannot or will not travel; and (5) Ohio's female labor laws are restrictive. To add insult to injury, 100 percent of the certified public accountants, engineers, and lawyers felt secretarial, clerical, and bookkeeping jobs were for women only. Some pointed out "few college women have good secretarial skills which could be useful to many in later life and for part-time jobs after marriage."[80]

In response to these various reports, Governor James A. Rhodes issued an executive order in 1969 creating a Women's Services Division within the Bureau of Employment Services. Nadine Cook Henninger was appointed director. Later that year, the Women's Division was renamed the Women's Services Section of the Employment Services Division, and in 1971 Emily L. Leedy became the director. Now called the Women's Division, Ohio Bureau of Employment Services, this division focuses on the employment and training needs of women. Since 1994, it has hosted biannually Kaleidoscope: A Conference for Women, and it also administers the Ohio Women's Hall of Fame, located in Columbus. The Hall of Fame "honors women who have played a significant role in Ohio's history through their trailblazing contributions."

The Governor's Task Force once again reported in 1978 on the status of Ohio's working women. The task force found, not surprisingly, that women were overrepresented at the lower levels of employment in state government. Women were paid substantially lower salaries than men in most categories, and they were less likely to advance or be promoted, especially in official or managerial positions.[81]

During the next twenty years, the gap did begin to close as more and more women entered the workforce and as legislation prohibiting discrimination was implemented. However, the gap still remains. WomenSpace, a women's group from Cleveland, noted that in 1990, 58.7 percent of all women in Cleveland worked outside the home, making up 45.2 percent of the workforce. Women now have greater access to professions but still make up a very small number of workers in positions such as electricians or machinists. Women are still clustered in the traditionally female occupations, and those women who do enter male-dominated professions continue to be paid less. In 1970 women's median annual income for full-time employment was 58.4 percent of men's. In 1990 it was 70.5 percent, and in 2000 it was 73 percent.[82] Ohio's women can be found in virtually every job and profession, but the obstacles to entrance into and equity within careers are still a challenge as the state enters its third century.

CHAPTER THREE

Women, Suffrage, and Politics in Ohio

ALTHOUGH ABIGAIL ADAMS admonished her husband, John, "not to forget the ladies," it appeared that the ladies, at least politically, had been forgotten in this country during the nineteenth century. Ohio was no exception. Even though women did not enjoy the political privileges allowed white males, they were political and social activists early in the nineteenth century. Many women were involved in the moral reform movement of the 1830s that grew out of the evangelistic religious movement of the same period. It was through women's intervention and hard work that schools and churches were started in the frontier communities of Ohio. They were also involved in the early temperance movement of the 1830s and the antislavery movement leading up to the Civil War.

Nationally and locally, women cut their political teeth within the antislavery movement, gaining experience as leaders, organizers, public speakers, and writers. Women such as Betsey M. Cowles of Austinburg, Frances Dana Gage from McConnelsville, Ann Clark of Deerfield, and Ann Eliza Lee of Randolph all held positions of responsibility in the antislavery societies. The sensibilities of the general public were shocked when these women and others, such as Abby Kelly, Lucy Stone, and Ernestine Rose, spoke in public forums before mixed audiences. The verbal abuse and garbage

Betsey Mix Cowles (Kent State University Archives)

thrown at these women was just the beginning of what they and others would endure as they embarked on the struggle for women's rights.

As the halfway point of the nineteenth century approached, more women had access to education through common schools and female seminaries. With this education came a realization, for many, of the subordinate position they held in society. Restrictions were put on women by organized religion, by strict rules of etiquette, and by the legal and political system.

One of the first groups in Ohio to demand woman's suffrage was the Universal Peace Society, founded in Mentor in 1848. Members of this group believed woman's suffrage was a means of abolishing warfare. They encouraged women only to attend churches that allowed them to speak, and they advocated a new courtship system that allowed women some say in whom they married and when.[1] To most in Ohio, including a majority of women, this seemed tantamount to heresy.

However, the same type of sentiments arose in other venues. Women writers, such as Margaret Fuller, in *Women in the Nineteenth*

Frances Dana Gage (Ohio Historical Society)

Century, pointed out the inequalities faced by women in society. Women's periodicals began to address the issue of the legal and political rights of women, as did many reform papers, including *The Anti-Slavery Bugle,* published in Salem, Ohio.

The Seneca Falls Convention in 1848 drew the attention of reformers around the country. Women in Ohio took the challenge to heart by beginning to point out the inequalities women faced under the law in Ohio and agitating for change. In 1850, the inheritance laws in Ohio stated that if no will was left, a widow received only one-third of her husband's estate. The law enumerated what household items were left for her and the children, and if the widow attempted to conceal any property she could be subject to fines and imprisonment. In addition, the will could stipulate a guardian other than the children's mother.[2]

Under Ohio law, married women had no right to their own earnings, or to jewelry or anything bought with those earnings. A mother had no legal control over her children except in the case of illegitimacy, and an abused wife could testify against her spouse only if she could swear that her life was in danger. Married women could not make contracts, file suit in cases of slander or personal injury, or serve on juries. And according to the state's constitution, women, along with criminals, the insane, and Negroes, were prohibited from voting.

Tired of these inequities and spurred by the Seneca Falls Convention of 1848, women in Ohio saw an opportunity to effect some change. In 1850, a small group of women began planning a convention dealing with women's rights, with the goal of bringing their concerns to the Ohio Constitutional Convention (which was scheduled for later that year). They issued a "call" on March 30, 1850, asking women to meet in Salem, Ohio, on April 19–20, 1850, for the purpose of securing equal rights and political privilege for women. The women issuing the call were Jane Elizabeth Jones, Emily Robinson, Mary Ann W. Johnson, and Sarah Coates (all from Marlboro). They were later joined by Ann Clark from Deerfield and Eliza Lee from Randolph. Soon after its founding in 1804, Salem had become a strong Quaker community. It seemed an appropriate venue for such a meeting, as it was an early center for antislavery reform and home to the *Anti-Slavery Bugle* for eighteen years. Many lecturers visited Salem.[3]

The format of the women's convention was similar to that of the antislavery conventions held at the time. One outstanding difference was that women controlled the meeting. The organizers allowed men to attend but not participate in the convention. The meeting convened at the Second Baptist Church with a standing-room-only crowd. The first order of business was to elect permanent officers of the convention, and Betsey M. Cowles was elected president. Cowles and other officers read letters from noted suffrage leaders, and the female attendees selected a committee of three to prepare an address "To the Women of Ohio."[4]

The afternoon session met at the Friends Meeting House on Green Street, a venue that could accommodate more people. It was estimated that five hundred were in attendance. Jane Elizabeth

Jones presented an address entitled "The Wrongs of Woman." The convention participants adopted twenty-two resolutions, including a suffrage resolution.[5] On the second day of the convention, the group affirmed the points in Jones's address and passed a memorial (a statement outlining the conditions endured by Ohio's women)that would be sent to the Ohio Constitutional Convention delegates. The meeting then adjourned with a resolution to continue such meetings in the future. A men's meeting followed that reaffirmed the sentiments of the women's convention, and the men present pledged to agitate until equal rights were attained.

Activists then held local meetings around the state to increase women's awareness of the memorial sent to the Ohio Constitutional Convention and to garner support through petitions. Supporters of the memorial held two meetings in Akron in May, and another in McConnelsville, headed by Frances Dana Gage, on May 29, 1850, which was entirely closed to men. Petitions poured into the Ohio Constitutional Convention—some advocating equal suffrage for blacks and women while others only asked for female suffrage. However, only two of the twelve counties sending petitions were from the southern part of the state.[6]

The Ohio Constitutional Convention convened on May 6, 1850, and lasted until March 10, 1851. During that time, no woman in the state could be found who would venture onto the floor of the convention to present the memorial that had been adopted at the Salem women's convention. Male supporters did present the memorial, but neither Negro suffrage nor female suffrage was passed. Negro suffrage went down on a vote of 12 yeas and 66 nays, while female suffrage lost by a vote of 7 yeas to 72 nays.

The women of Ohio were not deterred by this defeat. They, along with their counterparts across the nation, continued their efforts to educate women about their need for increased rights. A national women's rights convention was held in Worcester, Massachusetts, on October 23, 1850, in which several Ohioans participated. Another convention was held in Akron on May 29, 1851. Frances Dana Gage presided over the convention, and both men

*Caroline M. Severance
(Ohio Historical
Society)*

and women acted as officers of the convention and members of the committees.[7] A reform periodical, *The Genius of Liberty,* began publication in Cincinnati in October 1851. It focused its writing on the rights of women. Supporters in Massillon held the Massillon Women's Rights Convention on May 27, 1852. Attendees at this convention established the Ohio Woman's Rights Association. Its membership was "open to any person interested in equal rights for all human beings in all endeavors." The convention attendees also created a series of tracts, entitled the *Woman's Rights Advocate,* to explain to the public the purpose of the women's rights movement.[8]

With the establishment of a statewide organization, it was hoped that a more focused and far-reaching approach could be put into operation. Caroline Severance presided at the first state convention of the Ohio Woman's Rights Association, held in Ravenna on May 25, 1853. The convention attendees drafted a petition to be presented to the state legislature during the next session on April 1, 1854, and on that date Severance read the petition on the floor of the Ohio Senate.[9] However, Ohio's legislators passed no legislation granting women additional rights during that session.

More and more women stepped forward to demand their political rights. In Randolph in 1853, the Ladies Temperance Alliance went to the polls. Even though it was illegal, they cast their votes in a separate box in support of temperance in that community. In 1854, the voters of Lorain County elected Adeline Swift county supervisor, though she could not legally hold the position. In an address declining the office, she stated, "I presume that I am the first advocate of equal rights, temperance and abolition who has ever received your support."[10]

Ohio rightly claimed a prominent role in the national woman's rights movement. Movement leaders held a national convention in Cleveland on October 5, 1853, where participants elected Frances Dana Gage president of the convention. The national convention returned to Ohio again two years later, meeting in Cincinnati on October 18, 1855. This convention started a national petition drive led by Adeline Smith, and she along with other suffrage leaders presented almost four thousand signatures to the 1855–56 session of the Ohio Legislature.

Ohio's women were optimistic about the 1857 legislative session. They held local meetings to elect delegates to address the legislature. Governor Salmon P. Chase, an antislavery lawyer who was in the forefront of the legal battle against enforcement of the federal fugitive slave law, requested that the legislature consider extending women's rights—the first Ohio governor to do so. Approximately ten thousand people signed the petitions submitted to the legislature. The House Select Committee reported favorably upon the need to change Ohio's property laws. Changes were made in the law, allowing women to control their own earnings and, in certain cases, the earnings of their minor children. Further, widows had the same rights to property as did widowers. A *Report of the Select Committee of the Ohio Senate Concerning the Enfranchisement of*

Women was issued on February 6, 1857, asking the State Judiciary Committee to prepare a bill to amend the state constitution. The report ended by stating: "Resolved, That the Judiciary Committee be instructed to report to the Senate a bill to submit to the qualified electors at the next election for Senators and Representatives an amendment to the constitution whereby the elective franchise shall be extended to the citizens of Ohio without distinction of sex."[11] However, the committee's recommendation for a constitutional amendment was defeated in the Ohio Senate by a tied vote, 44–44.

No other successes could be reported until 1861, when the Republican-dominated legislature changed the amount of property a widow might keep if her husband died. The legislation also allowed a married woman to own real estate, to have complete control over her personal property and earnings acquired before or during marriage, and to make contracts for her own work if she was abandoned by her husband. In addition, a woman's property could no longer be confiscated to pay her husband's debts.[12]

The Civil War stopped the woman's rights movement in its tracks throughout the country. Activity did not resume in Ohio, and around the country, until the late 1860s. Activists organized the Cincinnati Equal Rights Association in 1868, followed by the American Woman Suffrage Association, which held its first annual meeting in Cleveland in 1869. Supporters in the Toledo area formed the Equal Suffrage Association of Lucas County on March 9, 1869, and it became very active. They hosted a state suffrage convention in 1873. Members continually attempted to vote in local elections, and the group refused to participate in the 1876 centennial celebration because half of the citizenry of the United States was denied the vote. They also instituted their own paper, *The Ballot Box*. By 1870, Ohio had thirty-one suffrage associations. The Ohio Woman's Suffrage Association (OWSA) formed at this same time, but there were no annual meetings of the group until Mrs. Rebecca Janney of Columbus called a convention in 1884. The OWSA was officially formed in Painesville in May 1885, but it refused to affiliate with any national group because it hoped to maintain a nonpartisan stance.[13]

Another opportunity for change presented itself when another Ohio Constitutional Convention was announced for 1873–74. Once again women began a petition drive, this time collecting eight thousand signatures from thirty-three counties. They lobbied for the appointment of a Special Committee on Woman Suffrage, which was accomplished. The committee's recommendation to put an amendment forward was accepted, but the legislature defeated it 49–41. They also defeated the proposed constitution. This response would continue again in 1888, 1889, 1890, 1897, 1898, and 1900.

Even though the suffrage amendment was not successful, other attempts at political participation were. In 1884 and 1887, legislation was passed allowing married women the right to sue and be sued, and to have absolute control over all the property they owned whether obtained before or during the marriage. In 1893, married women could legally be named as guardians, and in 1897, the law allowed them to serve as executors of wills. By the end of the century, the law allowed the state to appoint female physicians at all state insane asylums and required all cities to employ police matrons. In 1898, however, the Ohio Supreme Court declared a law allowing women to be notary publics unconstitutional because women were not electors.[14]

By the end of the nineteenth century, many state legislatures passed laws allowing women to vote in school board elections. Society had long considered women to be the primary educators of children. Now that most children's education occurred outside the home, it was considered necessary for women to continue to be involved in the education of their children. This they could do as members of the school board. In 1894, Mrs. Caroline Everhard, Ohio Woman's Suffrage Association (OWSA) president, and Mrs. Katharine Claypole headed a petition drive and lobbying effort to obtain the right for women to vote in school board elections. These efforts paid off when the Ohio House and Senate voted in

Harriet Taylor Upton
(Ohio Historical Society)

favor of the legislation. A case challenging the law was brought forward in Hamilton County in 1895, but the Ohio Supreme Court ruled the law constitutional. There was an attempt to introduce legislation, in 1898, to repeal women's right to participate in school board elections, but the Ohio House voted against its repeal.[15]

Several Ohio women associated with the woman's suffrage cause participated in school board elections, either as candidates or supporters. Harriet Taylor Upton, OWSA president from 1899 to 1908 and 1911 to 1920, won election to the Warren School Board in 1898 and served on the board until 1913. Pauline Steinem, OWSA president from 1908 to 1911, served on the Toledo School Board from 1905 to 1909. Columbus attorney Dora Sandoe Bachman won election to the Columbus School Board in 1909 and remained a member of the board until 1917.[16] Participating in an election campaign for school board, either as a candidate or supporter, provided women with experience in canvassing, polling, public speaking, and registering voters—all skills they would need in their fight to obtain the right to vote in all elections.

Pauline Steinem (Ohio Historical Society)

With these successes under their belts but with the major prize eluding them, women in Ohio refocused their efforts under the direction of Harriet Taylor Upton. Upton was elected president of the Warren Suffrage Club in 1891, and served as treasurer of the National American Woman Suffrage Association from 1894 to 1910. Ohio suffragists elected her president of the Ohio Woman's Suffrage Association in 1899, and she remained in that position until 1908. She served again from 1911 to 1920. Because of her involvement, the national headquarters of the National American Woman Suffrage Association was housed in Warren at the courthouse from 1903 to 1910. Besides these many responsibilities, Upton also edited a suffrage paper, *Progress.*[17]

It became obvious to those involved in the struggle that more local suffrage clubs were needed. Outside organizers were brought in with great success. Annual conventions were held, but still there was little to cheer about. Suffrage amendments never made it out of committee, and low voter turnout at school elections played into the hands of those who wished to continue to deny women the right to vote. Suffrage activities received little press, and the majority of members resided in the northern part of the state. A change in tactics was necessary. Open-air meetings were held in Cincinnati and Cleveland. New groups appealing to different groups of women emerged.

Maude Wood Park, a Radcliffe graduate, and Inez Haynes organized the College Equal Suffrage League (CESL) in Boston in 1900. The purpose of the group was to attract middle-class, college women and alumnae to the suffrage movement. Delegates from eleven CESL organizations gathered in Buffalo, New York, in 1908 and formed the National College Equal Suffrage League. Bryn Mawr president M. Carey Thomas led the group, which headquartered in New York City. Park came to Ohio in January 1909, and within one month organized three CESL alumnae groups in Cleveland, Columbus, and Cincinnati. Groups of college women organized at Oberlin, Western Reserve University, the University of Cincinnati, and Ohio State University.[18] Activist Florence E. Allen was a member of the Cleveland College Equal Suffrage League. She organized a group of young college women to participate in trolley trips to surrounding counties during Ohio's 1912 suffrage campaign. The CESL became an integral component of the urban suffrage movement.[19]

Carrie Chapman Catt organized a Woman Suffrage Party (WSP) in New York City in October 1910. The WSP used a very formalized organizational structure that grouped members according to wards and assembly districts. Special suffrage schools taught potential leaders organizational methods. The executive committee of the OWSA, at a meeting in Cleveland in November 1910, voted to "recommend the Women Suffrage Party plan of organization to all existing suffrage clubs in Ohio at once and to put it into operation everywhere as fast as we can."[20] After the meeting, a group of Cleveland women met and voted to develop such an organization.

They called a meeting for 3:00 P.M. on December 1, 1910, appointed a nominating committee to secure candidates willing to

Woman suffrage headquarters, Cleveland, summer 1912 (Ohio Historical Society)

run for office, and, at the meeting, organized a forty-five member committee to find women to serve as ward leaders and precinct captains. The group's goal was to "form an army rank and file and march solidly into the camp of the enemy, capturing said enemy and afterward conferring him to the woman's cause."[21] By October 1911, the Woman Suffrage Party of Greater Cleveland was Ohio's largest suffrage group, with more than one thousand members. This tremendous growth in membership was due, for the most part, to the hard work of Zora Dupont, who was the chief organizer for Cleveland's WSP from 1910 to 1914.[22]

Some suffrage clubs during this time attempted to include African American women in the suffrage movement. In 1903, Mrs. William Kline, president of the Lucas County Suffrage Association, organized a "colored woman suffrage club" This was the only

African American women's suffrage club in the state, and the OWSA gave it a "hardy welcome."[23] Though difficult to accomplish at the beginning of the twentieth century, the OWSA tried to be inclusive of black women who supported the suffrage cause. The OWSA parade committee, which was organizing Ohio's first woman suffrage parade on August 27, 1912, in Columbus, voted to integrate the county delegations instead of having a separate unit of black marchers. Black suffragists also entered two floats in the parade. In Dayton, during the 1912 campaign, suffragists spoke to black congregations and other organizations to gain support for their cause.[24] However, for most African American women, given the segregationist mentality and activities still present in this country, the woman's suffrage movement remained a predominantly white, middle-class movement that did not address the issues of racism and segregation present in society.

Between 1910 and 1920, a growing optimism among state suffragists allowed for a shift toward focusing on grassroots political activities. Another constitutional convention was slated for 1911–12, and the strategy for this assault was put forward by Harriet Taylor Upton. The city organizations were to be revitalized, the rural areas were to be saturated with the message concerning suffrage, and each candidate for legislative office would be asked his position on suffrage. Florence Allen, a Cleveland attorney, visited sixty-six of the eighty-eight counties during the summer of 1911. She and others spoke before farmers' groups and union locals. The Ohio Men's League for Woman Suffrage helped to interview legislative candidates. Emmeline and Sylvia Pankhurst, British suffragettes, visited the state.

At the start of the constitutional convention, it was determined that 56 of the 119 delegates favored suffrage. An Equal Suffrage and Elective Franchise Committee was appointed with William Kilpatrick, a known suffrage supporter, as chair. This committee began hearings on January 31, 1912. The convention president, Herbert Bigelow, was also a suffrage supporter. Registered lobbyists Elizabeth J. Hauser and Mrs. Myron Vorce worked endless hours visiting undecided delegates and legislators. The signs of a victory were promising. The convention voted on March 7, 1912, to let the electorate decide whether or not the clause "white male" should be eliminated from Section One, Article V of the 1850 Ohio Constitution. This amendment would be number twenty-three of forty-one presented to the voters.

The real battle was now underway. With only $23 in its treasury, the Ohio Woman's Suffrage Association began a fund-raising campaign—with limited success. Professional organizers such as Florence Allen, Zora Dupont, and Elizabeth Hauser canvassed the state. Fifty out-of-state suffragists arrived to help. Suffragists held open-air meetings throughout the state. A huge suffrage parade was held in Columbus, where integrated county delegations marched four thousand strong. Supporters printed and distributed thousands of pieces of literature to counteract the antisuffrage materials, and a well-publicized debate between Florence Allen and Lucy Price took place at the Men's City Club in Cleveland and was repeated at Gray's Armory.

Women were active throughout the state. In May 1912, Cincinnati women formed the Cincinnati Woman Suffrage Party. This caused some dissension between the new group and the Central Suffrage Committee, but by July the groups had "buried the hatchet," and the WSP took the lead in sponsoring events. The WSP of Montgomery County held its first meeting on June 11, 1912, and it immediately divided the city into districts, named district leaders, and appointed various working committees. Members elected Mrs. Oscar Davisson president of the group, a position she maintained until 1920.[25]

All this work, however, did not bring victory. On September 3, 1912, only one congressional district passed the amendment. Twenty-four counties, located in the northwest, northeast, and north, passed the amendment, but it failed in a popular vote of 249,420 to 336,875. However, the suffrage supporters were not disheartened. Harriet Taylor Upton, who led this struggle, summed up the feelings of many when she said:

It was the most remarkable campaign I have ever had anything to do with and I have financed a goodly number for
the National Association and know the workings of the
same. The splendid loyalty which all our women showed towards each other and the admiration, the courage which
they displayed at defeat; the amount of work which they put
in under circumstances which were not pleasant, surpassed
anything which has ever come under my observation.

I feel that if this campaign did nothing else and it did much
else, it showed us what the real womanhood of the state of
Ohio is and it also showed where women will stand and what
they will do when they come into their inheritance.[26]

Work began immediately on the next assault. A weekly publication focusing on suffrage, *Everywoman,* began publication in
Columbus. Local organizations continued fund-raising and increasing the number of members. Movement leaders decided that
a new tactic would be used this time. Instead of trying to have an
amendment adopted, the suffrage leaders decided to work through
the referendum process. The suffrage workers needed to gather
130,000 signatures in order to place an issue before the voters as a
referendum. Suffrage supporters were able to gather 131,271 signatures. The OWSA declared May 2, 1914, Woman Suffrage Day.
They organized a "pilgrimage" to Salem for June and held a massive suffrage parade in Cleveland on October 3, 1914.[27] The WSP of
Greater Cleveland attempted to attract new groups to the cause.
They opened a lunchroom in their downtown headquarters and
served inexpensive lunches in hopes of bringing working women
to the cause. They also organized auxiliary groups among Hungarian and Polish women, professional women, and even a junior
auxiliary for children.[28]

The main opponent of the referendum, the U.S. Brewers Association, helped it go down to defeat. Members of the U.S. Brewers
Association in Ohio stood to lose a great deal of money if the state

went "dry," and since the late nineteenth century, opponents of prohibition had tied woman suffrage and prohibition together—a logical assumption, since the Women's Christian Temperance Union supported woman suffrage. In 1912, the liquor industry used the slogan "Vote for Woman Suffrage and Help Make Ohio Dry," to deter voters and spent $620,000 to defeat the amendment.[29] The battle continued in 1914. Ohio's Prohibition Party endorsed the referendum, and subsequently opponents linked it to the Anti-Saloon League. The antiliquor groups promised the suffragists that there would be no prohibition campaign in 1914, and therefore the liquor industry could not tie the two causes together so readily. However, the U.S. Brewers Association began a petition drive asking Ohio voters to approve amendments that would permit "home rule" for cities on the question of liquor and abolish the county local option law. The antiliquor forces now felt compelled to organize a statewide campaign for prohibition, once again linking woman suffrage and prohibition and sealing the fate of the woman suffrage referendum.[30]

During this debate, other events around the country and around the world were capturing the nation's interest. Across the Atlantic, Europe found itself embroiled in "the war to end all wars." However, World War I, unlike the Civil War, did not stop the suffrage activity. In fact, the war added a new dimension to the effort and seemed to help it pick up momentum. Woman's suffrage groups were placing an increased emphasis on efforts at the national level, and an attempt to pass an amendment allowing for presidential suffrage (which would allow women to vote only in the presidential election) was garnering support. Ohio governor Frank Willis and perennial presidential candidate William Jennings Bryan supported such an amendment. The Reynolds Bill, allowing presidential suffrage, was introduced in the Ohio House and passed 72–50 on February 1, 1917. It passed the Ohio Senate on February 15, 1917, and was signed by Governor Cox on February 21, 1917. This victory was short-lived, however. A ruling by Ohio's attorney general allowed the issue to be submitted to the voters via an initiative petition, if petitioners filed the requisite number of signatures by May 20, 1917. The required signatures were collected, though a court battle soon followed over charges of fraudulent signatures. The state held a referendum on November 6, 1917, and the voters defeated presidential suffrage 568,382 to 422,262.

Suffragists in other states were more successful. In Illinois, suffragists campaigned successfully for a state constitutional amendment granting presidential suffrage to women in 1913. This amendment also granted statewide municipal suffrage to women. In 1917, North Dakota, Nebraska, Michigan, Rhode Island, and Indiana passed presidential suffrage amendments, and during the fall of 1918, South Dakota, Michigan, and Oklahoma were added to the list.[31]

Suffrage supporters, both in Ohio and throughout the nation, would not be stopped. Work for a federal amendment was moving forward. Suffrage was now a nonpartisan political issue. Both major parties had declared themselves in favor of suffrage in 1916. President Woodrow Wilson also supported the so-called Susan B. Anthony amendment, and on January 10, 1918, the U.S. House of Representatives voted 274 to 135 in favor of the amendment—one vote over the needed two-thirds. Only eight of Ohio's twenty representatives voted favorably.

The vote in the Senate was also expected to be close. Ohio's Senator Atlee Pomerene from Canton was opposed to the amendment. Senator Warren Harding from Marion held a meeting to discuss the issue with those interested. The Senate's vote was scheduled for October 1, 1918. President Wilson addressed the Senate on September 30, asking them to pass the amendment. The vote fell short of the needed two-thirds majority by two votes.

On February 5, 1919, the Ohio Legislature passed a resolution calling upon Senator Pomerene to change his antisuffrage vote, but Harriet Taylor Upton summed up the suffragists' views on Pomerene:

Ohio women feel that the Democratic Senator from Ohio has been the one man who has retarded the passage of the national suffrage amendment. He could no more be elected Senator today from the state of Ohio, if women voted, than he could fly and I have been wondering if anybody could tell him this. This is not anything to threaten him [with], this is not a promise that he would be elected if he would vote for it ... but it is perfectly safe to say that unless he votes for this amendment in this Congress, his days, politically, are numbered in Ohio.[32]

The amendment was defeated once again on February 10, 1919, by one vote. The Sixty-sixth Congress convened in special session on May 20, 1919, to once again consider the issue. The U.S. House passed the amendment, this time with only two Ohio representatives voting against it. On June 4, 1919, the roll call was held in the U.S. Senate with a vote of 66–30 in favor, thus sending the amendment to the states to be ratified. Harriet Taylor Upton was an observer in the Senate that day and years later she recalled:

As I rose to go with my companions, I thought how strange it is that my life battle is over and I am not moved. . . . I walked up the stairs leading to the hallway and Mrs. LaFollette reached her hand over the railing which separated her from me and said most feelingly, "Well, well, you were here to see it." I burst into tears and had to go stand by the window, look out at the Potomac and the trees and the flowers before I could trust myself to join the others. I wouldn't have had anybody know for the world that I cried. Why are people ashamed of tears? Twenty-five years or more fighting nearly every day. Not now and then but always; and fighting for a great principle. I remembered so well my first suffrage day and recalled those who were then with me. And now for different reasons I was alone. Why shouldn't there be tears? My later thought, however, was my best thought and it was a thought of joy. Joy that at last men and women together would fight on together and never again be separated as they had been separated in the past.[33]

The amendment was sent to Ohio for ratification on June 16, 1919. The Ohio House passed it 73–6 and the Ohio Senate passed it 27–3. Ohio was the fifth state to ratify the amendment. The legislature also passed the Reynolds-Fouts Presidential Suffrage Bill, ensuring that Ohio women would be able to vote in 1920 if the needed thirty-six states had not been obtained.[34] On August 25, 1919, Tennessee, through the lobbying efforts of Harriet Taylor Upton, became the thirty-sixth state to ratify the Susan B. Anthony amendment. The last one hundred years of work, by both Ohio women and scores of others, had finally borne fruit. Women were now allowed to vote.

Women activists in Ohio did not stop their demand for equal rights with the passage of the Nineteenth Amendment. Some women shifted their energies to the formal political arena, deciding to run for political office. Many others continued their activities by forming or joining civic organizations that had progressive political agendas.

Carrie Chapman Catt formed one such group, the League of Women Voters, in 1920, from the National American Woman Suffrage Association, an organization whose job was now complete. The league supported progressive reform legislation, believing that "women would bring a nurturing sensibility and reforming vision into the political arena."[35] Members worked within a broad range of reform organizations. The first tasks of the league nationwide were to educate voters and convince women to become engaged in the political process by voting. It held massive voter registration drives throughout the country. In April 1920, the Cleveland chapter was founded when the Cuyahoga County Woman's Suffrage party voted to disband. Belle Sherwin, a leader of the Cleveland League, announced a drive to register 50,000 women voters, and by the end of October 1920, 41,416 women were registered. The membership elected Sherwin as president of the National League of Women Voters in 1924, a position she would retain until 1934.[36]

Cleveland's League of Women Voters continued to support progressive reform legislation, fighting for a city manager plan as well as working for federal legislation dealing with child labor, a state minimum wage, and strict school attendance policies. Cleveland's league was the first to poll political candidates on the issues and publish their responses—an activity that would become common practice around the country.[37]

World peace was an issue central to many women's groups during the early twentieth century. Peace activists believed that women's perspectives as mothers, people who knew the value of life, needed to be heard in the international arena. After World War I, the League of Women Voters began to cooperate with the Women's International League for Peace and Freedom, the Women's Joint Congressional Committee, and the Daughters of the American Revolution to oppose militarism. However, the United States War Department began a red-baiting campaign against the Women's International League for Peace and Freedom in 1922, forcing women's groups to withdraw their support of this group. The League of Women Voters, under the direction of Carrie Chapman Catt, developed a new coalition with the American Association of University Women, the General Federation of Women's Clubs, the Young Women's Christian Association, and the Women's Christian Temperance Union to work for world peace.[38] The Cleveland league participated in a peace march in downtown Cleveland in 1924 with the Cleveland sections of these other groups.

Women in cities and counties throughout Ohio also joined in league activities. Some communities, like Norwalk, formed leagues in the 1920s. League members unanimously elected Marguerite Morris Rice Stewart director of the Ohio League of Women Voters in 1924, and she served as a delegate to nearly every league convention in the 1920s.[39] Other communities formed leagues throughout the next fifty years as need and interest arose, many not forming until the 1960s and 1970s. The League of Women Voters, through nonpartisan political activity, continues to take an active role in encouraging women to be involved in politics by voting and running for political office.

Another group formed prior to the passage of the Nineteenth Amendment was the Ohio Consumers' League. The National Consumers' League (NCL), formed in 1890 by Florence Kelley, a worker at Hull House, dedicated itself to improving the working conditions of women and children. The NCL sponsored a "white label" campaign, whereby manufacturers who met the NCL's standard could use NCL labels on their clothes. The organization's members also fought for maximum hour and minimum wage laws.[40] The Consumers' League of Ohio, founded at Goodrich House in Cleveland, affiliated with the NCL in 1900. This group intensified its political activities after the suffrage amendment was passed, becoming very active during the Great Depression. Elizabeth Magee, executive director of the Consumers' League of Ohio from 1925 to 1965, played an extensive role in shaping that organization's policy, both in the state and across the country. Under Magee's leadership, the Consumers' League of Ohio drew up a plan dealing with unemployment insurance, which became known as the Ohio Plan. Because of this work, Governor George White appointed Magee to the Ohio Commission on Unemployment Insurance in 1931, and to the National Committee on Economic Security in 1934. She continued her reform work at the national level in 1941, when President Franklin D. Roosevelt appointed her to the Women's Bureau of the Department of Labor. Her activities with the Consumers' League, however, did not end. She was general secretary of the National Consumers' League from 1943 to 1958 and also served as a lobbyist for the league. She fought for national health insurance as a member of President Truman's Commission on the Health Needs of the Nation.[41]

Many women chose to become politically active through women's clubs and civic organizations. For some it seemed a more acceptable way of entering the political arena—an alternative to running for office themselves. For others, these groups were a springboard into political office—a means of gaining political experience and supporters. Many of these organizations were founded well before the passage of suffrage and continued their "political" activities beyond suffrage in 1920.

Women concerned about the welfare of Cincinnati's citizens established the Cincinnati Woman's Club in 1894. In 1897, the organization formed a civic department that studied issues such as city charters, voting qualifications, and election procedures. In order to focus more directly on civic issues, reform-minded members established the Woman's City Club on March 6, 1915, with the intent "to establish a broad acquaintance among women through the common aim of service to their city; to provide a central meeting place where members may meet informally, and to establish an open forum for the discussion of all ideas of civic import."[42] The open forum concept, along with educating women on the issues, helped women develop the skills that would help them in the political arena.

The Woman's City Club (WCC) also helped to organize a movement to get mothers of school-age children to vote in school board elections in 1917 and 1919. It was the WCC's general policy to endorse not candidates but issues. Prior to 1913, there were no independent nonpartisan tickets for board of education elections—party machines elected the candidates. Election reforms took place in 1913, mandating that all candidates for school boards must be nominated by petition, and in 1913 and 1915, nonpartisan candidates stood for citywide election. However, in 1917 and 1919, there were attempts to return to the pre-1913 situation. The WCC, fearful that political parties were again trying to control the school board elections, asked its members to make an exception to its policy and support the nonpartisan tickets. In both elections, women overwhelmingly voted for the nonpartisan candidates.[43]

Through this struggle "to free the public education system from . . . the deleterious influence of ward politics based on the national political parties," women gained the skills necessary to run the

Cincinnati Charter Reform Movement.[44] An attempt to adopt a city charter based on municipal home rule and nonpartisan elections failed in 1914, but the movement did not die. In 1916, the WCC examined the issues involved in the proposed reforms and published its findings in the July/August *Bulletin* of 1916. In December 1916, the committee working on the new charter asked the WCC to participate, which they did. The voters adopted a new charter incorporating home rule in 1917, but it was not the version advocated by reformers. This did not deter the WCC. They began to investigate the possibility of holding nonpartisan elections.[45]

Ironically, even though the WCC was in the forefront of municipal reform, its membership was not open to everyone. African American women were not accepted as members until 1948. This exclusion did not sit well with all members, and the WCC revisited its position on this issue often. Because of this exclusion and a different civic agenda, African American women founded their own groups to support the needs of their community members. Essie Wooten was one of the founders of the Massillon Urban League and served as its president for many years. Bertha V. Moore of Summit County started the Tea Time Study Club. This organization sought commitments from local candidates on issues such as improved public accommodations and job opportunities in turn for the club's endorsement. The club also provided opportunities for candidates to appear before various community groups so that the candidates could be questioned about their views on improving public accommodations and job opportunities for Summit County blacks.[46]

While most politically active women confined their endeavors to the ballot box or civic organizations, a few women did venture into the political arena as office seekers. The first office available to Ohio women was a position on the local school board, and the highest percentage of female officeholders in the state were in these positions. Elizabeth Folger was elected to the Massillon Board of Education in 1895. Several women who would go on to be municipal and state office holders gained their initial political experience as school board members. In 1911, Edith Campbell became the first woman in Cincinnati to hold such an office. Campbell later became the director of the Ohio Vocation Bureau and in 1913 became a member of the Ohio State School Survey Commission. In 1933, Governor White appointed her to serve as the first woman trustee of Ohio State University. Others, like Evelyn E. Jenkins, made service to the local schools their lifetime endeavor. Jenkins served on the Macedonia School Board from 1920 to 1931 and served as its clerk from 1932 to 1941.[47]

Some women, such as Anne Case of Tallmadge and Norma Wulff of Cleveland, found themselves elected to leadership positions on their respective school boards. Case served as the first female president of the Tallmadge School Board for ten years and retired in 1957 after serving a total of twenty-four years. Clevelanders elected Wulff as the first woman president of the Cleveland School Board in 1937. Helen Arnold was the first black woman elected to the Akron Board of Education in 1978, and she eventually served as its president.[48] Mary B. Martin, a schoolteacher in Cleveland, became the first black woman elected to the Cleveland School Board in 1929. She was re-elected for a four-year term in 1933 and ran again in 1939, an election she won easily over her two male opponents. However, she died of a cerebral hemorrhage before resuming her duties for the term beginning in 1940.[49]

City and municipal offices, particularly city council positions, also held opportunities for women wishing to hold political office. In Cincinnati, ten women ran for city council seats in 1921, and two were elected—Dr. Bertha C. Lietze and Connie F. McCloskey. Elizabeth Cassatt Reid was elected in 1943, but from 1931 to 1961 the Republican party in Cincinnati did not run a single woman for city council. Dorothy Nichols Dolbey began her long political career as a council member. She was elected in 1953 and immediately chosen as vice mayor. The following year she became acting mayor, and served as chair of the Cincinnati City Council's City Planning and Boundaries Committee, along with serving on various other council committees throughout her career.[50]

Other communities also began electing women to council positions. Munroe Falls Village elected Julia Cowas as a city council member in 1927, and Mary Hartzell was elected treasurer in 1932. Tenth Ward voters in Akron placed Virginia Etheredge in office in 1938, over widely known labor leader Roy F. Wilkins. She won her Tenth Ward seat by winning the support of factory workers in her district and with the support of Labor's Nonpartisan League. She was re-elected and served until 1946. She became known as the "Tenth Ward Terror" because she was outspoken on civic issues, particularly those that had an impact on the relationship between employees and employers. She believed that Akron's city council must work out a plan to prevent labor violence in the city. Marie Wing and Isabelle Alexander announced their candidacies in Cleveland on August 20, 1920 — the day the suffrage amendment was passed — but both lost that election. Wing, the director of the Ohio Consumers' League, became the first woman elected to Cleveland City Council in 1923 and was re-elected in 1925. Women gradually increased their representation on that city council. By 1957, Cleveland voters elected six women (out of thirty-three seats) to city council positions — the most ever seated at one time. Three of these women were veterans of the council: Margaret McCaffery, Mary K. Sotak, and Jean Murrell Capers. McCaffery, elected in 1947, served until 1973. Sotak was elected in 1947 and retired in 1959, after being chair of the Parks and Recreation Committee. Capers, the first African American woman to sit on Cleveland City Council, served from 1949 to 1959.[51] Many other cities did not elect women council members until the 1970s and 1980s.

Other city offices also began to open up to women. In 1914, Dolly Spencer of Milford, Ohio, was the first woman in the United States to serve as a chief of police. Bernice Secrest Pyke was the first woman in Cleveland to be a member of the mayor's cabinet. She served as welfare director for Cleveland from 1923 to 1933. In 1934, President Franklin D. Roosevelt named Pyke a United States collector of customs. Amy Kankoner from Fairport Harbor became Ohio's first woman mayor in 1921. Forty years later, Albina Cermak became the first Cleveland woman to run for mayor, but she lost to Anthony J. Celebrezze. Mary Paul ran for mayor of Akron in 1929 but dropped out of the race. Catherine R. Dobbs was more successful in her quest, serving three terms as Barberton's first female mayor from 1956 through 1961.[52]

Even before the passage of the suffrage amendment, women were holding some offices at the county and township level. In 1866 and 1868, Emily Bronson Conger was elected deputy county treasurer of Summit County.[53] But even more opportunities opened up for women after the passage of the Nineteenth Amendment. Mary Kennedy of Boston Township served as its township clerk from 1922 to 1924. For some women this position became a lifetime commitment. Helen M. Schrader served as Springfield Township clerk from 1956 to 1992. Women also served as county treasurers, auditors, finance directors, and even justices of the peace. Margaret Conger of Boston Township served as justice of the peace beginning in 1922, as did Allison D. Houssley in Portage Township. Alison Price served as constable for Northampton Township from 1938 to 1947. Still others served as county court clerks. Mabel Marsh of Lorain County was elected in 1931, and Verna M. Shoemaker in Clark County was elected in 1934. In 1988, Florence C. Lenahan, M.D., of Delaware County, was the first woman in Ohio to be elected to the office of county coroner. She served as a mounted deputy sheriff for the Franklin County Sheriff's Department and became the first woman elected to the Columbus Society for the Scientific Detection of Crime. Katherine M. Crumbley of Belmont County was the first Ohio woman elected county sheriff, a position she held from 1977 to 1981.

Most of the political offices held by women in Ohio and nation-wide have been at the local level—city, county, or township. In 1922, Ohioans elected six women to the state legislature, four to the House and two to the Senate. Nettie Mackenzie Clapp from Cuyahoga County served three successive terms in the Ohio House, and Maude Comstock Waitt served four terms in the Ohio Senate, retiring in 1930. However, the first woman elected as the president pro tem of the Ohio Senate was Margaret Mahoney in 1949.[54]

A few women were able to complete long and successful careers in government at the state level. In 1976, Ethel G. Swanbeck became the first woman to serve in the Ohio House for ten consecutive terms (1955–76). Anna F. O'Neil was the first woman to serve in the Ohio House of Representative for ten terms, but only nine of those were consecutive (1932–34; 1937–54). While in office, she wrote Ohio's minimum wage law covering women and minors in industry, coauthored a bill during the Depression that allowed the state to provide matching funds to cities to buy food for the needy, and helped to organize the National Order of Woman Legislators. She also served as chair of the House Finance Committee. Blanche Eugenie Bruot Hower, who defeated O'Neil in 1934, was known as the "Mother of the Ninety-first General Assembly." In time, women did move into leadership positions in the legislature. Democrats elected Representative Francine M. Panshal majority whip in 1978, and Republicans elected Representative Dona K. Pope minority whip.[55]

During the last three decades of the twentieth century, women began to hold executive positions in state government. Gertrude W. Donahey was elected state treasurer in 1970, becoming the first woman to be elected to a state office. In 1994, Nancy Putnam Hollister, a former mayor of Marietta, became the first woman lieutenant governor and governor; Betty Montgomery became the state's first female attorney general (December 28, 1998–January 11, 1999); and JoAnn Davidson became the first woman Speaker of the House.[56]

Women also moved slowly into positions in the judicial branch of government, often serving in a capacity that allowed them to work with women and children. Mary Belle Grossman was elected a municipal court judge in Cleveland in 1923, a position she held until 1959. In 1926, she organized and headed a morals court that was to hear cases regarding domestic violence, vice, and prostitution. She was one of the first two women admitted to the American Bar Association in 1918.

Gertrude Donahey and JoAnn Davidson, ca. 1995 (Ohio Historical Society)

A leader for women in the Ohio judicial system was Florence E. Allen, a suffrage advocate and lawyer. Allen was appointed assistant county prosecutor in Cuyahoga County and was the first woman admitted to the Ohio Bar Association in 1919. In 1920, she was elected to the common pleas court, thus becoming the first woman in the United States to be elected to a judgeship. She was

*Supporters of Judge Florence Allen's bid for the United States
Senate, 1926 (Ohio Historical Society)*

elected to the Ohio Supreme Court in both 1922 and 1928, the first
woman in the United States to serve in such an office. Franklin D.
Roosevelt, in 1934, appointed her to the United States Sixth Circuit
Court of Appeals in Cincinnati, where she presided over the de-
cision regarding the constitutionality of the Tennessee Valley
Authority.[57]

The types of judgeships women were appointed and/or elected
to began to change in the 1980s and 1990s. Joyce George served as
a judge in the Ninth District Court of Appeals from 1981 to 1990.
Governor James Rhodes named Ann Aldrich the first woman
judge in northern Ohio's Federal district in 1980.[58]

Very few Ohio women have served in elected federal offices. Victoria Claflin Woodhull, who lived in Canton for several years, was
the first woman to run for president of the United States. She did

so in 1872, nominated by the Equal Rights Party. Not only was she defeated, but she was also threatened with imprisonment for her illegal candidacy (women were excluded from running for office) and for attempting to vote in the election. Ohio's first woman to serve in the U.S. House of Representatives was Frances Payne Bolton from Cleveland. Bolton inherited her husband's seat in 1939. She subsequently won the seat on her own and retained it until 1968. She gained an expertise in foreign affairs and in 1953 became the first congresswoman to be appointed to the United Nations General Assembly. Ohio voters did not elect another woman to represent them in the U.S. House until 1976, when Mary Rose Oakar, a former Cleveland City Council member, won a seat. She served until 1992, when she was defeated after allegations of impropriety.[59]

Some women did receive state and federal appointments, as noted with Judge Florence Allen, Judge Genevieve Rose Cline, Bernice Secrest Pyke, and Elizabeth Magee. Maud McQuate was appointed to the Cleveland Civil Service Commission by the mayor of Cleveland in 1935, and the governor made her the first female member of the Ohio Liquor Commission. In 1949, Governor Lausche appointed Representative Anna O'Neil to the Ohio Children and Youth Commission. He named Margaret Mahoney director for the Department of Industrial Relations of Ohio in 1953, and she served in that position through 1957. Governor Michael DiSalle appointed Frances McGovern to the Ohio Public Utilities Commission in 1960 and reappointed her in 1961 for a six-year term, the first woman in the United States to receive such an appointment. Other women receiving federal appointments were Zelma W. George, delegate to the United Nations General Assembly in 1960, and Donna M. Pope, director of the United States Mint in 1981.[60] In 1993 Cleveland native Donna Edna Shalala was selected by President Bill Clinton to be Secretary of Health and Human Services. Women's appointments at the state and federal level continued to grow as the twenty-first century approached.

Women's participation and growing leadership in the two domi-

Ohio Council of Republican Women, May 1928 (Ohio Historical Society)

nant political parties reflected their gains in political and appointed offices. Mrs. Effie Rheinoche organized the Democratic women in Massillon, while Mrs. Hale Richter organized the Massillon Women's Republican Club. Lethia C. Fleming became a leading figure in the Cleveland Republican party and the African American community. She campaigned in 1920, 1924, 1928, and 1936 for Republican presidential candidates, served on the Cuyahoga County Republican Executive Committee, and organized the National Association of Republican Women. Albina Cermak served as a Republican precinct committeewoman from 1925 to 1953 and on the County Board of Elections from 1948 to 1953. She also served as a delegate to the Republican National Convention in 1940, 1944, and 1952. Harriet Taylor Upton from Warren served as the vice chair of the Republican National Committee in 1920, the first woman in the United States to hold such a position with any political party.

Katherine Kennedy Brown served as the Republican National Committeewoman for Ohio for more than thirty-five years, beginning in 1932. She was vice chair of the Republican National Committee from 1949 to 1952. She served as a delegate to the Republican National Convention in 1932, 1944, 1948, 1952, 1956, 1960, and 1964. She was the only woman named to the National Strategy Committee in 1944, 1948, and 1952.[61]

Bernice Secrest Pyke became the first woman, in 1920, to be chosen as a delegate to the Democratic National Convention. Frances McGovern was elected a delegate to the Democratic National Convention in 1960 and 1964. In 1960, Democratic party leaders named her the Ohio Democratic Woman of the Year. Jane Quine, chair of the Summit County Democratic party in 1991, coordinated John Seiberling's campaign in 1974, and chaired the mayoral and congressional campaigns of Tom Sawyer in 1983 and 1986.[62]

Women's political participation, either as officeholders or voters, did not guarantee equal treatment for women. Legislative and executive action continued throughout the twentieth century to protect women's rights. In 1923, the Ohio Constitution was amended to permit women to qualify as electors, making them eligible to serve on juries. In 1965, the Ohio General Assembly authorized the Legislative Services Commission to make a comprehensive study of the status of women in Ohio. Governor James Rhodes created the Ohio Governor's Committee on the Status of Women on March 30, 1966. In response to this report and federal legislation, the Ohio General Assembly passed House Bill 610 in 1973, prohibiting discrimination on the basis of sex in employment, public accommodations, and housing. During the same year, Elizabeth Boyer and Audrey Matesich organized Ohio's Coalition Plan to gain ratification of the Equal Rights Amendment. Ohio ratified the amendment in 1974, but it died in 1979 when the required number of states needed to ratify it did not materialize.[63]

Toledo native Gloria Steinem strove to bring to the attention of the American public the inequalities faced by women. Steinem, along with Betty Friedan, Bella Abzug, and Shirley Chisholm, founded the National Women's Political Caucus in July 1971. They hoped to provide a political forum for the issues facing women and to provide monetary support for female candidates running for political office. President Jimmy Carter appointed Steinem in 1977 as one of the commissioners to the national committee on the Observance of International Women's Year.

Ohio's women continued to strive to participate in the political arena. The 123rd General Assembly in 2000 included twenty-three women out of ninety-nine members in the Ohio House of Representatives and three senators out of thirty-three in the Ohio Senate. Women from Ohio occupied three out of the state's nineteen seats in the U.S. House of Representatives.

Ohio's women continue to play a significant role in addressing the economic and social issues facing Ohio, through their presence on boards, commissions, and task forces, both at the local and state levels. The desire to continually improve their communities is still as much a motivating factor for women's involvement as it was in the nineteenth and twentieth centuries.Throughout the state's history, Ohio's women have committed their time, energy and expertise to advancing the good of its citizens through political participation. As we move into the twenty-first century, women will continue to play a prominent role in state and national political life.

CHAPTER FOUR

Ohio's Benevolent Women

SOCIETY'S EXPECTATIONS DEFINED women's role in the nineteenth century. Women were to remain in the private sphere of the home—raising children, tending to domestic duties, and maintaining the moral fiber of America. But these expectations, along with the religious fervor that gripped Americans during the early nineteenth century, actually propelled women into the public sphere, albeit through church and charitable activities.

The second Great Awakening, a period of revivals beginning in the late eighteenth century and lasting about fifty years, was at its peak in the 1820s, in towns in upper New York. During this revival movement, women participated in greater numbers than men, and the theological doctrines put forth by revivalist preachers reflected women's concerns and attitudes. Several preachers, such as the Reverend Charles G. Finney, came from New York to Ohio, carrying their message of universal salvation and forgiveness. This message embodied the feminine values honored by society—loving, forgiving, suffering, and sacrificing for others.[1]

Women, like most converts, felt compelled to express their new faith through the practice of good works, thus hoping to convert others. Both men and women formed national (and local) benevolent societies and reform groups. These groups, based on Christian morality and duty, led women outside the home and into a more public arena that would provide them with opportunities to form networks with other women and develop organizational skills.[2] As the revivalist spirit began to lessen in the 1830s, women took their newly developed skills, experience, and values into a more secular arena, led by women who maintained the moral fervor and religious tone of the second Great Awakening.

Ohio's women experienced this call to reform society. Many of the activities women became involved with related to the well-being of women and children. As more people moved into growing urban areas, societal problems—unemployment, overcrowding, lack of affordable housing, poverty, and alcoholism—increased. Women took it upon themselves, as an extension of their domestic role, to help alleviate these problems through church organizations and, in time, secular groups. Women in Ohio also responded to political crises of the day. However, by becoming involved in issues such as abolition and temperance, they were much more likely to receive society's criticism and condemnation.

The antislavery issue was one that continued to become more controversial as the nineteenth century progressed. With the abolition of slavery in the northern states, there was a growing sentiment that slavery was morally wrong. Antislavery societies enlisted members, and women joined in record numbers. As the antislavery movement grew, so did the moral indignation of its members. Most antislavery groups became abolitionist in nature, demanding the immediate freeing of the slaves with no monetary remuneration to their owners. The American Colonization Society, whose solution to slavery was to free all slaves in the United States and transport them to their own colony or country, founded branches in Warren, Cleveland, and Ravenna in 1826. These groups included both men and women. In Cincinnati, women's and children's auxiliaries were formed.[3]

As the number of antislavery societies grew, women became a significant segment of the membership and in some instances formed their own organizations, such as the Cleveland Anti-Slavery Society, formed in 1833. Opportunities for leadership and the development of the skills necessary for such leadership became available when they formed their own organizations. Several women who took the lead in Ohio's antislavery movement stepped into other political arenas, such as temperance and women's rights, after gaining experience in the antislavery movement.

Betsey Mix Cowles was one such woman. She helped to form the Ashtabula Female Anti-Slavery Society and served as its secretary in 1835. She also served as the corresponding secretary for the Austinburg Female Anti-Slavery group. Cowles urged women throughout Ashtabula County not only to form township societies, but also to work together under one county banner. She helped coordinate the numerous small groups and sometimes helped them obtain speakers for their meetings. She also circulated a petition calling for immediate emancipation of all slaves. The petition was to be submitted to the Ohio Anti-Slavery Society (OASS) meeting in Granville, Ohio, on April 27–28, 1836. Of the twelve female antislavery groups attending the OASS meeting, the Ashtabula County Female Society was the largest, with 437 members. The Ashtabula group was also the second-largest antislavery society in the state. The next largest women's society was the one in Portage County, with 300 members.[4]

In the early 1840s, Cowles became involved with the antislavery movement on a national level. She became one of the group's preeminent speakers, drawing praise wherever she spoke. Frederick Douglass suggested Cowles as a suitable person for the position of female agent to head an antislavery office in Rochester, New York, and abolitionist educators offered her a seminary teaching position in Iowa to "sow the seeds" of the antislavery movement. But many Americans weren't ready to accept a woman in such a public leadership role. Female abolitionist speakers often faced ridicule for daring to step out of the domestic sphere. Speaking in public and in front of mixed audiences was seen by many as shocking behavior. Other female speakers were criticized for traveling unchaperoned, or for traveling with men who were not relatives. When Cowles returned to Ohio, she organized antislavery fairs in 1846, 1847, and 1849 to raise needed funds. She realized the necessity of such endeavors, but constantly reminded society members that their main goal was to agitate collectively on behalf of the slaves.

She again served as secretary of the Ashtabula County Female Anti-Slavery Society and was appointed to the Western Anti-Slavery Society Business Committee in 1848. In 1849, she became its recording secretary.[5]

Funds from the Ashtabula County Female Anti-Slavery Society financed the paper *Plea for the Oppressed*, a monthly publication that appeared from December 1846 to February 1847. Cowles edited and Jane Elizabeth Hitchcock Jones published the paper. In it, Cowles questioned the motive of those in Ohio who professed to support emancipation but denied 25,000 free blacks the right to vote. She also condemned the Ohio Legislature for listening to the neighboring slave states and denying free blacks the right to vote.[6]

Even the most progressive communities did not always welcome outside agitators. Salem, Ohio, a Quaker community, was the home of a number of strong antislavery proponents. However, when Abby Kelly, a national antislavery speaker, came to Salem, along with William Lloyd Garrison, Frederick Douglass, and Giles Stibbens, she was denied access to the largest church in Salem. The trustees were blunt: "We think the principles of the lecturer are dangerous to our common country." So a tent was pitched in the south end of town for the speakers and their audience, and the lecture was held without incident.[7]

Jane Hitchcock and Benjamin Smith Jones came to Ohio in 1845, after a lecture tour in the East, to organize antislavery societies. At the time she came to Ohio, at the age of thirty, she was a veteran abolitionist lecturer. She and Smith Jones established the Garrisonian newspaper, *The Anti-Slavery Bugle*, in the Salem area. Soon after, they were married, and they remained as co-editors of the paper until June 1849. Jane Hitchcock Jones continued to be active in the Western Anti-Slavery Society, running a book and pamphlet agency from her home and giving lectures throughout the state. The Joneses left Salem in 1861, when they heard a rumor that a mob was intent on tarring and feathering them for their radical views on the social equality of blacks and whites.[8]

Many other women were not as visible in their support of the antislavery effort for a good reason. Ohio served as an important link in the Underground Railroad. Many slaves crossed the Ohio River with the goal of making it to Canada via several debarkation points on Lake Erie. Women were instrumental in supplying fugitive slaves with food, clothing, and shelter along the way. Mrs. James Lee provided shelter to runaways in Hartland, Huron County, as did Mrs. Lydia Foster Hawkins in Rockport, Cuyahoga County. Mrs. Mush of Champion, Trumbull County, cooked meals for the fugitives, and Mrs. Julia Morley Gillet opened her home not only to runaways but also to prominent abolitionists such as William Lloyd Garrison and Frederick Douglass.

Some women even worked as conductors. Mary Bushnell was given the task of leading a group of fugitives from her father's home in Hartford, Trumbull County, to the next township, Vernon. There Mrs. Levi Sutleff (née Mary Plumb) joined her, and they continued on to Andover, Ashtabula County, until the fugitives could be brought to Ashtabula Harbor and taken to Canada.[9]

After the passage of the 1850 federal Fugitive Slave Law, antislavery positions in Ohio solidified. More people became involved in the movement, and more stops on the Underground Railroad were recorded. Women continued to act as protectors and guides. Mrs. Judd of Ravenna, Portage County, allowed her farm to be added to the stations along the route.

Several African American women, especially in the Cincinnati area, were active in the antislavery movement. Elizabeth Coleman and Sarah Ernest led the Anti-Slavery Sewing Society, which provided clothes for runaways. Eveline Cooper was an officer of the Ohio Female Anti-Slavery Society, and Jane J. Jackson and Mary Gibson chaired a committee that put on a fair for the benefit of the Ohio Anti-Slavery Society in 1858.[10] Women attended conventions held by Ohio's African American community between 1849 and 1858. At one of the earliest meetings they demanded their right to participate fully in the proceedings. The women in attendance passed the following resolution: "Whereas we the ladies have been invited to attend the Convention, and have been deprived of a

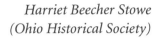

*Harriet Beecher Stowe
(Ohio Historical Society)*

voice, which we the ladies deem wrong and shameful. Therefore, Resolved, That we will attend no more after tonight unless the privilege is granted."[11] The resolution passed with little opposition.

The publication of *Uncle Tom's Cabin* in 1852 by Harriet Beecher Stowe, a seventeen-year resident of Cincinnati, had a tremendous impact on people's response to slavery, both in the North and South, as the country moved toward the brink of civil war. Americans purchased 300,000 copies of the book within its first year of publication, and it sold 1.5 million copies in England. The book's heart-rending story of the slave Eliza trying to save her child made more converts to the antislavery cause than any previous lectures and pamphlets. The story pointed to the real evil of slavery, "it thwarted and repressed the maternal bond, separating mother and child, brother and sister, husband and wife, eroding the emotional fabric of the black family in the name of the vested property right of white slaveowners."[12]

At the same time that slavery was a national issue, the use and abuse of alcohol was also coming under scrutiny. Many women who were involved in the antislavery movement were also involved in the early temperance movement and for the same reason—morality. On the Ohio frontier, distilled alcohol served as a cash crop and a salable commodity. The distillation of alcohol was common, and many women used alcohol to barter in exchange for needed household items. Alcohol was served at all social functions, such as land clearings and barn raisings. This was the customary payment (along with the meals provided) given to those who helped with these community projects. However, after the religious revival of the second Great Awakening, the use of alcohol came under attack as being immoral, or at least leading to immoral behavior. As this attitude grew, so did the attempts to limit or ban the use of alcohol.

Evidence of women advocating temperance in Ohio can be found dating back to the early nineteenth century. Rosamon Harris (Mrs. Levi Sargent) came to the west side of Cleveland in 1818 and said it was easier to get a gallon of whiskey than a gallon of rainwater. And Emaline Bidwell Merlan from Madison, Lake County, endured her neighbors' criticism when she refused wine at weddings. Soon after, Ohioans organized more formal responses. In 1826, Trumbull County residents established a temperance society in Vienna. Members prepared a pledge and Eliza Woodford and Phebe E. Merrieth were the first signatories.[13] Citizens of Summit County organized another society, with its own constitution, in 1829 in Copley. Mrs. Lawrence Moore was the only woman from Copley to join the society. Other societies sprang up randomly throughout Ohio in the 1830s, but no formalized network for organized activities existed. Not until the 1850s would a centralized organization develop.

Rebecca Rouse, a leading figure in Cleveland's many benevolent societies, supported the cause of temperance in northeast Ohio. In 1850, she helped to organize the Cleveland Ladies' Temperance Union. On June 27, 1850, they issued a pledge stating, "intoxicating liquors should not be used as a beverage nor as an article of entertainment." The directors of the union were Rebecca Rouse (Mrs. B. Rouse), Mrs. J. G. Harris, and Mrs. J. Lyman. By January 1, 1853, the union had a significant number of members (reports ranged from 140 to 700).[14] Women in Cincinnati organized the Daughters of Temperance Union, and they hosted a meeting in September 1851 for women interested in the temperance cause. Mrs. Mary B. Slough, "Grand Presiding Sister" of Ohio's Daughters of Temperance Union, chaired the meeting. Political alliances were attempted when the group promised the firemen of Company No. 1 that if they would agree to vote for temperance candidates, the women would work to raise funds to buy them a new banner.[15]

Temperance supporters held a Women's Temperance Convention on January 13, 1853. Mrs. Henry Cowles, a noted abolitionist, presided, and Mrs. Josephine Bateman, editor of the "Ladies Department" of the *Ohio Cultivator,* and Mrs. Mary A. Bronson served as vice presidents. Jane Elizabeth Jones, the noted abolitionist, served as one of the secretaries, as did Josephine Griffing. Conventioneers adopted a constitution for a state society, thus forming the Ohio Women's Temperance Society. Josephine Bateman served as the society's first president. All the women's auxiliaries of the Women's State Temperance Association held a meeting at the Ohio State Fair in Dayton later that year.[16]

However, as with most reform activity, the outbreak of the Civil War halted this growing organized effort to ban the use of alcohol. Only after the cessation of hostilities did Ohio's women commence efforts to curb the use and sale of alcohol. By the late 1860s and 1870s, as they perceived that the alcohol problem was growing worse, the activists became much more radical. Because of this, the women who participated in the temperance movement were subjected to the criticisms, jeers, and even physical abuse of their critics. Forming organizations, sponsoring speakers and drafting and circulating pledges was acceptable in most Ohio communities; taking to the streets was not.

As urban areas grew in this country after the Civil War, so did the problems. The number of people in poverty increased, housing problems intensified, and children worked in factories or roamed the streets. The number of immigrants grew, increasing the unskilled labor pool and driving down wages. Criminal activity was also on the rise. A significant number of nineteenth-century Americans attributed these growing problems to the increasing abuse of alcohol. Many reformers believed that if alcohol was not readily available, the social ills of the country would lessen dramatically. The goal of the temperance movement was to close the saloons and obtain people's pledges that they would abstain from the use of alcohol.[17]

Women were the frequent victims of alcohol abuse, and they received no protection under the law from this abuse. Husbands, fathers, and sons could drink away the family income, leaving the family destitute, but the women and children affected by this had no legal recourse. Prior to the Civil War, women who participated in the early temperance movement tried to combat the problem largely through moral suasion—by setting a good example. However, after the Civil War, when the temperance cause moved to the political arena, women also had to move into that arena if they were committed to the fight. Many women rationalized this step by asking, "If the saloon was a threat to home and hearth, was it not a woman's duty to invade the public sphere to defend what was universally acceded to be her special area of responsibility?"[18]

Ohio women led this nationwide crusade for temperance. An opportunity for reform came with the 1873–74 Ohio Constitutional Convention, which debated the liquor license and regulation of liquor traffic issues. At this time, the state did not license liquor dealers, and the law forbade the selling of hard liquor in saloons, permitting only wine and beer to be sold there. Also, saloonkeepers and liquor dealers could be prohibited from selling to a person if that person's relatives asked that he not be served. The liquor industry wanted the constitutional convention to allow for liquor licensing and the sale of hard liquor in saloons. The temperance forces were adamantly opposed to both issues.[19]

The war against alcohol and drunkenness commenced in 1873, in Hillsboro, Ohio, and soon spread throughout the state and nation. During the last six months of 1873, 76 barrels of whiskey, 52

Eliza Jane Thompson of Hillsboro, leader of the "Women's Crusade" (Ohio Historical Society)

kegs of wines and liquor, and 903 kegs of beer had been delivered to saloons in Hillsboro.[20] Women of the town were determined to stop this traffic in spirits.

In 1873, after hearing an impassioned speech by Dr. Diocletian Lewis, a homeopathic physician and ardent temperance advocate who admonished women to take to the streets and close the saloons through prayer, Eliza Jane Trimble Thompson and seventy-five other women held a march through the streets of Hillsboro. They marched to the twenty saloons and prayed for the souls of those corrupted by alcohol. The marchers demanded that the saloonkeepers sign a pledge promising not to serve alcohol. Hillsboro's citizens met nightly at either the Presbyterian or Methodist church to hear about the day's activities and to encourage further participation.[21] One reporter described attendance at the meetings: "all denominations are represented; all parties, all classes, all colors, are represented. The leading spirits are the women of our most influential families, and with them march, and work, and kneel and pray, the representatives of every circle in our village society."[22]

The tactic proved successful in the short term and soon spread to other towns and cities. Marches were held in 130 Ohio towns. Activity increased during 1874. Mrs. Monteith, the leader of the crusade in Elyria, talked and prayed with saloonkeepers. On one occasion, she stood on an empty beer keg to get people's attention and spoke strongly in favor of temperance. In New Vienna, the women laid siege to the local saloon, forcing it to close. In Piqua, two hundred women gathered on February 18, 1874, to pray and discuss the temperance issue. They divided into six groups and took to the streets. Over the next six weeks, they visited local saloons and were met by buckets of cleaning water thrown by irate saloonkeepers.[23] Parades and demonstrations grew in size, but often the public railed at the women marchers for their "unladylike" behavior. In cities such as Columbus, Cleveland, and Cincinnati, city leaders passed ordinances to prevent parades, on the grounds that the marchers were obstructing traffic. Ministers and town leaders criticized women for their unladylike activities. The *Cincinnati Enquirer* noted that "women should pray in churches and not upon sidewalks or in beer saloons." But politicians began to take note of the movement. Mills Gardners, C. W. Rowland, and E. D. Mansfield marched with the women.[24]

Temperance women established a state league at Springfield, Ohio, in January 1874. The guiding spirit of this group was Eliza Stewart from Springfield, whose care of wounded soldiers in hospitals and on battlefields during the Civil War earned her the title "Mother." Stewart traveled throughout Ohio, the United States, and Europe fighting against the sale of alcohol. Clifton M. Nichols, editor of the *Springfield Daily Republic,* described her as "one of the first of the world's women to rise the banner of revolt, and so great was her zeal, and so robust and boundless her courage, that she accompanied her prayers and her marchings upon the streets with an attack—with the gospel in one hand and the law in the other—upon the saloon-keepers themselves."[25]

Women's Temperance Crusade, Waynesville, ca. 1875 (Ohio Historical Society)

In early November 1874, the Women's Temperance League of Cleveland reorganized; it joined forces with the Women's Christian Temperance Union on November 20, 1874. The Women's Temperance League in Cleveland established a number of inns throughout the city. These inns served as temporary shelters for the poor and provided temperance workers bases from which to work. The first such inn was the Central Friendly Inn, opened in 1875. Soon others were opened. At these inns temperance workers planned strategies, gave aid to those in need, counseled mothers, and provided job training for young women. The Central Friendly Inn had a reading room, an industrial school for girls, and lodgings for men.[26]

The 1873–74 crusade was volatile but short lived. In August 1874, Ohio's voters defeated the liquor licensing amendment. The campaign was most successful in small villages, but the Women's Christian Temperance Union continued its work throughout the state, particularly in urban areas. The "drink problem" remained a hot political issue throughout the rest of the nineteenth century and into the twentieth century. The Nonpartisan Woman's Christian Temperance Union in Cleveland split from the national Women's Christian Temperance Union in 1885, when the national group endorsed the Prohibition Party. Temperance Republicans organized the Prohibition Party in Cleveland in 1869, when they nominated a slate of candidates for the March 1869 municipal elections. Soon after, temperance supporters organized both state and national prohibition parties. The Prohibition Party gained support from a small number of Ohio voters in every election from 1860 to 1914.[27] The goal of the Prohibition Party was to pass legislation making the manufacture, sale, and distribution of alcohol illegal—a step beyond the goal of the temperance movement. It was a position that would solidify the liquor industry's position as a strong political enemy of the prohibition movement in the late nineteenth and early twentieth centuries.

The Women's Christian Temperance Union continued to operate temperance inns, and founded the Open Door Home for unwed mothers, the Training Home for Friendless Girls, and the Mary B. Ingersoll Club for Working Girls. The work of the group became more secular in the early twentieth century. The inns offered geography and mathematics classes for boys and cooking classes for girls. The Central Friendly Inn opened a babies' dispensary, a kindergarten, a tuberculosis dispensary, and a public bath. The Inn became a settlement house in 1924, cutting its ties with the Nonpartisan Women's Christian Temperance Union.[28]

Some Women's Christian Temperance Union chapters continued their activities into the 1950s. Over a period of twenty-seven years, Mrs. Minnie Goode Jameson served as president, vice president, and treasurer of the Lucy Thurman Union of the Women's Christian Temperance Union, the largest African American union in the United States. She was a lecturer for the Ohio Women's Christian Temperance Union beginning in 1903, state superintendent from 1903 through 1920, and state director in 1927.

Many Ohio women, though concerned about the problems they saw resulting from the use of alcohol, decided not to take to the streets but to address the issue through religious or secular charitable groups. These activities were more in keeping with the "traditional" types of activities with which Christian ladies should be involved. For some, this was a continuation of earlier charitable works. One of the earliest known women's charitable groups was the Female Society of Cincinnati for Charitable Purposes. In 1815, it reported its expenditures as follows: missionaries in Louisiana, $20; for purchase of Bibles, $59; for the Theological Seminary at Princeton, $60; and for tracts, $5.[29]

Another early group was the Female Moral Reform Society, whose purpose was to promote and sustain moral purity amongst its own and amongst those who "wandered from the path." Oberlin's chapter was founded in 1835 and continued through 1859. Between 1835 and 1840, the Oberlin Female Reform Society had 308 members, and by 1837, it was the fourth largest society in the country. Young women attending Oberlin were strongly encouraged by Mrs. Alice Welsh Cowles, principal of the Female Department, to join the group. The implication was that if they did not join the organization, their character was less than moral.[30]

Members of the society insisted on strict standards of behavior between the sexes, required modest dress, decried dancing, and abhorred the reading of novels. In 1842, the Oberlin Female Moral Reform Society passed the resolution "That in view of the wrong views of human life instilled—the time wasted—the hopes wrecked—and the souls ruined by novel reading—it would greatly promote the well being of society, if this style of literature was banished from our world."[31]

Several chapters of the Female Moral Reform Society were formed in Ohio during 1837–38. Women from these chapters met in Cleveland in 1840 and reorganized the society, with Mrs. Lathrop as its first director. In October 1842, a convention was held to discuss issues pertinent to them, including temperance.[32] At this convention, the participants decided to begin gathering petitions to present to the state legislature asking them to "suppress licentiousness." As a result of these petitions, supporters introduced a bill in the Ohio legislature providing "That a man or woman who shall live or cohabit in a state of adultery, shall be deemed guilty of a crime, and on conviction there of shall, each, be imprisoned in the penitentiary, and kept at hard labor, for a term not exceeding three years, nor less than one year."[33] The bill was killed by an unfavorable report from the Committee on the Judiciary in the Senate. In the 1850s and 1860s, many of these women would turn their efforts toward benevolent societies.

Mrs. Rebecca Elliott Cromwell Rouse, the "mother of the Baptist churches and founder of the Woman's Christian work in Cleveland" spent her life working to relieve the plight of the poor. She organized the Martha Washington and Dorcas Society in 1842. This group of two hundred women, initially linked to the Washingtonian temperance movement, soon extended its base to address the broader needs of the poor. During 1848, 231 families applied to the society for assistance. Such assistance might consist of gifts of meat, flour, sugar, coffee, rice, tea, meal, candles, clothing, bedding, and wood. Rouse also organized support for the Protestant Orphan Asylum, which opened January 22, 1852. Mrs. Stillman Witt provided the money to purchase a building, and Sophia L. Hewitt offered her services as matron and teacher.[34]

Another church-related group was the Ladies Bethel and Mission Aid Society, organized in Cleveland on November 14, 1867. The Ladies Bethel and Mission Aid Society was the female arm of the Bethel Union, a group organized on January 31, 1867, as an auxiliary of the Western Seamen's Friend Society. The group initially operated out of Bethel Church on West Ninth Street, but in 1868 they purchased and renovated a building dedicated on January 27, 1869, as Bethel Hall. The Ladies Bethel and Mission Aid Society's goal was to visit the poor, ascertain their needs, and help them if possible. In 1870, they solicited door to door for donations and clothing. These donations were distributed to the poor, but only if after visiting their homes it was determined that they were truly in need.[35]

A similar group, Union Bethel, formed in Cincinnati and was one of the earliest charitable agencies. It grew out of a well-furnished barge that was docked at the public landing. This barge provided ship hands with a place to attend worship services. The group later turned its attention to helping the unemployed in the area. Union Bethel ran a Sunday school, sewing and cooking schools, and a kindergarten. Medical and dental facilities were available for the poor, as well as a bath and a laundry. Union Bethel also housed various clubs for young and old, male and female. The poor received relief in the form of clothes, shoes, groceries, and rent money.[36]

The most active Protestant women's organization was the Cleveland Woman's Christian Association (WCA), formed in 1868. Members chose Sarah E. Fitch as president, an office she retained until 1893. During that time, members were busy with proselytizing efforts, going to homes, jails, hospitals, and the city infirmary in search of converts. The WCA established a boardinghouse in 1869 for working women, along with the "Retreat," a home for "erring and unfortunate women." Women staying at the "Retreat" were taught a skill that would enable them to support themselves and their children. In 1876, they opened a Home for Aged Women and in 1884, the Eliza Jennings Home for Incurable Invalids.[37]

Other religious groups also carried out charitable activities. Jewish immigrant women from Germany organized the Jewish Ladies' Benevolent Society in 1860 in Cleveland. This group sponsored fund-raisers to help the poor within their community and raised funds for the Jewish Orphan Asylum that opened in 1868.[38] The Cincinnati chapter of the National Council of Jewish Women had a membership of seven hundred. This group devoted itself to "the work of social betterment through religion, philanthropy and education." The Episcopal Diocese in Ohio supported Saint John Orphanage for Girls Ages Four through Eight in Cleveland. Catholic women's groups were also busy. In 1851, the Ladies of the Sacred Heart of Mary opened Cleveland's first orphanage, St. Mary's Female Asylum for Young Girls, and in 1863, St. Joseph's

Sarah Worthington, noted Cincinnati philanthropist (Ohio Historical Society)

Orphanage for Older Girls. The Sisters of Charity of St. Augustine opened St. Vincent's Orphan Asylum in 1853.[39] Sarah Worthington King Peter, a leading Catholic citizen of Cincinnati, was responsible for bringing the Little Sisters of the Poor to the city, along with the Franciscans and Claires, to establish convents and continue the work among the city's poor.[40]

Individual women and secular groups were also concerned about the needs of the poor, in particular the children. Charity Rotch of Massillon, who died August 8, 1824, designated that after family bequests, the remainder of her estate should be used as a trust to set up a school for orphans.[41] Sarah Worthington King Peter helped found the Protestant Orphan Asylum in Cincinnati in 1831, and Catharine Fay Ewing is credited with establishing the first children's home in Ohio near Marietta. Concerned women organized the Columbus Female Benevolent Society on January 5, 1835, with the explicit purpose "to seek the poor in the city of Columbus and provide them relief, and, instruction or employment, as may be deemed best." Mrs. Charlotte Degmeier of Cleveland developed the School and Relief Society in 1853. This was followed in 1857 by the Children's Aid Society, which would be incorporated under state law in 1865. Mrs. Eliza Jennings gave her home to the Children's Aid Society in 1868.[42] In Piqua, women started the first city-wide organization dedicated exclusively to charity work, the Union Relief Society, in 1858. Members of the society worked to provide poor children with clothing and promoted their attendance at Sabbath and day schools. Even Lucy Webb Hayes, when she was the First Lady of Ohio, became interested in the plight of Ohio's children. With her aid, reformers raised money to buy land near Xenia in 1869 for a soldiers' orphans home. In April 1870, the Ohio Senate converted the home into a state institution.[43]

Many women were also interested in the care of the sick. Church members opened the Trinity Church Home for Sick and Friendless in Cleveland in 1856, with Mrs. Philo Scovill as president of its board of managers. Also in Cleveland, the Ladies Society of the First Presbyterian Church established a Home for the Friendless in 1863. This home started out as a small medical facility and in time became the Wilson Street Hospital. The Sisters of Charity of St. Augustine opened St. Vincent's Charity Hospital in 1865, Cleveland's first permanent general hospital. Women's groups in other cities would organize similar facilities.

Another problem that came to the attention of women during this time was the treatment of female criminals, especially young women. There was little opportunity for rehabilitation, either through vocational or religious training, prior to 1869. In 1869, the state bought White Sulphur Springs, a health resort near Delaware, and turned it into a home for "wayward" girls. In 1872, the institution, by that time housing 153 residents, was named the Girls Industrial School.[44]

The Civil War provided women in Ohio with a different focus for their charity work. Local benevolent and charity groups quickly converted to soldiers' aid societies. Maria Parson Harmon, president of the Benevolent Society of Warren, became the president of the Soldiers' Aid Society of Warren in 1861. In Elyria, women elected Mrs. H. G. Blake president of the Elyria Soldiers' Aid Society, an office she held for ten years. Every township in Lorain County organized branch societies. Society members gathered and sent boxes of clothes, bandages, socks, lint, and jellies to the soldiers. The Piqua Soldiers' Aid Society decided to focus its efforts to aid the families of veterans. Society members raised money to buy firewood and extra rations of meat for those affected by the war.[45]

The Cleveland Branch of the Soldiers' Aid Society organized at Chopin's Hall, April 20, 1861, with only women members. In October, the members offered to become one of the receiving and distributing branches of the United States Sanitary Commission. In November, the women changed its name to Soldiers' Aid Society of Northern Ohio. They elected Mrs. Rebecca Elliott Cromwell Rouse president and Mary Clark Brayton secretary. The women organized fund-raisers and set up their own hospital at Union Station in October 1863 to care for the ill or injured soldiers arriving by train. Commission members then organized a soldiers' home. In May 1865, they tried to help returning soldiers by running an employment agency. Between 1861 and 1866, the women collected and dispersed money and goods totaling $1,133,405.09. In recognition of these efforts and, in particular, the efforts of Mrs. Rouse, her likeness is included on the Soldiers' and Sailors' Monument on Cleveland's Public Square. This organization remained under the management of women—unlike the Cincinnati and Columbus societies, which were organized and run by men with the assistance of women's auxiliaries.

Thousands of state branch societies collected supplies and funds and sent them to one of the central agencies. Mrs. Elizabeth Mendenhall, vice president of the Cincinnati society, was in charge of the Great Western Sanitary Fair, which raised $200,000 for the National Sanitary Commission's use. The fair opened on December 21, 1863, and ran through April 21, 1864. The fair featured numerous lectures, concerts, and other entertainments, along with an art gallery. Sixteen committees and 70 subcommittees made the

U.S. Sanitary Fair, Cleveland, February 22, 1864 (Ohio Historical Society)

arrangements for all the activities, more than 150 organizations participated, and the railroads and express companies provided free transportation for the goods consigned to the fair.[46] The Cincinnati group was one of the most productive in the country, sending large amounts of material goods to distribution centers and establishing hospitals.

The need to focus the North's manufacturing and business activity on the war effort provided opportunities for women to use and obtain skills that usually would not be open to them. Jobs involving sewing skills expanded due to the materials needed— uniforms, tents, and canvas products. Women also filled the role of nurse at home and on the battlefield, a job that received the praise of the public. Among the most famous of the Civil War nurses was Mary Ann (Ball) Bickerdyke from Knox County. "Mother" Bickerdyke, as the soldiers called her, was lauded for saving many lives at Shiloh through her care and skills. Nursing sisters, such as Sister Anthony O'Connell of Cincinnati, worked in the field hospitals,

"Mother" Mary A. Bickerdyke (Ohio Historical Society)

and many women, such as Lucy Webb Hayes and Eliza Daniel Stewart ("Mother" Stewart), spent time visiting and comforting the soldiers who were recovering or dying in their cities.[47]

The continuing needs of soldiers and their families after the war led women's groups once again to refocus their charitable activities. Kate Brownlee Sherwood of Lucas County organized the National Women's Relief Corps (NWRC), an auxiliary of the Grand Army of the Republic (GAR), and many communities that had had soldiers' aid societies now formed branches of the NWRC. The Buckley Relief Corps No. 23, under the leadership of Sarah M. E. Battels, provided relief services for veterans and their families. This group remained active until the 1930s.[48]

Other groups such as the National Alliance of Daughters of Veterans and the Ladies of the GAR in Massillon formed to keep alive and honor the memory of Civil War veterans. On January 25, 1885, Bertha Martin of Massillon organized the Daughters of Union Veterans of the Civil War, serving as its vice president. The group was responsible for marking historical sites in the Massillon area. In 1906, the national group was formed, and Martin became its president.[49]

As the United States recovered economically from the post–Civil War recession, industrialization and urbanization raced forward. The country's population increased dramatically, with millions of immigrants pouring into its major cities. City planning was virtually unheard of, or at least not practiced, and the problems facing urban dwellers increased, not the least of which were corrupt municipal governments. Women embraced opportunities offered to them to help clean up society.[50] This led to a greater public role for women, which eventually contributed to women's attempts to gain the right to vote. It also led many women to continue to work through organizations specifically organized to improve the community.

The women's club movement is a prime example of women coming together to better the quality of life of those living in their communities. This movement began in New York City in 1868 when a group of professional women were not allowed to attend a dinner for Charles Dickens at the New York Press Club. The women formed their own club, Sorosis, and a precedent was set. The initial clubs were devoted to "self-culture" and often provided middle-class educated women with the means for intellectual stimulation, upward mobility, and the training for public activity.[51] These clubs were conservative in nature, but they led women to participate in civic and philanthropic causes.

The General Federation of Women's Clubs, founded in 1890, brought together groups of women from around the country into an umbrella organization. The Cincinnati Woman's Club was organized on March 26, 1894, at a meeting called by Mrs. S. P. Mallon, Miss Annie Laws, Mrs. J. J. Gest, Mrs. H. C. Yergason, Mrs. H. B. Morehead, Mrs. Fayette Smith, and Miss Clara C. Newton. The members elected Miss Laws its first president. The goal of the organization was to provide an "organized center of thought and action among women to promote their social, educational, literary, and artistic growth, and to do "whatever relates to the best interests of the city." The group established a civic department in 1897 to study good city government. They were interested in issues such as city charters, voting qualifications, school board membership, and the separation of national and municipal elections.[52]

The Piqua Federation of Women's Clubs formed in the 1890s and soon affiliated with the state and national organizations. Pauline Steinem became president of the Toledo Federation of Women's Clubs in 1901. She headed a joint committee of the Toledo Federation and the National and International Council of Women to establish and run a vacation school program. The program, financed entirely by women, was a success. Members of various women's clubs organized the Federation of Women's Clubs of Greater Cleveland in 1902, which included eighteen clubs with seven hundred members. By 1910, however, the federation included sixty clubs with over four thousand members. The federation provided clothes for poor children at Christmas and thousands of school lunches to children in Cleveland's public schools. By 1902, the Ohio Federation of Women's Clubs had more than 289 club affiliations with more than ten thousand members. The state federation worked for changes in the school code and labor laws, helped finance a traveling library, investigated factories, and promoted art in the schools.[53]

The women's club movement would continue to grow after women achieved the right to vote. In 1919, the Massillon Woman's Club was organized with more than four hundred in attendance. Mrs. P. N. Geiger was elected president. In October 1924, a home was donated for their use, and this home is still the meeting place of this and other women's organizations. Similar groups continued to develop through the 1950s. The Woman's Club of Wadsworth was organized on March 6, 1958, and affiliated with the state and national groups soon after.[54]

Race was a barrier to the unification of women's groups during this period. African American women were not allowed to join the clubs formed by white women. In response to this, the National Association of Colored Women organized in 1896. Clubs filled a tremendous need in their communities by founding homes for the elderly, orphanages, kindergartens, and day nurseries. Lethia C.

Fleming and Dorothy Chestnut spearheaded the activities of African Americans in Cleveland. By 1924, black women in Cleveland had formed the Cleveland Council of Colored Women, and the group continued to press for funds from Cleveland's many charities.[55] Cincinnati also had a very active club, which in time did join with the white women's clubs in supporting like causes. The racial barrier, however, would not be easy to overcome.

Many other women's organizations developed to address the broad range of women's needs. By 1915 in Cincinnati, women's groups included suffrage organizations, professional clubs, benefit groups, mothers' clubs, and religious organizations. Among these were the Hamilton County Woman Suffrage Association, the Graduate Nurses Association, the Woman's Press Club, the Progressive Benefit Society, the Kennedy Heights Mothers' Clubs, and the Ladies City Missionary Society. Piqua's women formed the Fortnightly Club in 1889 in order to expand their knowledge of world events, and many others followed their lead. The women of Germantown formed the Twentieth Century Club in 1900 for the purpose of "attainment of intellectual, cultural and social enjoyment." They raised funds in 1907 to furnish the new library, and they conferred with the village council in 1915 on how they might help promote the construction of a new waterworks. They also distributed food baskets at Christmas. In 1912, the Junior League of Cleveland was formed, and all members were required to volunteer in a social service agency, public health facility, or settlement house. They administered League House, a home for working women, from 1919 to 1946. Mrs. Dudley Blossom and Mrs. Chester Bolton donated the property for this home.[56]

Women continued to be concerned about the plight of women and children they considered less fortunate than themselves. Many of the causes they had supported during the 1840s and 1850s still needed attention, especially as urban areas continued to grow, wages for the poor stayed low, and substandard housing proliferated. Added to this was an attempt by members of middle- and upper-class society to force their values on the poor. Many women and men involved in charitable work believed that urban poverty was due to the individual failings of the poor themselves, not the result of economic or structural problems in American society. Many reformers also believed that the urban poor would benefit from interacting with their "moral" superiors. This could be accomplished by female reformers visiting the homes of the poor and by establishing homes for single, young women who did not have the protection of middle-class family values.[57] Women visiting the homes of the poor were told, "we must keep at work continually, season after season, pulling up the weeds of degradation and destitution, cultivating the thrift, self-dependence, industry, virtue [and] health, as well as the intellectual and social natures of our poor friends."[58] Thus the social service agencies and settlement houses that reformers established during the late nineteenth and early twentieth centuries reflected the assumptions and values of middle-class white Ohioans.

Middle- and upper-class women in Columbus concerned about the morals of working-class women established a home for prostitutes in 1869–70, with the express purpose of the reformation of "fallen women." This goal continued with the establishment of the Florence Drittenton Home in 1901 and the Friends Rescue Home by Evangeline Reams in 1905. A similar home for African American girls, known as the Columbus Home for Girls, was opened through the efforts of the Circle of the King's Daughters. In 1931, the institution's name was changed to the Phillis Wheatley Home.[59]

One of the major concerns of women who wished to improve the lot of the "deserving " poor was the welfare of the city's children, particularly those whose mothers worked outside the home or who were employed to do piecework at home. The development of day nurseries and kindergartens received a great deal of attention. Flora Stone Mather helped to establish the Day Nursery and Kindergarten Association in Cleveland, along with the Children's Aid Society. While in Akron, Margaret Chapman Barnhart worked to obtain funding, space, and equipment for children's playgrounds. She also managed the campaign to build a new children's home in

Women's Department, Cuyahoga County Jail, 1889 (Ohio Historical Society)

Akron and helped to found the Juvenile Court and the Detention Home. In Cincinnati, Agnes Senior Seasongood was involved with the establishment of day care centers and was president of the Children's Psychiatric Center. Helen Trounstine, who had spent time at Hull House and in New York City, organized the Juvenile Protection Association, an organization devoted to the welfare of children, when she returned to Cincinnati. Women were able to undertake some of these endeavors because in 1913, the Ohio Constitution was amended to allow women to serve as board members for departments and institutions involving the care of women and/or children.[60]

Because of their longstanding interest in health issues, Ohio women continued to be involved in the development and management of hospitals. In 1888, several women served on the board of trustees of Cleveland's Lakewood Hospital. Only women served on the Board of Managers, which raised funds and managed the daily affairs of the hospital, including the hiring of staff. In 1893, the Sisters of Charity of St. Augustine opened St. Ann's Infant and Maternity Asylum for unwed Catholic mothers. The Young Ladies' Hebrew Association, later named the Jewish Women's Hospital Association, sponsored the funding of Cleveland's Mt. Sinai Hospital in 1892. In Huron County, Mrs. Ada Gates Stevens, along with other family members, donated money to build the Gates Hospital for Crippled Children. Massillon's hospital also had a "board of lady managers" who collected jams, jellies, and canned foods and vegetables to be served at the hospital. In the 1930s, they supervised the Volunteer Service League and it, like many of the above-mentioned groups, was converted to a hospital auxiliary in the 1950s.[61]

Reform-minded women also addressed the issue of care for elderly women. A number of women met in Salem in 1886 in hopes of establishing a home for aged women. The main problems were finding a place and funding its operation. Both obstacles were overcome with a $1,000 donation from Mrs. Eliza Jennings and a considerable donation from the estate of Tacy Wilson. Mrs. Rhebe Gruell donated her services as matron during the first year; Mrs. Eliza Marple then succeeded her. The Pauline Home for the Aged, a home for German widows, opened in Columbus in 1888. In 1895, Mrs. E. Ainsworth and Mrs. Rounds established the Old Ladies' Home in Lodi and endowed it with $20,000. Flora Stone Mather of Cleveland was a major benefactor of the Home for Aged Women in that city. Also in Cleveland, under the direction of Eliza Bryant, African American women raised funds for the Cleveland Home for Aged Colored People that opened in 1896. Most of the trustees and officers of this home were women.[62]

The most significant development regarding the care of the poor was the settlement house movement that spread through cities in the United States in the 1890s and continued into the twentieth century. Settlement houses provided a means for immigrants to assimilate into American society. Settlement houses provided adult education, vocational training, day care, kindergartens —all the things needed by immigrants to become "good" Americans and to pull themselves out of poverty. They also provided "women's space" for the young, college-educated women who filled most of the positions at these centers, as well as space for immigrant women visiting and using the services.

Many such settlements were established in both Cleveland and Cincinnati, two cities with large immigrant populations. The Methodist Episcopal Deaconess Home, opened in 1890 in Cleveland, was a precursor to the settlement house. The Deaconess Home served as a residence for women reformers dressed in a distinctive garb or dark dresses and white caps, who visited the sick and proselytized in the neighborhood. The first settlement in Cleveland was Hiram House, which opened in 1896. Three of its original founders were women, and its first headworker was Maude Thompson. Goodrich House, sponsored by Florence Stone Mather and others, opened in 1897 and offered various social services. Many of its early activities were aimed at women and young girls. Goodrich House had a public laundry and baths, two kindergartens, a visiting nurse, a gymnasium, and a public reading room for men and boys. It sponsored several clubs for girls—Busy Bee Girls Club, Rosebud Club, Villet Club, Little Women Club, Florence Nightingale Club, and the Martha Washington Club. Workers led the drive to obtain legal aid for the indigent, worked for clean streets, and encouraged the formation of a consumers' league. In time, Goodrich House would serve as the home of the Legal Aid Society and the Ohio Consumers' League. The Sunbeam School for Crippled Children and Cleveland Boys' Farm in Hudson both had their origins at Goodrich House. Alice B. Gannett served as its director from 1917 through 1947, and it is now known as Goodrich-Gannett.[63]

In 1899, the Cleveland branch of the Council of Jewish Women established the Council Educational Alliance, formalizing the services it was already providing to recently arrived eastern European Jews. By 1910, the alliance was conducting religious services and citizenship classes and teaching traditional Jewish trades such as cloak making. In 1900, Alta House opened in the Little Italy neighborhood of Cleveland. The building, donated by John D. Rockefeller, housed day care facilities for children whose parents worked in the vineyards outside of Cleveland. In 1911, Jane Edna Hunter established the Phillis Wheatley Association for young black women. Hunter, a graduate of Hampton Institute and a trained nurse, arrived in Cleveland in 1905. Seeing first-hand how difficult it was for a young black woman to find a place to rent, she set out to change the situation. She organized the Working Girls Home Association and rented a house to provide lodging for young black women. In 1917, she was able to purchase a three-story building in which to carry out her dream.[64] At about the same time, 1915, Russell and Rowena Jelliffe were working to establish their dream. They set out to help all poor youngsters, no matter their race or nationality, learn about the arts and drama through various classes and programs. They also hoped that by performing together these children would discover their similarities. Thus the Jelliffes established the Playhouse Settlement, later renamed Karamu House, in 1915. It became the oldest interracial performing arts center in the nation. A contemporary called the Jelliffes the "Banner Bearers in the field of Negro White relations in the American Settlement House Movement."[65]

The only Catholic settlement house in Cleveland opened in 1919. Merrick House, funded by the National Catholic War Council, provided services for neighborhood children, including day care and camping. It served as a training site for students from the Western Reserve University School of Applied Social Sciences.

There were several settlements in Cincinnati also, many of which were organized homes for working girls. The Cincinnati Union Bethel Society opened the Anna Louise Inn and the Protestant Episcopal Church ran the Eleanor Lodge. The Emanuel City Mission Methodist Episcopal (M.E.) Church operated the Emanuel Girls Home, and the Woman's Home Missionary Society of the M. E. Church ran the Esther Home for Girls. The Woman's Home Missionary Society of the M. E. Church operated the Friendship Home for Colored Girls. Martha House was a privately owned home. Columbus also had a home for working girls. The Women's Educational and Industrial Union opened in 1886, providing rooms for twenty-five regular boarders along with a day nursery and kindergarten.[66]

Another women's organization that arose to deal with the needs of working women was the Young Women's Christian Association (YWCA). The YWCA's goal was to provide for the "temporal, moral and religious welfare of women, especially the young, who are dependent upon their exertions for their support." Women adhering to this goal organized a branch in Cincinnati in 1870. The branch soon purchased a house that could accommodate ninety girls. It opened an Industrial Institute to provide training in various trades in 1872. That same year, Mrs. L. B. Reakert provided funding for the building of a summer cottage so that the young women would have a chance to get out into the country and enjoy the fresh air. In 1883, the branch opened a Woman's Exchange that provided a market for the goods made at the Industrial Institute.[67]

In Cleveland, the YWCA opened a boarding house in 1896 and soon began running classes. In 1903–4, it offered classes in English, typing, stenography, sewing, dressmaking, physical education, and Bible study. Factories in Cleveland held educational meetings and religious services conducted by members of the YWCA for women employed at the Central Knitting Mills, R. B. Biscuit, American Cigar, and United Knitting. By 1919, the Cleveland YWCA had a membership of 46,046, including 7,000 non-English-speaking women who were being taught English. The organization provided accommodations for 5,151 women.[68] After World War I, several branches of the YWCA could be found in smaller towns throughout Ohio, providing a new dignity and respectability for working women.

An issue that most women struggled to find information about was birth control. The settlement workers realized the implications of a large family on the health and lives of the women they provided services for. But the Comstock Law forbid them to disseminate information on birth control or family planning. Margaret Sanger, among others, challenged this law nationally, and there were many women in Ohio who also stood up and spoke out against such laws. Mrs. Charles Brush and Mrs. Brooks Shepard decided to give out birth control information at the prenatal clinic where they volunteered in Cleveland. In response, the clinic's board members forced both women to leave the clinic. In 1923, they helped organize the Maternal Health Clinic, and they tried to persuade the city's hospitals to pass out contraceptive information at their out-patient clinics. However, local ordinances and public outrage prohibited this. In 1928, they formed the Maternal Health Association and opened an independent clinic, which Rosine Valk and Dr. Ruth Robishaw Rauschkolb staffed. Initially, the clinic offered its services only to married women, but in time it extended its services to others. In the 1930s, Valk and Rauschkolb opened a clinic on the west side of Cleveland.[69]

With the nation's involvement in World War I, women's philanthropic work was once again turned toward wartime activities. Organizations were developed throughout the state to address the needs of the soldiers and their families. Mrs. George Zimmerman of Fremont served as chairwoman of the Women's Committee of the Council of National Defense for Ohio. Mrs. Zimmerman was succeeded by Miss Belle Sherwin of Cleveland. Sherwin had organized a National Defense Unit in every township of Huron County. The women of Massillon also mobilized for war. In the fall of 1917, the Massillon Women's Committee named Bertha Martin chairwoman. One of the group's main activities, prompted by the policies of the United States Food Administration, was to enlist the help of the women in the community in the conservation of food. Martin organized a door-to-door solicitation in which approximately three hundred women participated; in addition, she established markets where surplus food from liberty gardens could be sold. The Civics Club in Vinton made and packed kits for the Red Cross that would be sent to soldiers serving overseas.[70]

Clubs that had been formed for other purposes changed their focus during the war. The Sorosis Club sold war bonds and knitted clothes for military personnel. The Federation of Woman's Clubs

World War I nurses (Kent State University Archives)

organized victory gardens and sold and purchased liberty bonds. The YWCA in Cleveland housed members of the Women's Land Army, whose job it was to plant crops to feed United States and Allied troops. Thousands of women across the state volunteered at the Red Cross.

Some women played a much more direct role in the war effort. Dr. George W. Clark of Lakeside Hospital in Cleveland led a team of volunteers to serve in France in 1915. The unit, initially named the U.S. Army Base Hospital No. 4 but later renamed the Lakeside Unit, had 26 medical officers and 64 nurses. These medical personnel were transferred to Rouen, France, in May 1917 to staff a British hospital. In August 1918, 61 members of the unit staffed a hospital near the Meusse-Argonne front. By the end of the war, the unit had 124 nurses who had been organized and supervised first by Grace Allison and then Elizabeth Folckemer.[71]

At the opposite end of the state, Laura Logan recruited one hundred nurses to staff the Cincinnati Base Hospital No. 25. She served as chief nurse until the unit was running smoothly. In 1918, the Ohio Council of Defense named her chair of its Committee on Nursing, where she successfully recruited more than 200 nurses for war service in the United States and overseas.[72]

The ordeal of the "war to end all wars" led many Americans to embrace a burgeoning peace movement. The women in Ohio were no exception. The YWCA, League of Women Voters, Consumers League of Ohio, and the Cleveland Women's City Club organized the Women's Council for the Prevention of War. On May 18, 1924, these groups staged a march of 5,000 women calling for world peace. Delegates from more than 200 organizations participated. The Woman's City Club of Cincinnati set up the International Good Will Committee, chaired by Amy Roth. They focused most of their energy on the education of school-age children about the prevention of war.[73]

During the two decades after the 1919 Paris Peace Conference, one popular aim of peace advocates was disarmament. In the 1930s, the Woman's City Club of Cincinnati became a leader in the advocacy of such a policy. Ruth Neely France, Clara Grueninger, and Setty Swarts Kuhn led the club's work in this area during the 1930s. Kuhn was named "Public Citizen #1" among Cincinnati women in 1935. She helped establish the Geneva Scholarship Fund of the University of Cincinnati, which sent local students to Geneva, Switzerland, to study world politics. She served as the executive secretary of the Foreign Policy Association, which was the predecessor of the World Affairs Council. Ruth Neely France helped to organize the Cincinnati Peace League and worked with the Foreign Policy Association. She served as a delegate to a national peace demonstration held in Chicago in the summer of 1932 during the Democratic and Republican National Conventions.[74] This concern for peace was not relegated to those in the cities. Olive A. Cotton was one of the founding members of the Lucas County Council on the Cause and Cure of War.

The 1930s also found women directly confronting the effects of the Great Depression. Women's organizations once again assumed much of the burden of helping to provide for the needs of Ohio's residents. Ohio's unemployment rate in 1930 was 13.3 percent, and it rose to 37.2 percent by 1932. Some cities, such as Cleveland and Toledo, experienced unemployment rates of over 50 percent. Wage reductions averaged 30 percent, and "Hoovervilles" sprung up in Ohio's major cities.[75] The Cincinnati Woman's Club, like many others, raised funds for the unemployed. They hosted a Fellowship Fete and raised $6,000. In 1931–32, they sponsored a milk drive and supplied 86,970 quarts of milk to the city's children. During 1935–37, they raised money for the victims of one of Ohio's worst natural disasters, a flood that only added to the woes of those caught in the throes of the Depression.[76] The Columbus Chapter of the American Red Cross cut and sewed a total of 80,297 garments between October 1932 and April 1933.

Cleveland Associated Charities, formed early in the twentieth century, was the largest distributor of direct relief to the poor in Cleveland between 1928 and 1933. In 1928, it provided aid to 1,379 families, while in 1933, it provided aid to 28,929 families. Helen W. Hanchette served as Cleveland Associated Charities' associate general secretary from 1917 to 1934. In 1935, she continued her career as its first woman executive secretary, a position she held until 1953. When Clevelanders implemented President Franklin D. Roosevelt's relief policies, Cuyahoga County established its County Relief Agency, an organization staffed mainly by women from the Cleveland Associated Charities. In 1935, the Cuyahoga County Relief Agency returned the responsibility for direct relief back to the city.[77]

Another world conflagration led Ohio women to mobilize as they had in 1917. With the entrance of the United States into World War II after the bombing of Pearl Harbor, women's charitable work once again turned to providing United States soldiers with needed items and services. Earlier in 1941, the women of Massillon formed the "Bring the Boys Home for Christmas Club" whose goal was to provide transportation money for all local servicemen to come home from various training camps for Christmas. However, with the bombing of Pearl Harbor, the club was reconstituted on December 8, 1941, as the Victory Mothers' Club. The response was just as quick at other sites around the state. The Fourth General Hospital, Lakeside Unit, the successor to the Lakeside Unit of World War I, set up the first American hospital overseas seventeen days after Pearl Harbor. Seventy-two Cleveland nurses served in this unit, which found its way to the southwest Pacific theater, serving first in Melbourne, Australia, then New Guinea, and finally Manila.[78]

The Cincinnati Woman's Club raised $2,000 for the purchase of fifty hospital beds. The organization purchased war bonds and stamps, sold defense bonds, held classes and knitted for the Red Cross, and made surgical dressings. They also baked seventeen thousand cookies for the soldiers of Fort Thomas and purchased a movie screen for the fort's theater. Their efforts also provided books for the Soldiers' Service Clubs. They recruited nurses, nurses' aides, and volunteered at General Hospital.[79]

In Cleveland, the local section of the National Council of Jewish Women urged its members to volunteer at the Red Cross, USO, and hospitals, along with conserving gasoline and electricity. They encouraged poorer women to save paper, rags, and old metal in order to buy war bonds. In May 1943, forty-six women's groups in Cleveland reported on their members' war activities: 4,690 worked at the Red Cross; 8,000 bought or sold war bonds, 824 worked in civilian defense; 974 volunteered at the USO, and others volunteered at draft or ration boards. In recognition of this work, the Fourth Annual Festival of Freedom, held on July 5, 1943, honored Cleveland's "women at war."[80]

At the conclusion of the war, women were forced to deal with societal changes such as the introduction of nuclear weapons and the demands for civil rights by both blacks and women. As previously noted, racial barriers divided charitable activities in which women participated. But it was obvious that not all women were comfortable with this barrier, and many wished to establish ways to work together. The Woman's City Club of Cincinnati had organized a race relations committee in December 1927, which formulated a plan to keep this issue in the forefront of the club's issues. The club's City Planning Committee, concerned over the deplorable living conditions of many of Cincinnati's black residents who lived in the city's west end, began to look for a solution through planning initiatives. Elsie Austin, the only black female attorney in Cincinnati, addressed the Woman's City Club Race Relations Committee in January 1934, asking them to support the Wagner-Costigan Anti-lynching Bill that was pending in Congress.[81]

During World War II, the Woman's City Club Race Relations Committee kept a watchful eye on those unions who discriminated against blacks and noted the lack of employment of black women in war industries. In the late 1940s, the Woman's City Club committed itself to building an interracial movement. The Race Relations Committee sponsored a tea in March 1947 and invited thirty black women known to be interested in civic affairs. After a discussion of the racial problems in Cincinnati, club members decided that this group should meet regularly. The group formed Fellowship House. One of its most popular educational programs, the "speaking trios" composed of representatives of the black community, the Jewish community, and the white community (the three major racial groups in Cincinnati) addressed civic groups throughout the community about their experiences in facing prejudice and discrimination. By 1949, the club reported that one hundred trios had spoken to over eight thousand people. Finally, in February 1949, two black women, Johnnie Mae Berry and Reber Cann, joined the Woman's City Club, but integration would continue to be a thorny problem.[82]

Ohio's heritage of increasing segregation forced African Americans to establish their own charitable organizations. The Colored Big Sisters organization was formed in Columbus on June 26, 1926, with an interracial board. The goal of this group was to help girls adjust to and surmount problems in their homes and schools, secure employment, and provide general supervision of activities. The Cleveland branch of the National Urban League was formed in 1918 as the Negro Welfare Association, a social service agency created to help largely rural southern blacks in their transition to the urban north. Cleveland's league focused on housing and employment needs. Women served as officers on the board of trustees, but the first woman director, Anita Polk, was not appointed until 1970. By 1946, all league committees had black and white female members.[83]

The National Association for the Advancement of Colored People (NAACP) was the most prominent group that worked for the rights of blacks, both nationally and in Ohio. The Cleveland NAACP chapter formed a women's auxiliary in 1916, and by 1946, Cleveland's was the sixth largest chapter in the country. Many of the membership chairs were women, and in 1945, Dovie D. Sweet was credited with bringing in 500 new members; in subsequent years, she would bring in 150 to 300 members. Women did serve on the chapter's executive committee, and in 1918, members chose Eleanor Alexander as vice president. She became the first woman president in 1930–31. Pearl L. Mitchell, president in 1934, organized an antilynching rally in support of congressional legislation. She became one of the directors of the national organization and headed successful membership drives throughout the country. In 1960, she led the successful fight to integrate the Ohio Soldiers' and Sailors' Home. In 1961, as a national vice president, she attacked the segregation of Cleveland's public schools.[84]

Another group working in Cleveland, though not as actively as the NAACP, was the Congress of Racial Equality (CORE). The chapter president in 1946, Juanita Morrow, led a demonstration protesting the segregation of Euclid Beach Park. Police beat members of Morrow's group as they picketed. Roena Rand and John McCloud revived the chapter in 1962, and in 1963, Ruth Turner became the first executive secretary.[85] The riots during the 1960s in Cleveland, Dayton, and Cincinnati caused people to take a closer look at the social conditions that fomented the riots. With the appointment and election of blacks to state and local offices and a visibly growing black middle class, black advancement became a reality.

Women's rights again took center stage during the 1960s and 1970s, this time focusing on the feminization of poverty, reproductive rights, and equal pay. In 1957, 3,192 families received Aid to Families with Dependent Children (AFDC), and in 1969, 24,817 Cleveland families, of which 13,870 were headed by women, had incomes below the poverty level. With continued cuts in AFDC payments and other types of public assistance during the 1970s, a welfare rights movement developed that centered on women and children. Among the many recipients who became activists was Lillian Craig, a native Clevelander, who founded the National Welfare Rights Organization and was co-author of *The Welfare Rights Manual*.[86]

Various chapters of the National Organization of Women in Ohio supported the Equal Rights Amendment, feminist political candidates, employment of women in male-dominated professions, and the protection of women's reproductive rights. Rape crisis centers opened in Ohio's major cities. The Cleveland Rape Crisis Center opened in 1974. Another group, Women-Together, opened a shelter for battered women in 1975. This was a place where abused women could find not only a safe haven but counseling and job training. As a show of strength, the Greater Cleveland Congress of International Women's Year was held October 25–27, 1975. The International Women's Year was supported by the United Nations with the objective "to define a society in which women participate in a real and full sense in economic, social, and political life and to devise strategies whereby such societies could develop." Cleveland's event was the largest in the nation, attracting approximately fifty thousand people. During the final preparations for this event, the plans for a women's center were completed. WomenSpace opened in spring 1976 and continued to serve as a focal point for women's activities in Cleveland for more than twenty years.[87]

CHAPTER FIVE

Building Ohio's Culture

Arts, Entertainment, and Leisure Activities

WOMEN PLAYED A significant role in providing for the cultural development of Ohio. Many wealthy women served as patrons of the arts, an accepted role for women, utilizing many of their organizational skills to develop world-renowned museums, symphonies, theaters, and schools. Along with their enthusiasm, time, and organizational skills, many upper-class women donated funds, their own collections, and buildings to house museums. Still other women stepped outside their accepted societal roles and onto the stage to become noted artists, vocalists, instrumentalists, and actors.

Mrs. Sarah Worthington King Peter of Cincinnati organized the Ladies' Academy of Fine Arts in 1854 to "aid the cultivation of public taste." The Ladies' Academy of Fine Arts was composed and managed entirely by women. During its first sixty days, it hosted four projects that raised five thousand dollars. Mrs. Peter then went to Europe to purchase *copies* of European masters that could be displayed in a permanent collection. She was successful in her endeavor and returned to Cincinnati with reproductions that were displayed in the Ladies' Academy of Fine Arts gallery until 1864, when the association was disbanded. In the interest of modesty, however, Mrs. Peter had fig leaves applied on the paintings where appropriate. The Ladies' Academy of Fine Arts was one of the first groups in America to meet the goal of bringing art to the people.[1]

A group of men and women met in Cincinnati on March 12, 1877, and established a committee to develop an Art Museum and Training School. A few weeks later, on April 28, 1877, the Women's Art Museum Association (WAMA) was founded with Elizabeth Williams Perry as president. The group's goal was the "cultivation and application of the principles of art to industrial pursuits and the establishment of an art museum in the City of Cincinnati."[2] In 1878, the group presented the Cincinnati Loan Exhibition, attended by more than thirteen thousand people during its six-week run. The WAMA located its exhibition in the south wing of the Exposition Building in 1879. Soon thereafter, they raised enough funds through subscriptions and donations to build an art museum, and on March 8, 1881, the Cincinnati Museum Association was organized. Five years later, on April 3, 1886, the WAMA transferred its collection of art objects and furniture to the Museum Association. On May 17, 1886, the Cincinnati Art Museum was dedicated and opened to the public. Annie Sinton Taft and her husband, Charles P. Taft, presented their home, paintings, and porcelains to the city as a museum, the Taft Art Gallery, and in time others continued the tradition. Mary Emery added her collection to the Fine Arts Wing of the Cincinnati Art Museum; Miss Mary Hanna erected another wing in memory of her father, and other substantial donations were made by J. G. Schmidlapp in honor of his wife and by Mrs. Frederick Alms.

Cleveland's women also served as patrons of the arts, but initially they were geared more toward the promotion of the arts. In 1878, a group of wealthy women organized, within their own circle, an exhibition of locally owned collections as a fund-raiser for local hospitals. In 1883, Mrs. Liberty E. Holden persuaded her husband, owner and publisher of the *Cleveland Plain Dealer,* to buy a collection of Italian Renaissance paintings and house them in a gallery on their estate in Bratenahl. The Cleveland Sorosis, a ladies' cultural club, was founded in 1891 and had as its goal the pursuit of "the higher things of life, culture, responsibility and service." However, it wasn't until the beginning of the twentieth century that wealthy Clevelanders turned their attention to providing the community with an art museum. The Cleveland Museum of Art was incorporated in 1913, and in 1916 it opened on University Circle. There were no women who served on the board of trustees in its early years, but a few of its major donors were women. Mrs. Holden purchased the James Jackson Jarves collection of Italian primitives and donated it to the museum. Elisabeth Severance Allen Prentiss, daughter of Louis H. Severance and widow of Cleveland surgeon, Dr. Dudley P. Allen, donated her collection of seventeenth- and eighteenth-century European paintings and decorative arts. Mrs. Henry Norwell, wife of a diplomat, donated her pre-Columbian art collection. Norwell was one of the first Americans to be interested in such art.[3]

Other communities also showed their love of the arts. In 1912, the Dayton Art Museum, a gift of Mrs. Harrie Gardner Carnell, was organized with Mrs. Henry Stoddard as president. The Marion Art Club was organized in 1921 with Mrs. James Craumer serving as its first president. Toledo, through the support of Edward Libbey, the prominent glass manufacturer, developed a first-class museum. During the latter half of the twentieth century, Columbus, Youngstown, and Akron supported growing art centers and collections.

Music was an early form of entertainment and culture on the Ohio frontier and would continue to increase in importance as the state emerged and grew. From local singing schools to world-class orchestras, Ohio's citizens showed their love for good music.

Cincinnati women, such as Mrs. Charles P. Taft and Mrs. William H. Taft (née Helen Herrone, daughter of a prominent Cincinnati civic leader), among others, decided to form the Ladies' Musical Club in 1893 for the purpose of establishing a symphony orchestra. Mrs. William Howard Taft served as president of this group's board and worked with the group for seven years before leaving Cincinnati to accompany her husband, whom President McKinley had appointed head of the United States Commission, to the Philippines. Annie Sinton Taft then took over leadership of the group.

Later the Tafts, along with Cora Dow and Dolly Louise Cohen, would leave significant bequests to the Cincinnati Symphony.

Adelia Prentiss Hughes was the guiding force behind the development of the Cleveland Orchestra and is often referred to as its "mother." After graduating from Vassar College, Hughes returned to Cleveland and became an accompanist for visiting artists at musical benefits. She was a member of the Fortnightly Club, a group founded in 1894 that sought "to advance the interests of music in Cleveland by sponsoring recitals by members and concerts by visiting performers."[4] In 1898, Hughes began a new career as a booking agent that would culminate in the founding of the Cleveland Orchestra. She brought to Cleveland various world-renowned artists and in 1915 formed, with a group of businessmen, the Musical Arts Association, which would continue to help with this endeavor. In 1918, Hughes and the association, with funding from John L. Severance, a wealthy industrialist, founded the Cleveland Orchestra. The orchestra made its first tour in 1920 and moved to its current quarters, Severance Hall, in 1931. Adelia Prentiss Hughes served as the orchestra general manager until 1933.

Women also supported the training of talented artists and musicians, especially women, in their home state. They were able to provide the funds and organizational abilities that led to the development of schools of design, conservatories, and other facilities that offered world-class training.

Clara Baur, founder of the Cincinnati Conservatory of Music, arrived in Cincinnati from Germany in 1849, where she kept house for her brothers and taught piano and voice. In 1867, she established a music studio in conjunction with a fashionable girls' school, and within two years she had enough students to employ a dozen teachers. By 1896, the conservatory had 800 students, 747 of whom were female. Upon her death in 1912, her niece, Bertha Baur, took over the running of the conservatory. Originally, Bertha had come to the conservatory to study with her aunt, but she had gradually assumed responsibility for recruiting students in the United States and Europe. She became associate director in the 1880s and became director in 1912, a job she filled until 1930. At that point, she gave the conservatory to the Cincinnati Institute of Fine Arts.[5]

Sarah Worthington King Peter attempted unsuccessfully in 1854 to establish a school of design in conjunction with the Ladies' Gallery of Fine Arts in Cincinnati. However in 1869, a bequest to the City of Cincinnati by Charles McMicken, an entrepreneur and real estate investor, funded the McMicken School of Design, which became part of the University of Cincinnati in 1871. The school established the Practical Art Department in 1873, and Agnes Pittman, a noted potter, volunteered her services. The McMicken School of Design began offering a class in china painting for young women in 1874 and exhibited examples of the students' work at the Sixth Annual Exhibition of the School of Design the same year. In February 1884, the McMicken School of Design was transferred to the Cincinnati Museum Association and was renamed the Art School of Cincinnati, which was generously funded by Nicholas Longworth. The school was renamed the Cincinnati Art Academy in 1887 when it moved into a new headquarters funded by Reuben Springer and David Senton.

One of the most significant factors in design reform of the late nineteenth and early twentieth centuries was the Arts and Crafts Movement. It began in Great Britain as a rebellion against an increasingly industrialized and mechanized society, and the movement soon made its way to the United States. The goals of the Arts and Crafts Movement were to revive handcraftsmanship, to establish working conditions that allowed for the draftsperson to have more control over the creative process, to cultivate an aesthetic of simplicity, and to elevate the decorative arts to the status of the fine arts. The belief that the decorative arts were equal to the fine arts greatly benefited women, since it bestowed dignity to crafts and provided an avenue to professionalize women's skills.[6]

In 1882, Sarah Kimble, along with Mrs. Stevenson Burke, Mrs. Liberty E. Holden, and others, began the Western Reserve School of Design for Women. Due to the popularity of the Arts and Crafts

Movement for women, the school's objectives were to "'teach the principles of Art and Design as practically applied to artists and industrial pursuits' and to exhibit works of art."[7] The School of Design was incorporated with Western Reserve University in 1888, but because of its vocational objectives it did not fit well within academe and the merger ended in 1891. In 1891, the school became known as the Cleveland School of Art, and Georgia Leighton Norton served as its head. It underwent another name change in 1948, when it became the Cleveland Institute of Art.

The institution that gave women the greatest access to artistic training, creative potential, and renown was Rookwood Pottery in Cincinnati. As mentioned previously, the Arts and Crafts Movement, beginning in the late 1870s and continuing through the 1880s, provided women with an acceptable artistic outlet. In Cincinnati, this movement focused on pottery and porcelain. In preparation for the nation's centennial celebration and the Centennial Exposition in Philadelphia, the Women's Centennial Committee was formed, with Mrs. Elizabeth Williams Perry as president. It was decided that the ladies of Cincinnati would exhibit examples of their artwork in Philadelphia, including woodcarving and china painting. Ben Pittman hired Miss Marie Eggers as a teacher of china painting, and she had a class of about two dozen women. They painted facsimile signatures of George and Martha Washington, along with American flags, on china cups. These cups were the first china decorated by unpaid women amateurs outside of a home setting in the United States.[8]

In September 1875, Mary Louise McLaughlin, an exhibitor at the Centennial Exhibition, became intrigued with what she saw there and began experimenting with underglaze painting techniques. She was founder and first president of the Pottery Club, which started on April 1, 1879. Other charter members were Clara Chipman Newton, Alice Belle Holabird, Minerva Engart Dominick, Florence Leonard Kebler, Mary Rhodes Ellis, Henrietta D. Leonard, Abbie Taylor Field, L. M. Merriam, Mrs. Mary Virginia Keenan, Clara Fletcher, and Agnes Pittman. The Pottery Club held its first exhibition on May 5, 1880, and later that month received national attention with an article in *Harper's Weekly.*[9]

Upon returning from the Centennial Exposition, McLaughlin began to experiment to reproduce the underglaze technique she saw exhibited by Haviland Company of Limoges, France. Her first successful piece with the underglaze painted faience was taken from the kiln in January 1878, and on May 6, she displayed several pieces at the Cincinnati Loan Exhibition. Later that year, she sent representative pieces to an exhibition in New York and to the Paris Exposition Universelle, where she received an Honorable Mention. In order to continue her work, McLaughlin paid for a kiln to be built at the Frederick Dallas Pottery in Cincinnati that would be devoted exclusively to the firing of underglaze painting. She also branched out into decorative metalwork and won a Silver Medal at the Paris Exposition Universelle in 1889 for her overglaze decoration with metallic effects. McLaughlin also wrote books concerning the various techniques she used. These included *China Painting—A Practical Guide for the Use of Amateurs in the Decoration of Hard Porcelain* and *Pottery Decoration under the Glaze.*[10]

Maria Longworth Nichols (later Storer), upon her return from the Centennial Exposition, began to incorporate Japanese designs in her work. In May 1879, she began working in wet clay at the Frederick Dallas Pottery, but in 1880, she founded her own pottery company, the first in Cincinnati to be owned by a woman, naming it Rookwood after her childhood home. The first kiln was drawn on Thanksgiving Day, and one of the pieces to come from it was the Aladdin Vase decorated by Nichols. In 1882, Nichols was awarded a Gold Medal at the Tenth Cincinnati Industrial Exposition for her white-tinted ware. She continued her experiments and was awarded a patent in 1887 for the process of "chromatic ornamentation of pottery by the incorporation of color or pigment in the body material or in the glaze in addition to applying color to the surface of the vase itself."[11]

Clara Chipman Newton was hired as Rookwood's secretary, and the Pottery Club took up residence at Rookwood in July 1881. Soon after, Rookwood expanded its facilities and Laura A. Fry, Henrietta (Harriet) Wenderoth, Fanny Auckland, and three men were employed as decorators. Rookwood continued to prosper and opened an exhibition room in fall 1882 under the direction of Kate Wood. At the same time, it employed a traveling salesman. In late 1885, Rookwood began to gather examples of its early pieces to be added to the Cincinnati Art Museum's permanent collection. By 1889, Rookwood was self-supporting. Maria Nichols Storer retired the following year, signing the operation over to her manager, William Walter Taylor, and spent most of her time studying at the Cincinnati Art Academy. Rookwood continued to provide a training ground and creative outlet for some of the country's greatest ceramic artists.

Other women in Ohio were also working in this medium. Evelyn Elizabeth Shultz Wentz worked in enamels, glazes, and stained glass in Fostoria. During the Depression, as part of the Works Progress Administration, Emilie Scrivens, Elizabeth Seaver, Grace Luce, and Edris Eckhardts, a graduate of the Cleveland School of Art, created ceramic figures for children's libraries.[12]

Society's acceptance of women's involvement in the Arts and Crafts Movement did not extend to the theater. It took almost a century beyond statehood for Ohio to begin to develop strong repertory theaters. Frances Trollope's opinion on theaters, expressed in 1828 as she visited Cincinnati, held sway for a long period of time: "They have a theatre, which is, in fact, the only public amusement of this triste little town, but they seem to care little about it, and either from economy or distaste, it is very poorly attended. Ladies are rarely seen there, and by far the larger proportion of females deem it an offense against religion to witness the representation of a play."[13] However, by the beginning of the twentieth century women became more involved with theater—both in its promotion and as actors. In 1916, the Play House Campaign was formed in Cleveland, which would become the Cleveland Playhouse, the oldest continuously running repertory company in the country.

Russell and Rowena Jelliffe established Playhouse Settlement in Cleveland in 1915. It had the usual settlement house activities for children and young adults, both black and white. It soon began to emphasize theatrical activities, and in 1917 the house staged *Cinderella* with an integrated cast. The Jelliffes noted that this opportunity for people of different races to work together and learn about each other's cultural heritage was significant. After attending a Pan African Congress in Paris in 1921, the Jelliffes became very interested in African art, and this became an integral part of the settlement's programs. In 1927, a newly renovated theater named "Karamu" opened at the settlement, and in 1941, the Playhouse Settlement was renamed Karamu House. The Jelliffes directed Karamu House until their retirement in 1963.[14]

Society expected genteel ladies of the nineteenth century to have some skill in painting or drawing, appropriate pastimes for women. However, some women were able to take it beyond a pastime and pursue a career with their artwork—some on a local level, but others developed international reputations. In light of the numerous women artists in Ohio, this discussion will review only a few of the early prominent artists. Mrs. Clark was a noted watercolor artist in Piqua in the 1840s; at the same time, Mrs. Lois Mansfield from Poland had her paintings exhibited in public and private galleries. Miss Lily Martin Spencer (1822–1901), with the financial support of Nicholas Longworth, was able to study art in Cincinnati. She showed early promise in the use of charcoals and later exhibited her works in New York. Some of her most significant works include "Self Portrait" (about 1848), "The Cook" (1854), and "The Pic Nic or the Fourth of July." Miss Cleveland, who painted in watercolors, is believed to be the pioneer artist in Cleveland. Little is known about her except that her studio was already in operation when Miss Caroline L. Ormes Ransom opened her studio in Cleveland in 1860, after studying in New York and Germany. Ransom was the most financially successful of the female artists of the late nineteenth century. She developed her reputation by painting large oil portraits of political leaders and other nota-

The War Spirit at Home—Celebrating the Victory at Vicksburg, *painting by Lily Martin Spencer, 1866*

bles. One of her paintings, a portrait of Joshua Giddings, the prominent Western Reserve congressman, was the first work of art by a female artist purchased by the United States government. And in 1895, Elizabeth Nourse of Cincinnati was the first American woman elected to the Société Nationale des Beaux Arts.[15]

Women artists continued to flourish during the early twentieth century. Alice Archer Sewell James of Urbana found her paintings hanging on the "walls of Paris salons and [the] Carnegie Institute."[16] Dayton artists included Annie Campbell, Juliet Burdoin, Mrs. Jess Brown Aull, Rosalie Loury, and Martha K. Schauer. Grace V. Kelley was a well-known member of the Cleveland art community, and Alice Schille and Josephine Klippert influenced the

Columbus art community. Klippert founded the Ohio Water Color Society and was its president for many years.

Government-sponsored artistic endeavors by women characterized the 1930s. Many female artists were employed by the Works Progress Administration during the Great Depression. Gladys Carambella painted murals of children's fairy tales for the children's wards of City and Sunny Acre Hospitals in Cleveland, along with several elementary schools. Women also used their artistic skills in other endeavors. Edwina Dunn invented the cartoon characters "Cap Stubbs" and his dog "Tippy," and Caroline Williams did sketches for the *Cincinnati Enquirer.*[17]

Sculpture was another area within the arts in which women participated. Anna Eugenia Felicia Morgan, one of the earliest sculptors in Ohio, worked in this medium in 1845 while attending Oberlin. Evelyn B. Longman, born in 1874 in Winchester, Adams County, was the best-known Ohio woman sculptor and the first woman sculptor to become a member of the National Academy. Another notable sculptor was Mary Elizabeth Cook, who was born in Chillicothe in 1881. The American and French governments honored her unique work during World War I—she sculpted six hundred life masks for the reconstruction of faces of American soldiers killed during the war. Other sculptors of note included Frances Grimes of Braceville, Anna M. Valentine of Cincinnati, Ruth Maurer Yates of Greenville, Harriet A. Ketcham of Scio, and Katherine Schmidt of Xenia.

Photography was another area in which women excelled artistically. One such woman, Nell Dorr (Nellie Becker) was born in Cleveland in 1895, but she became interested in photography when her family moved to Massillon. She went to the Florida Keys to take photographs, and then moved to New York City to pursue her art. Her first book, *In a Blue Moon,* published in 1939, included the pictures she took in the Florida Keys in 1929. Another book, *Mother and Child,* appeared in 1954 and was reissued in 1972. By 1954, she was acknowledged as one of America's great women photographers; the Corcoran Gallery in Washington, D. C., honored

Dorr by naming her as one of its "Ten Best Women in Photography." She believed that "a woman can live in photography and have it reflect her home, her family, her children, and leave a document of her time."[18]

Another noted photographer was Berenice Abbott, born in Springfield, Ohio, on July 17, 1898. She attended Ohio State University, moved to New York City and then to Paris to study sculpture. While in Paris she became interested in photography and worked as a darkroom assistant. She opened her own studio where she made portraits of such people as James Joyce, Edna St. Vincent Millay and Marcel Duchamp. Abbott returned to New York in 1929 and began documenting the Great Depression through photographs. These photographs were published in the book *Changing New York*. At the time of her death in 1991, her photographs were exhibited in galleries throughout the world.[19]

Music was a particularly important form of expression and entertainment for women. It was an area in which all women, with or without formal training, could participate by singing in local groups, church choirs, accompanying singing groups, playing an instrument (preferably the piano), or even performing on stage. Singing schools, popular institutions on the Ohio frontier, provided a social outlet for both women and men. The leader of a singing school would travel from cabin to cabin directing the vocal and instrumental efforts of its residents. These singing schools provided one of the few appropriate places for young men and women to meet under the watchful eyes of the community. Church choirs often served the same purposes. Phebe Carr organized the first choir in Ridgefield Township in Huron County, and on August 13, 1855, the Columbus Beethoven Association was formed. Men and women who could "read and perform church music properly and were of good moral character" were eligible to join.[20] Other choral societies developed throughout the state. The Cincinnati May Festival, which began in 1873 through the efforts of Maria Storer, provided an opportunity for many of these groups to come together to perform. A woman's choral group was formed in 1899 in Cleveland,

and from 1907 to 1910, Estelle Ford, a trained vocalist from the Cleveland Conservatory of Music, served as its director. Even during the Depression, one of the federal musicians projects included a choral group in Cleveland that performed *The Mikado*.

Ethnic groups also developed singing societies to keep their cultures alive. In 1849 in Cincinnati, several German singing societies met to establish an organization to "foster good fellowship and folk songs of the fatherland." The first German Sängerfest in the United States was held in Cincinnati June 1–3, 1849. Singing societies competed for prizes, and intense rivalries emerged between groups and towns.[21] Cleveland also had its singing societies, and these groups held five Sängerfests in Cleveland between 1855 and 1927. These events included such activities as picnics, torchlight processions, dinners, and balls—all designed to keep the ethnic heritage alive.[22]

Many other talented Ohio women received formal training and pursued careers either as vocalists or instrumentalists on the stages of Europe and the United States. Cornelia Cowles, a professional musician, performed in Reverend Aiken's church in Cleveland in 1837, and in 1838 sang at St. Peter's Episcopal Church in Brooklyn, New York. She became the talk of the town for her "conspicuous" parts in public performances. Adelina Patti sang in Walcutt's Hall in Columbus in 1851. She was accompanied by her sister, Madame Strakosch. Theresa Parodi sang Mendelssohn's *Jerusalem* at Neil's Hall in Columbus in 1854.

More opportunities were available for women to study and perform music after the 1870s. Lillian Bailey Henschel from Columbus studied voice in Paris, and in 1878 appeared with the London Philharmonic. Rachel Walker Turner, an African American soprano, began her career as a teacher in the Cleveland public schools. In the mid-1890s, she went to New York for formal voice training and began touring the United States in 1895–96 as a soloist with white musical companies. She later went to London for further study. She appeared in several European venues, but returned to Cleveland after the outbreak of World War I.[23]

Many Ohio women graced the stages of the world's opera houses. Jean Osborn Hannah, born in Wilmington in 1873, joined the Chicago Opera Company as a soprano. Cyrena Van Gordon, born in Camden in 1896 and ultimately recognized as one of the great contraltos, performed with the Chicago Opera Company. Rose Bampton, born in Cleveland in 1909, an Ohio resident until the age of seventeen and thereafter a resident of Buffalo, New York, began her operatic career with the Chautauqua Opera Company in 1928. She was given a Metropolitan Opera contract and sang mezzo soprano roles for five years. On May 5, 1937, she made her second Metropolitan Opera debut, but this time singing soprano. After her marriage, she and her husband made the first paid tour to South Africa.[24] Grace Divine, born in Wyoming, Ohio, and Queens Mario from Akron also became Metropolitan Opera stars. Other Ohio stars of the early twentieth century included Marjorie Squires, Ruby Mercer, Helen Jepsen (who later signed with Samuel Goldwyn Productions), Lila Rebeson, Mary Van Kirk, and Alma Jean Smith. Smith was born in East Cleveland, attended the Cleveland Music School Settlement and Oberlin Conservatory, and made her Metropolitan Opera touring company debut in Cleveland's Public Hall in 1974. Betty Allen, who made her operatic debut in Kansas City in 1966 in Purcell's *Dido and Aeneas,* had toured with the Wilberforce Singers, as did her classmate, Leontyne Price.[25]

Ohio women also gained reputations locally, nationally, and internationally for their abilities as instrumentalists. In the early years, the piano was the instrument deemed most appropriate for women. Emilee Pardee Hanchet of Wadsworth was one of the first settlers to have a piano on the Ohio frontier around 1820. When that town's Presbyterian church was dedicated, the piano was taken to the church, a very unusual occurrence, and Hanchet led the song service. Cynthia Shannon Dutton of Youngstown stepped beyond the bounds of custom and played the violin. Criticized for performing in public, she played in the garret of her home for her own pleasure. Her daughter, Jane Dutton Wick, was also musically talented but chose to play the piano. When she returned from school in the East, her father purchased for her the first pianoforte ever brought to Youngstown.[26]

More opportunities for women instrumentalists appeared by the turn of the century. Fannie Bloomfield Zeisler and Julia Rivé-King from Cincinnati were noted pianists, as were Madame Ninn Romaine of Toledo, Vera Barstow from Celina, Josephine Forsyth Myers from Cleveland, Pauline Harrison from Massillon, and Lue Alice Keller from Findlay. In 1901, the Cleveland Federation of Musicians began to admit women, and by 1910, thirty-five female instrumentalists were registered.

Some instrumentalists were also composers, such as Julie Rivé-King (1857–1937) of Cincinnati, who wrote virtuoso piano pieces. Local songwriters included Julia Marlowe, Clara Morris, and Ella May Smith. Ruth Crawford Seeger (1901–1953) of East Liverpool in 1930 was the first American woman to receive a Guggenheim Fellowship to study in France and Germany. She is considered among the most significant female composers of the twentieth century. Her influence extended beyond classical music to folk music collecting and cultural activism.

Other talented women turned their energies to teaching. Madame Rostel was teaching piano in Cincinnati as early as 1817. As previously noted, Clara Baur founded the Cincinnati Conservatory in 1867. Music was taught in the public schools in several Ohio cities, and many women were able to earn a living teaching in public classrooms. Others gave instrumental or vocal lessons in private institutions, such as the Cleveland School of Music, which opened in 1875. Ida Frances Horton was an instructor in instrumental music at Wilberforce College in 1914. Dorothy Richard Starling taught and performed throughout her life, and upon her death in 1969, her husband established the one-million-dollar Dorothy Richard Starling Chair in Classical Violin Music at the College Conservatory of Music in Cincinnati. Women continue to teach at all the major music schools and departments in the state at both private and public institutions.

The theater and, in later years, the silver screen, attracted many Ohio women, even though societal norms viewed this type of public performance by women even more harshly than those previously discussed. As Mrs. Trollope pointed out, Christian women (i.e., "good" women) shunned attending such activities in the early years of statehood. The noted actress Jenny Lind did play Cincinnati and Columbus in 1851. One of the earliest female actors in Ohio was Pauline Hall of Cincinnati, who was popular during the last years of the nineteenth century. Cincinnati was also home to Delia O'Callahan, whose stage name was Trixie Friganza. The most popular female actor of this time period, however, was Elsie Janis from Columbus. She went to France to entertain the troops during World War I and was called "the Sweetheart of the A.E.F." (American Expeditionary Force).[27] Rae Samuels from Youngstown starred in the Ziegfield Follies, as did Marilyn Miller from Hancock County. Miller, who made her acting debut in Dayton in 1903, starred in the plays *Sally* in 1920 and *Sunny* in 1925. She was one of the leading glamour girls of the era. Julia Marlowe (Sarah Frostin England) lived in Ironton and Portsmouth and made her stage debut at the age of twelve using the name Frances Brough. She would become one of the great Shakespearean actors of the late nineteenth and early twentieth centuries.[28] Amelia Bingham, born in Hicksville in 1869, left Ohio Wesleyan University to pursue a stage career, and she was soon traveling throughout the United States. A few women were employed by the Works Progress Administration in theater projects during the Great Depression. Two federal theater projects were located in Cleveland. Successful productions of *The Loving Newspaper* and *Triple A Ploughed Under* employed a few women.

Some women utilized their skills by directing theater productions. Amelia Bingham became a producer after having a successful acting career. She took over the Bijou Theatre in New York City and in January 1901 opened in her own production of Clyde Fitch's *Climbers*. Other successful productions followed. Bingham is thought to be the first American actress to succeed as a producer.

Elsie Janis, "The Sweetheart of the A.E.F." (Ohio Historical Society)

Cheryl Crawford, another producer, was born in Akron in 1902. After a brief acting career she turned her attention to directing. In 1932 she founded the Group Theatre with Harold Churman and Lee Strasberg. She established the American Repertory Theatre in 1945 and helped to found the Actors' Studio in 1947 with Elia Kazan and Robert Lewis. Crawford produced the Broadway revivals of *Porgy and Bess* in 1942 and *Brigadoon* in 1943, along with the works of Tennessee Williams and Berthold Brecht.[29]

By 1915, however, a new form of theater, the moving picture, was introduced, and this innovation gave actors another medium for their talents. There are probably no greater silent film stars than the Ohio-born Gish sisters—Dorothy and Lillian. The Gish sisters were originally stage actors. Lillian made her debut in Rising Sun, Ohio, in a play called *In Convict's Stripes*. Dorothy had a part in a melodrama *East Lynne*. They continued to occasionally appear on stage but were more and more engrossed with the movie industry. They played the leads in many popular films between 1915 and 1930, including *Birth of a Nation, Broken Blossoms, Orphans of*

Actress Lillian Gish
(Ohio Historical Society)

the Storm, and *Way Down East.* In 1984, at the age of ninety, Lillian received the Life Achievement Award from the American Film Institute.[30]

Other early movie stars included Theda Bara, born Theodosia Goodman in Cincinnati, the first "vampire" of film; Marguerite Clark from Cincinnati; and Alice Calhoun of Cleveland. Eleanor Whitney of Cleveland became a dancer in the movies, and Charlotte Louise Shockley, a contralto soprano with the Cincinnati Symphony Orchestra, appeared in a supporting role in the movie *Mau Mau Drums.* Perhaps one of the most hated and loved faces in the movies is that of the Wicked Witch of the West in the *Wizard of Oz.* The face belonged to Cleveland native Margaret Hamilton. The first black woman to win an Oscar nomination for best actress was also a Cleveland native, Dorothy Dandridge. Dandridge was nominated for her performance in *Carmen Jones* in 1954. Dandridge died at the early age of forty-two in 1965. Doris Day (born Doris van Kappelhoff) was born in Cincinnati in 1924. After an accident ended her career as a dancer, she turned to singing and became a successful band singer with Les Brown. In 1948 she embarked upon her movie career as a replacement in *Romance on the High Seas*. She was a hit in movie musicals and comedies during the 1950s and 1960s, starring with Cary Grant. During the late 1960s and 1970s, Day hosted television programs.[31]

A few early Ohio playwrights were women. Among these were Florence H. Morgan of Cleveland, born in 1861; Dorothy Kuhns Heyward, born in Wooster in 1890; and Alberta Pierson Hannum, born in Condit, Delaware County, in 1906.

Other forms of entertainment allowed for women's participation both as entertainers and spectators. The image of the western frontier with its rough ways fascinated many "Easterners" and because of this, "Wild West" shows drew large crowds wherever they played. One of the highlights of most of these shows was the riding and shooting skills of the show members particularly if they were female. One such early entertainer was Emma Lake. Lake, who grew up in Cincinnati, eloped with the clown when the Robinson and Eberts Circus performed there in 1845. She entered show business and spent eleven seasons with the Floating Palace, a circus in Cincinnati. She and her husband then opened their own circus. After her husband was shot and killed in Granby, Ohio, for refusing to admit a man who had no ticket, Lake continued operating and supervising the day-to-day affairs of the business. She also continued her riding. It is said that Buffalo Bill thought her to be the best equestrian in the country.[32]

Another Buckeye native made her name a common household word through her abilities to entertain. Phoebe Ann Moses of Darke County, a native of Woodington who spent her early years in an orphanage, discovered at the age of fourteen that she had a great ability to accurately shoot a rifle. Moses earned her living by hunting and selling game to markets in Cleveland. In 1875, she visited a local shooting club and beat professional marksman Frank Butler. Phoebe and Frank married in 1876 and decided to use Phoebe's skills in a more lucrative manner. She took the stage name Annie Oakley and toured in vaudeville shows, including

Annie Oakley (Ohio Historical Society)

Spring festivities, Kent State University, ca. 1920 (Kent State University Archives)

Buffalo Bill's Wild West Show, for eighteen years. She was given the name "Little Sure Shot," and in 1887, she was presented to Queen Victoria. Both Annie and Frank died in 1926. Adele von Ohl Parker, an adopted Ohioan, replaced Annie Oakley in Buffalo Bill's Wild West Show, revitalizing it in North Olmsted.[33]

As technology changed, so did the acceptable roles for women. Women soon became involved in other areas of the entertainment industry. Radio provided women with new opportunities. Early radio entertainers from Ohio included Vera Van (Marion), Carolyn Dies (Dayton), Connie Gates (Cleveland), Margaret Speaker (Columbus), Genevieve Rowe (Fremont), Eileen Ellsworth (Cleveland), Helen Nugent (Cincinnati), Loretta Clemens (Cleveland), Hortense Rose (Coalton), and Grace Donaldson (Columbus). Marjorie Yost Marimer hosted a cooking program on WFMJ radio

Margaret Zilla, Kent State University archery student, 1947 (Kent State University Archives)

in Cleveland in 1951, and with the advent of television in 1953, she hosted the television program *Kitchen Corner.* Another Ohio woman, Paige Palmer, hit the national television scene as one of the first female fitness experts to host a syndicated program in the 1950s.

Women were also engaged in physical pursuits, even though throughout most of the nineteenth century physical activity was discouraged for being too stimulating for women. Mrs. Susan Hooff of Vernon did not take this to heart and found her favorite pastime in the early nineteenth century to be fishing. She was considered an expert angler, and other women would accompany her on her excursions to the Pymatuning River. Mrs. Hooff does seem to be an exception. For the most part, women's opportunities to participate in physical activity were limited to a few "ladylike" sports such as croquet and lawn tennis. In time, cycling and skating would be added to the list of acceptable activities.

Early in the twentieth century, team sports developed for women but generally not in a competitive framework. Most were engaged in exhibitions. Young female gymnasts performed on the uneven bars during a holiday exhibition in 1912; others ran track at Lake Erie College. The female garment workers at Richman Brothers in Cleveland played baseball, the national pastime, while on their lunch break. Women formed equestrian clubs, and golf and field hockey eventually became sports available to women.

The passage of Title IX legislation in 1972 by the federal government provided opportunities for women to engage in competitive sports such as volleyball, basketball, and soccer in high schools and colleges. Ohio's schools responded by adding competitive team sports for women at the secondary and postsecondary levels. This opened the way for the development of professional sports for women. The Cleveland Brewers of the Women's Professional Football League formed in 1979, and the Cleveland Rockers of the Women's Professional Basketball Association formed in the 1990s. Today, girls and young women throughout the state compete in volleyball, soccer, basketball, track, gymnastics, swimming, softball, and field hockey, giving them the opportunity to develop physically and pursue leisure activities.

Women's opportunities to engage in public activities that spotlight their skills and talents have increased tremendously throughout the past two hundred years. Most of these opportunities have been of their own making, and through their initiative and energetic activities, they have provided the citizens of Ohio with world-class orchestras, art museums, and theaters and have expanded the horizons for the young women following in their footsteps.

CHAPTER SIX

Women's Contributions in Religion, Education, and Literature

DURING THE NINETEENTH century, women's roles were prescribed in every segment of their lives. Women's participation in religion and education were well defined and were tied directly to the ideology and expectations of "republican motherhood" and the "cult of domesticity." A woman's duty, in this developing republic, was to educate her sons to be moral and virtuous citizens who would sacrifice their individual advantage for the common good. Women were seen as more virtuous than men, because they did not have to work in the public sphere (politics or business). Therefore, women were responsible for nurturing children, caring for the home, and upholding social morality. However, in nineteenth-century Ohio, "morality" was typically defined from a white, middle-class perspective, and this definition of morality helped determine the efforts of reformers and missionaries.[1] Both of these arenas eventually allowed women increasingly greater commitments outside the home through access to higher education, professional education, and professional occupations beyond the prescribed societal boundaries. Not only did women use their greater opportunities to interact with the world outside of their homes, but they also showed the outcomes of these interactions through their participation and leadership in church-related activities, the development of and participation in female education, and their literary achievements.

The wave of religious revival meetings known as the second Great Awakening that began in the late eighteenth century reached its height in the 1820s. This movement, along with the ideals of "republican motherhood," further shaped women's sense of duty and moral obligation. Revivals encouraged women to participate in public events by praying in mixed audiences, even though they were condemned by some for doing so. For some women, this participation was the first step toward acting on their beliefs without the approval of men. Their religious and moral commitments helped to bring their activities out of the private sphere and into the public sphere.[2]

As discussed in chapter 1, women figured prominently in the establishment of churches during the frontier period. Women like Rebecca Rouse set the tenor for Ohio's communities. Rouse, along with her husband, came to the Western Reserve at the request of the American Sabbath School Union in 1830. Within one month, she had organized the Ladies Tract Society of the Village of Cleveland, an auxiliary to the parent society in New York. She was also one of the founders of the First and Second Baptist Churches. Margaret Dow Gebby, who resided near Bellefontaine, Ohio, recorded in her diary that the Presbyterian church she belonged to allowed women to vote on an equal footing as men on important issues such as the election of a pastor. Women in the Wesley Chapel of the Methodist Church in Columbus protested the requirement that the sexes separate upon entering church, and as a result "promiscuous seatings" were allowed in 1854.[3]

The support of foreign missions was another important activity for many women, and missionary work would lead some women to places unknown. Foreign missionary work took women to places such as India, the Philippines, and Africa. Usually they accompanied their husbands, who were also missionaries. Single women who wished to engage in missionary work often did so among the

Native American tribes, accompanying brothers, fathers, or family friends. Most Protestant denominations formed missionary aid societies that supported the work of the missionaries financially and provided items such as Bibles. Through participation in these societies, women who could not leave home to be missionaries felt that they were contributing to a vital cause. Mrs. Mary H. Severance of Cleveland helped form the first organized Foreign Missionary Society in that city. The society began with about a dozen women from the First Presbyterian Church, and Severance filled the role of secretary for twenty years. Even before this, church sewing circles from within various denominations were providing missionaries both at home and abroad with needed supplies. Cleveland's churchwomen formed the first ecumenical group in 1832, with Mrs. Richard Lord serving as its president. Women possessed the managerial skills that allowed these organizations to run effectively. However, the value of these managerial skills to women's ability to organize to fight for their own rights was often overlooked. As Margaret Dow Gebby pointed out in her journals, it was not an uncommon occurrence for the regional Presbytery (church governing body) and Women's Missionary Society meetings to be going on simultaneously. While providing meals for more than one hundred people, the women were still able to conduct the business of the Missionary Society.[4]

Oberlin College helped educate women for missionary work. Oberlin sought to train "a band of self-denying, hardy, intelligent, efficient laborers, of both sexes, for the world's enlightenment and regeneration."[5] Women were to be educated to help bring about the salvation of the world. Achsah Colburn, who attended Oberlin from 1837 to 1841, explained her decision to attend the college in this way: "I wish to go where not only the intellect but the moral principle will be cultivated, disciplined, and trained for active service in the vineyard of the Lord."[6] By 1900, more than one thousand Oberlin graduates had been, or were, missionaries in Canada, Jamaica, the west coast of Africa, and among the Native American tribes in northern Minnesota.[7]

Other women became missionaries, most accompanying their husbands to various outposts. Martha Sturtevant of Painesville married Reverend Horace S. Tyler and accompanied him to southern India, where they stayed for many years. Besides helping her husband with his work, she raised their family. Sarah Blackly became interested in the foreign missions while a student at Oberlin College. After her marriage to Dr. Bradley, a missionary, she returned with him to Thailand in 1850. In a unique situation, Isabella Thoburn, born in Belmont County, went to India in 1870, sponsored by the Woman's Foreign Missionary Society of the Methodist Episcopal Church. She was the first unmarried American woman to become a foreign missionary. She founded the Isabella Thoburn College of Lucknow University in India. After her return to Cincinnati, she founded the Elizabeth Gamble Deaconess Home and Training School. Mary Reed, after contracting leprosy while working as a missionary in India, returned to India in 1891 as superintendent of the leper asylum near Chandag. Even though her leprosy went into remission, she left Chandag only three times in fifty-two years. She died in 1943 and six years later the Mary Reed Memorial Hospital was build in Chandag by the American Mission to Lepers. Catherine Fay Ewing became a missionary to the Choctow Nation, but it is unclear if she was unaccompanied. Others, like Lillian Digel, aspired to become missionaries but did not succeed. Digel enrolled in the Shoufner Missionary School in Cleveland but was unable to continue. She returned to Massillon, however, and started training classes for Sunday school teachers. She also established one of the first vacation Bible schools.[8]

If women missionaries were few in number during the nineteenth century, women preachers or ministers were even fewer and less well received. Some groups, such as the Quakers, were more forward-thinking in their ideas concerning religious equality. Because they believed in the religious equality of all people, Quakers allowed women to preach and conduct services. Quaker women were allowed to preach and were expected to speak out in meetings. In 1804, a log meeting house was built in Warren Township in

Belmont County, and Ruth Boswell delivered the first sermon. Sarah Caroline Harlan Hadley, another Quaker preacher, held services every Sunday at the Olive Branch Church in Warren County and at Clarksville in Clinton County. She took part in Quaker meetings in other states and continued to preach after her marriage to Miles Hadley of Wilmington. Sarah Ann Linton was another ordained Quaker preacher.[9]

Outside the Quaker religion, it is difficult to find ordained women ministers in the nineteenth century. Antoinette Brown Blackwell, an Oberlin graduate, in 1835 became the first woman in the United States to be ordained a minister. However, she soon left Ohio. Melissa Terrell was ordained at the Ebenezer Church in Clark County on March 7, 1867. Terrell, a member of the Southern Ohio Christian Conference, was originally listed as a "female laborer" in the conference directory. After her ordination she was given her credentials and accepted as a member in good standing. The Reverend Florence Buck and the Reverend Marion Murdock served as co-ministers of the Unity (Unitarian) Church in Cleveland from 1893 to 1899. In 1895, Mrs. M. S. Lake was the pastor of the People's Spiritual Alliance in Cleveland. The city directory listed several women as Christian Science readers.[10]

In some instances, formal religious ideology as it was preached by male clergy rang false to some women. After working side by side with fathers and/or husbands to establish a home and business, some women were unwilling to accept the idea put forth by most clergy that women were inferior to men and should have no say in church matters, business decisions, or politics. Some women were beginning to speak out when they believed that the clergy were issuing pronouncements about activities outside the religious sphere. Liwwat Boke, a German farmer's wife, wrote a letter to Bishop Purcell on August 25, 1844, complaining that the local Roman Catholic priest, Cleve Henry Herzog, was preaching against sex in marriage. Boke's letter very explicitly defended sex in marriage, stating "Sex with the one we love is not just an appealing option, like reading a book with someone, or singing or praying with

*Antoinette Brown
Blackwell, an Oberlin
College graduate, the first
female ordained minister in
the United States (Ohio
Historical Society)*

another. Rather we would so much like to start sex with this person that it is a raw need inside our body. It is like hunger after a fast day, or like the need to sleep after thirty hours of hard work. When the need is fulfilled the contentment *can* and *does* permeate our whole being . . . similar to a good meal after hunger."[11] One can only imagine the look on the bishop's face after reading this letter. Another outspoken woman was Mary Rowland, president of the women's auxiliary of the Parnell Land League in Cleveland. The Parnell Land League was an Irish nationalist group, and Bishop Gilmour on May 14, 1882, condemned this group and warned the Catholic women of Cleveland not to join it. The group did not disband, and on June 1, 1882, the bishop excommunicated those who belonged, stating, "The Catholic woman must live within the modesty of the home; she must be the ornament of the family circle, and her womanly delivery and gentle nature shall not be tainted with the noisy brawl of the virago. Women must be women; women shall not be permitted to unsex themselves and be at the same time, within the limits of the diocese of Cleveland remain members of the Catholic church." If such activity made them un-Catholic, Rowland responded, "then we are proud to be called heretics."[12]

Many of the utopian religious movements of the nineteenth century found followers in Ohio and, as has been shown by the Quakers, some believed and even practiced equality between the sexes. In 1821, Ralph Russell organized a Shaker Society in Warrensville, Cuyahoga County. Mother Ann Lee, the founder of the Shakers, taught that God embodied both masculine and feminine traits. Both men and women carried on ministry. Women participated equally in the governance of the community and in political decisions. However, gender roles were traditionally differentiated, with women doing the work indoors and men doing most of the heavy outdoor work.[13] For a while the community flourished, owning 1,300 acres of land, a grist mill, a sawmill, and a woolen mill. The Shaker sisters manufactured fabrics that sold well. But the number of members of the community began to decline. Shakers believed in celibacy, and therefore membership grew only through conversions. The group was eventually forced, out of necessity, to sell its property and join with another group near Dayton.

Another group, the German Baptists or Dunkards from Ashland County, allowed women to participate in church services and to vote on all issues that came to the lower councils. However, they could not participate in the deliberations of the denomination's national conference.[14]

Spiritualism had an increasing number of followers from the 1870s through the 1890s, many of whom were women. Spiritualists communed with the dead and some foretold the future. These included Victoria Claflin Woodhull, the first female presidential candidate, born in Homer, Ohio, in 1838. Madeline Kline, a spiritualist and leader of the Society of the Faithful, came to the United States in 1851 and soon after to Ohio. Kline called herself a Christian Spiritualist and delivered lectures twice a week. She also published a book on her beliefs, *The Everlasting Gospel*, in which she described the first visit she received from the "Justice Band" whose mission was to induct her into the position of medium for their group. In 1874, Kline organized the Society of the Faithful, and in 1893, the society was chartered by the State of Ohio as the First Society of Christian Spiritualists.[15]

A few religious groups in Ohio found themselves systematically targeted for their religious beliefs. A small number of incidents related to witchcraft were reported. Around 1800, in Clermont County, members of the Hildebrand family accused Nancy Evans, one of their neighbors, of being a witch. There was no statute in Ohio against witchcraft, but a local justice of the peace decided to adjudicate the matter by weighing her against the Bible. A rude scale was made, with the Bible placed at one end and Nancy at the other. If she was a witch, the justice of the peace pronounced, she would be compelled to tip the beam. Obviously Nancy was too heavy for the Bible, and she did tip the beam; however, her fate was not recorded. The only recorded court case in Ohio that touched on witchcraft was *State of Ohio v. Abigail Church* in May 1823, when prosecutor Samuel F. Vinton accused Abigail Church, a fortune-teller, of fraud. Since Church did not claim to know the future, Vinton argued, she was perpetrating a fraud by accepting money for her fortune-telling services. As with witchcraft, there was no law in Ohio against fortune-telling, but Vinton tried to get the jury to believe that Church was claiming to be "divinely inspired," and thus was engaging in behavior that put her in league with the devil. Her attorney Richard Douglass showed that Church did not solicit customers, nor did she claim to know what would happen in the future. She only answered the questions people asked. The jury found her not guilty of the fraud charge, thus dismissing the covert suggestion that Church was a witch.[16]

The Mormons were another group targeted for persecution by Ohio's citizens because of their unorthodox beliefs. Mormon missionaries arrived in Kirtland, Ohio, in 1830, and were soon followed by a large number of settlers. They set about establishing themselves in the community and began building a temple. Kirtland's residents did not accept these new settlers or their ideas.

Many businessmen refused to employ Mormons, hoping to drive them away. When this was unsuccessful, they resorted to violence, burning farms and businesses. Hepzebah Richards wrote: "I care not how soon I am away from this place. I have been wading in a sea of tribulation ever since I came here. For the last three months we as a people have been tempest tossed, and at times the waves have well nigh overwhelmed us; but we believe there will yet be a way of escape."[17] That escape came in 1838, when most Mormons left Kirtland for Missouri.

Roman Catholic nuns were one group of religious women who were allowed to be autonomous within certain parameters and develop successful managerial skills. Beginning in 1824, nuns from Europe came to Ohio and began their work in education. Later, their efforts would expand to medical and charitable works. The Sisters of Charity arrived in the archdiocese of Cincinnati on October 27, 1829, and began their work. The Convent of the Precious Blood Sisterhood was established in 1849 at Marysville, Union County. In 1852, this convent opened a boarding school in Menster. They also founded the St. Joseph's Orphan Home in Dayton, and in 1931, the order was transferred to Salem Hills, near Dayton. The Sisters of Notre Dame also founded an academy and convent in Dayton, and the Sisters of the Poor of St. Francis started a hospital. In 1850, five Ursuline nuns from France arrived in Cleveland. They taught at the Cathedral School, along with several other schools in the city. In time, they opened their own boarding school and academy. Other religious orders, such as the Daughters of the Immaculate Heart of Mary, the Sisters of Holy Humility of Mary, and the Sisters of the Society of Mary, also came to the Cleveland area. In 1854, a convent and St. Ursula's Academy was established in Toledo. By 1858, it had 8 nuns and 160 pupils. In 1879, the convent opened the first kindergarten in Toledo, and the nuns received a dispensation allowing them to teach in parochial schools outside the convent grounds and to teach male students. The Sisters of Notre Dame de Namur came to Columbus in 1855, where they opened St. Patrick School on September 3, 1859. The Sisters of the

Poor of St. Francis started St. Francis Hospital in 1862, and the Sisters of the Holy Cross opened Hawkes Hospital of Mt. Carmel in 1886. Sisters of the Blessed Sacrament began their missionary work to African Americans in 1912, and the Sisters of Saint Dominic opened a college, St. Mary's of the Springs, in 1924.[18]

The success and autonomy that these women religious enjoyed was not always appreciated by the male hierarchy of the Catholic church. Bishop Richard Gilmour of the Cleveland diocese wanted greater control over church property, and he demanded that the Sisters of Charity of St. Augustine and the Sisters of Charity of Montreal turn over the orphan asylums they owned and operated to him. Gilmour believed that because the orphan asylums depended on the financial contributions of generous Catholics, he as legal representative of Catholics in the diocese should hold title to these institutions. The sisters rejected his argument, and a quarrel ensued. As one nun said, "we shall always make it a duty to submit to Your Lordship's Control of the Asylum and Hospital of Toledo" but that control did not mean "donation of property."[19]

Receiving an education served as an impetus for women to step outside the role defined by society and begin to define that role for themselves. Educational opportunities for women on the Ohio frontier were very limited, and most were of an informal nature. Mrs. Horace Townsend (née Sophia Case) from Huron County was recognized as a good scholar by her neighbors. Once she was able to read, she educated herself by reading everything that she could find, especially historical works. Mrs. Rebecca Gilman (née Ives) was educated by her grandfather. She was taught from the British classics, could read French, and was often the arbitrator of "intellectual" disputes among visitors to her home. Fanny Hayes, Rutherford B. Hayes's sister, read voraciously. She had memorized all of *The Lady of the Lake,* and by the age of twelve had read most of the plays of Shakespeare.[20]

The limited access to formal education prompted some women to either begin their own schools or bring a teacher to the area. Small neighborhood schools could be held in a teacher's house, where a woman would teach her own children, plus perhaps five or six neighbors' children. In some cases, neighbors banded together to bring a teacher to the area. In about 1816, Nancy Zane McCulloch started the first free school in Logan County, hiring a teacher for her children and those of the neighbors. Amy Easton established a school in Weathersfield, Trumbull County, that also provided accommodations for students traveling a distance. She had been educated by her father and had graduated from Granville Seminary. She also helped to prepare the local young men for their entrance to Allegheny College, an institution to which she was denied access. Some women, though not actively engaged in teaching, involved themselves in education by making regular visits to the local schools to evaluate their effectiveness, and they did become directly involved in the selection of teachers.[21]

As more settlers moved into Ohio, particularly from New England, a region that valued intellectual and moral development, the expectations concerning female education began to change. The development of one's moral and intellectual capacities was an essential expectation of those raised in the value system of New England Puritanism, even women. Many young women received their education at "female seminaries." At these seminaries, instructors taught courses in needlework, painting, drawing, music, French, and penmanship, all skills deemed appropriate for women who performed a decorative role in society. Little did those who founded the seminaries realize that for some women, the opportunity to attend these institutions would open the door to questioning the societal expectations that were thrust upon them. Tuition was charged to attend these schools, thereby making them available only to those women whose families were able to afford such a luxury.

Miss Dioneria Sullivan's Private School for Girls was one of the first such schools in Ohio. It opened in 1815 in the west central part of the state. Others in the area soon followed: The Female Seminary in Delaware, 1820; Urbana Female Seminary, 1824; Maria Harrison's School for Young Ladies, 1832; and Select School for Young Ladies, 1838.[22] It was not unusual for these privately funded schools to be open for only a couple of years. Other areas in the state also began to respond to the need for female education. Mrs. J. D. Parmlee was matron of the prospering Geauga Seminary in 1831, and Miss Marsh ran a private school in Columbus.

One of the better-known early female seminaries was the Steubenville Female Seminary, founded in 1829 by Reverend and Mrs. Charles C. Beatty. This seminary, besides the subjects usually seen as appropriate for young women, had a curriculum similar to what young men of the day were studying, including botany, chemistry, astronomy, algebra, philosophy, and religion. Cincinnati had several such schools. The Cincinnati Female Academy was opened in 1836, along with the Cincinnati Female Institution and A. Truesdell's Female Academy. In September 1824, the Sisters of Mercy established the first convent school for girls in Ohio, and other religious schools soon followed. The H. Thane Miller School for Girls was founded in 1857, and with a few name and location changes, it continued to operate well into the twentieth century. In 1900, the consolidation of The Bartholomew English and Classical School for Girls with Miss E. Antoinette Ely's School formed the Bartholomew-Clinton School.[23]

The residents of Cleveland were not far behind those of Cincinnati in establishing schools for local young women. One of the earliest female academies was Mrs. Day's School, opened in 1841. By the 1850s, the two leading schools for the daughters of the rich were the Young Ladies Institute and the Cleveland Female Academy/Seminary. The latter, run by Linda T. Guilford, emphasized the role each of these young women would assume upon marriage but also tried to emphasize that marriage did not end a woman's activities in the community. Besides being a wife and mother, the nineteenth-century woman would need to contribute to her community through participation in benevolent and religious organizations. The school was reincorporated in 1871 under the name Cleveland Seminary for Girls, but it was forced to close in 1883 due to financial problems.[24]

Later in the nineteenth century, three college preparatory schools

Cleveland Female Seminary, Woodland Avenue, 1865 (Ohio Historical Society)

for girls opened in Cleveland. The first was Miss Mittleberger's School, located originally in the home of its founder Augusta Mittleberger. In 1881, the school moved to a property donated by John D. Rockefeller. The school closed in 1908 when Mittleberger retired. Brooks School for Ladies opened in 1876 and was an adjunct to Brooks Academy, a school for boys. The school was renamed for its third owner, Anna Hathaway Brown, who sold the school in 1890. In 1905, the school moved to East 100th Street to a property donated by Flora Stone Mather, and in 1927 it moved to Shaker Heights, where it continues its reputation as a prestigious girls' school. The third school began in the home of Jennie and Warren Prentiss in 1896. Soon after it started enrolling boarding students, it became known as the Wade Park Home School for Girls. In 1904, the school was sold to Sarah E. Lyman and was renamed Laurel School. It too moved to Shaker Heights in 1927 and continues its goal of providing a quality education for young women.[25]

For those young women who did not have access to a female seminary, either because of geography or finances, secondary public education was available in some areas of Ohio by the mid-nineteenth century. Cleveland established public schools in 1836. By the 1837–38 school year, eight schools—four for boys and four for girls—enrolled 1,840 students. In 1845, boys' and girls' senior departments were merged. And in 1846, Central High School, the first public high school in the state, opened, admitting only boys. However, because of community pressure, girls were admitted during the summer of 1847. One of the first graduates was Laura Spelman, the future wife of John D. Rockefeller.[26]

"Union high schools" were located in various communities throughout the state. These schools were coeducational, and the curriculum and structure was determined by local norms. Some localities provided a "ladies department," allowing girls to attend classes in the same building as boys. The tuition for these schools was minimal, and by 1851, cities with union schools offering a "ladies department" included Massillon, Sandusky, Ashland, Warren, Cleveland, Columbus, Cincinnati, and Perrysburg. The success of these schools prompted the Ohio legislature to investigate the feasibility of opening a high school in each township.[27]

It appears that the curriculum in these schools was similar for boys and girls. Disciplines included were algebra, arithmetic, American history, chemistry, philosophy, reading, penmanship, vocal music, and bookkeeping. In one locale, educators prohibited young women from studying algebra beyond quadratic equations; in another, they were allowed to take chemistry but not to do experiments. In the 1880s, public schools started offering home economics classes, including sewing and cooking.

Parochial schools provided an alternative to public school education for those Catholic immigrants who perceived the public schools to be too "Protestant." These schools also provided a more affordable education than many private academies. Parochial schools tended to segregate the sexes, and some large parishes were even able to maintain separate buildings for boys and girls. By the turn of the century, there were more than sixty Catholic schools in Cincinnati. Other schools responding to specific needs of the community also opened. Helen Horvath, a Hungarian immigrant, opened a language school in 1902, believing that immigrants needed to learn English and Americans needed to learn the cultural backgrounds of their new residents.[28]

With greater access to a high school education, whether through public or private means, there was a larger demand by women for access to "higher education." Some female seminaries had fulfilled this need, but institutions on par with male institutions were needed. The Oxford College for Women, which opened in 1830, became part of Miami University in 1928. On February 28, 1834, the Ohio Legislature granted the Oberlin Collegiate Institute its charter "to confer on those whom they may deem worthy, such honors and degrees as are usually conferred in similar institutions." According to one of its early brochures, among Oberlin's objectives were "to give the most useful education at the least expense of health, time and money; and to extend the benefit of such education to both sexes and to all classes of the community, as far as its means will allow." In 1834, the college admitted women to a special "Ladies Course," which provided them instruction in the "useful branches" of study, but these courses were not college level. But in 1837, four women were deemed eligible to enroll in the collegiate department, making them the first women to matriculate for a regular college course of study. Thus, the first coeducational college in the country began.[29]

The Western College for Women in Oxford, Butler County, opened its doors in 1853, and Lake Erie College in Painesville opened in 1856. Oakland Female College, founded in Hillsboro in 1839, became Hillsboro Female College in 1859. It admitted males in 1888, burned in 1894, was rebuilt, but closed soon after. Glendale Female College, an Episcopalian school near Cincinnati, opened in 1854 and closed in 1929. Xenia Female Academy opened in 1850, changed its name in 1854 to Xenia Female College, and in 1863 changed its name to Xenia College.[30] Antioch College, begun in 1852, was the first institution to graduate women on the same platform as men. Otterbein began admitting women in the 1850s, and at the same time a female seminary in conjunction with Wittenberg University in Springfield, Ohio, was under construction. Ohio Wesleyan Female College opened in 1853 and united with Ohio Wesleyan University in 1877. By 1862, it is estimated that twenty-two "female colleges and seminaries" were operating in Ohio.[31]

In 1872, Western Reserve University's Adelbert College opened its door to women undergraduates, and by the 1880s women made up more than 30 percent of its student body. But in 1884, the Western Reserve faculty voted to deny women access, and this policy took effect in 1886. The new president, Hiram Collins Hayden, was permitted to open a separate college for women as long as it was self-supporting. The College for Women of the Western Reserve University opened September 1888, due to the generosity of Flora Stone Mather's family, who provided funds for building rental. President Hayden established an advisory board for the college and gave it ultimate responsibility for developing the college. The board, made up of local women, solicited funds for a library and furnishings for the classrooms. Mrs. Mather contributed $75,000 for a dormitory in 1892 in honor of Linda Guilford, a noted educator who had supported and provided women's education for years.[32]

During the early twentieth century, several Catholic women's colleges opened in Ohio. Notre Dame College for Women opened in 1922; during the same year, Bishop Stritek established Mary Manse College as the Diocesan Women's College. Other institutions included Ursuline College and Sisters College in Cleveland, and Our Lady of Cincinnati and St. Mary's of the Springs in Columbus.

Other institutions began to recognize the need for single women to be able to support themselves. In 1846, a coeducational facility opened in Albany, Ohio, that focused on manual training and provided a work-study arrangement for its students. Oberlin College initially operated with a manual labor department for males and females. Oberlin's founders believed in educating the "whole man," and in so doing felt that manual labor was necessary. For women, they believed that "housekeeping, the manufacture of wool, the culture of silk, the appropriate parts of gardening, particularly raising and fitting seeds for market, the making of clothes, etc., will furnish them employment suited to their sex, and conducive to their health, good habits, and support."[33] This was considered such a critical part of the program that women applicants had to certify "their ability and disposition to perform domestic labor."[34] The idea of educating the "whole man" was adopted by male and female industrial schools (i.e., reformatories) in Ohio during the nineteenth and early twentieth centuries. Learning a trade was part of the mission of the Girls' Industrial Home located in White Sulphur Springs, just as it was at the Girls Opportunity Farm in Cincinnati, established by Elsie Herzog in 1915 for delinquent girls.[35] The settlement house movement also incorporated trade training in its programming. Not only were job skills provided, but along with the skills came an infusion of white, middle-class values, including the Puritan work ethic.

With more women attending female institutions of higher learning, more female faculty members were needed. Many women upon graduation became faculty members at their alma mater or at a nearby institution. Mrs. James Dascomb (née Marianne Parker) became the first principal of the ladies department at Oberlin College after receiving her education at Ipswich Academy in Massachusetts. In 1835, Mrs. Henry Cowles (née Alice Welch) became principal at Oberlin, a position she held for five years. Eliza Blakesly, a graduate of Oberlin College, began teaching at a select school for girls in Poland in 1840. Later she taught at the Academy and then at the Seminary in Poland. Marian Ann Adams graduated from Oberlin College in 1839. She served as its assistant principal for three years, then served seven years as its principal. Rebecca M. Pennell became the first woman professor to be accorded the same privileges as her male counterparts at Antioch College. Wilberforce College, the first college in the country for

Hallie Quinn Brown, a faculty member at Wilberforce College, active in the struggle to obtain the vote and in the Republican Party (Ohio Historical Society)

blacks, employed a large number of African American women as faculty members. Sarah C. Bierce Scarborough was professor of natural sciences from 1877 to 1884, professor of French from 1884 to 1892, and principal of the normal school department from 1887 to 1914.[36]

However, as more institutions became coeducational, it was more difficult for women to obtain faculty positions, particularly in areas not traditionally defined as female. Faculty positions in nursing, teaching, or home economics provided women with some opportunities. Helen Norman Smith, a faculty member at the University of Cincinnati, was a pioneer in women's health and physical education both nationally and locally. She was head of the Women's Athletic Association, and in the 1930s was instrumental in establishing coeducational physical education classes. Elizabeth Dyer was dean of the College of Home Economics at the University of Cincinnati in the 1930s. It was her hope that the status of women would be elevated if home economics was seen as a scientific study. Mabel Maxine Riedinger dedicated forty years of her

professional life at the University of Akron to improving secondary education, retiring in 1971. Thelma Irene Schoonover held a
full professorship and chair of the psychology department at Cap-
ital University in 1954, while Margaret Ann Barnes was an associate
professor and chair of the sociology department at Western College for Women. Dr. Ruth Bartlett Buttoff Lewis accepted the position of assistant professor of rhetoric and public address and
director of forensics at Oberlin College in 1961, the first woman
hired in that position. Again, once these facilities became coeducational it was difficult for women to move into administrative positions. Having once run the entire institution and directed the
faculty, now they were relegated to positions of little power. Only
in recent years has this begun to change. Exceptions were Edna
Arundel, dean of the Rio Grande College in Rio Grande, Ohio,
from 1927 to 1936; Christine Yerges Conaway, dean of women at
Ohio State University in 1944; and Olive Parmenter, dean at Tiffin
University from 1954 to 1965. By way of contrast, in 1993, four
women held the position of university president in Ohio: Peggy Elliott at the University of Akron, Carol Cartwright at Kent State
University, Claire Van Ummersen at Cleveland State University,
and Jerry Sue Owens at Cuyahoga Community College.

Women also found it difficult to have their scholarly work
taken seriously by the academic community. However, a few were
recognized for their contributions. Lintonite, a variety of Lake Su-
perior sandstone, was named for Laura Linton, its discoverer.
Mary Emilee Homes was the first woman member of the Geologi-
cal Society of America. Debra Salter Bacon from Tallmadge was
the original proponent of the Baconian theory of the authorship of
the plays of William Shakespeare. Her work, *The Philosophy of the
Plays of Shakespeare Unfolded,* was published in 1857. Annie Wormley from Columbus became the first woman in the United States to
join the First Congress of International Scientific and Medical
Men in 1876. Wormley provided the drawings of poison crystals
that her husband, T. G. Wormley, was studying. These steel plate
etchings were said to be the "finest set of microscopic plates ever

produced in Europe or America." Another Columbus resident, Eliza Griscolm Wheeler Sullivant, also became famous for the drawings she provided for her husband's research in moss identification. Her drawings are at Harvard University and Ohio State University, and her name was given to an Ohio moss, Hypman Sullivantiae.[37] Esther Boise Van Deman from South Salem published the seminal work "Methods of Determining the Date of Roman Concrete Monuments" in 1912. Her methodology became standard procedure in Roman archaeology. Constance M. Rourke's book *American Humor: A Study of the National Character* was named by the American Library Association in 1931 as one of the most outstanding volumes written by any women in a hundred years. The Ohio Academy of Science named Mildred Ray Bowman a Fellow in 1956.

The increased interest in female education went hand in hand with the acceptance of teaching as a professional occupation for single women. This also led to a demand for better academic preparation for teachers. The answer to this demand was the development of normal schools (institutions dedicated to the education of teachers). Betsey Mix Cowles, abolitionist and women's rights activist, a graduate of Oberlin (1840) and a noted educator in Ohio, was chosen in 1856 as the person to head the experimental Model School in conjunction with McNeely Normal School in Hopedale. She began her position as principal of the Model School and teacher in the McNeely Normal School in August 1856. However, she was there for only one year before taking a position at the Illinois State Normal School in Bloomington, Illinois. Normal schools continued to proliferate throughout the state, and in time would be incorporated into the state's collegiate education program.

Certainly earlier teachers had no such training. A few of the first teachers in Geauga County were Lucinda Walden, Elect Clapp, Miss Patkin, Melissa Talbot, Mrs. H. M. R. Tracy, Asenith Mastick, and Mary Williams. Harriet Whitney was the first woman schoolteacher in Toledo, where she began her career in 1830 at the age of sixteen, teaching until she married three years later. Miss Calista Cummings taught in Summit County in 1836, and Hannah Fisher and Judith Townsend were the first teachers in Salem. Two select schools for young ladies also operated in Salem during the 1840s, along with the public school where Mrs. Helen M. Beatty was one of the first teachers. Miss Mary Ann Adams, who graduated from Oberlin in 1839, was the first teacher to teach in the first Wellington school building, built in 1849.[38]

Some women, like Mrs. Milla Hainly, Betsey Mix Cowles, and Lavina Marr, devoted almost their entire lives to teaching. Hainly began teaching at the age of eighteen in Ridge Township, where she taught for two terms for the salary of $1.50 per week. She was then "called" to Van Wert, where she was in charge of one of the city schools for several terms. She then went to Washington Township (Van Wert County) and taught for two terms. After the death of her husband, she returned to teaching. She taught two terms in Tully Township (Van Wert County) and then in 1868 moved to Van Wert, where she opened a select school. By the next year, however, she was employed in the union school (public school) in Van Wert, where she was in charge of the primary grades for twelve years. She was also very active in the temperance movement and was a property owner. At the time of her death, she owned three residential properties in the city of Van Wert.[39]

Betsey Mix Cowles began her teaching career at the Portsmouth Female Seminary in 1842, where she received a salary of $25 per month. While there, she started a Sabbath school for both black and white children. Many of the white parents withdrew their children when the school became integrated. This, however, did not deter Cowles. She kept the school open, and it continued to function after her departure. For the next few years she devoted herself to the abolition movement, but she returned to teaching in 1848. At that time, the new union school in Massillon opened. Besides being one of the first union schools to open in Ohio, it was also one of the first graded schools that grouped students based on their age and ability (primary, grammar, and high school). In 1848,

Cowles became a teacher and principal in the grammar department, and she received $300 per year plus board. She resigned in 1849 in opposition to the enforcement of the "black laws." The "black law" in education allowed for black children to attend school with white children only when no white parents complained. White parents complained, and Cowles quit. She did continue her work in the Massillon area, however. She helped organize the Stark County Common School Association and presented lectures at teachers' institutes. She was appointed superintendent of the girls' grammar and high school in Canton. During the 1850s, she turned her attention to women's rights. After her brief sojourn with normal schools, she was offered the superintendent position of Painesville schools in 1858 for an annual salary of $550. She was one of only two women to serve in the capacity of superintendent in Painesville.[40]

Lavina Marr graduated from Massillon High School in 1897 and attended the new normal school the state had opened in Kent. After this, she taught at a "subscription" kindergarten. In 1915, she taught math and tutored children in her home. The Massillon Board of Education gave her a commission in 1923 to start a class for "irregular and retarded" students, along with those who needed to learn to speak English. In 1925, she also established a class for physically handicapped children, many of whom were victims of polio. Seeing the special needs these children had, Marr realized one classroom could not deal with the problem. She began to lobby the local board of education and the community for funds. Massillon's Opportunity School was the result of her efforts. This school remained open until the State of Ohio began to provide funding for classes for children with special needs. Marr retired in 1940.[41]

Over time, the "black law" was enforced more consistently throughout the state. With the establishment of the "separate but equal" ruling by the 1896 U.S. Supreme Court in the *Plessy v. Ferguson* case, more schools for black children developed and the demand for black teachers increased. Jennie Davis Porter was the first black woman to earn a doctorate from the University of Cincinnati. She was a leader in the black community and championed the idea that blacks were intellectually equal to whites. Porter was a fervent believer that quality education was the key to improving the plight of blacks in society. She was a proponent of all-black schools with all-black faculty, and in 1914 she became the principal of Harriet Beecher Stowe School, the first black woman to hold such a position in Cincinnati. Other African American women championed the importance of education to the black community. Maribodine Busey was the youngest African American woman to receive a master's degree at Ohio State University in 1934 and the only one to receive one in physiological chemistry until that time. She went on to teach at Garfield School in Columbus. Ruth Moore received her bachelor's and master's from Ohio State University, and in 1933 she earned her doctorate. She went on to be a faculty member at the Medical College of Howard University.[42]

In 1926, Marybelle Burke Early became the first black woman to graduate from Kent State University's College of Education. She began her teaching career in Monongalia County, West Virginia, but returned to Cincinnati in 1948. She received her bachelor's degree from Kent State University in 1937 and a master's degree from Ohio State University in 1942. Upon her return to Cincinnati, she found more segregation there than she had encountered in West Virginia. She taught in segregated schools until 1970, and she retired in 1975. Anna Hughes, the first African American pupil enrolled in the Clinkenbeard School of Dramatics and Expression in Columbus, received her teaching certificate in 1911. She was the superintendent and executive director of the Ohio Avenue Day Nursery in Columbus for twenty years.[43]

Throughout the nineteenth century, teaching became a more and more feminized occupation, especially at the elementary level. In 1847, there were 1,988 female teachers in Ohio. By 1854, there were 6,413 female teachers in the common schools and sixty-three in the high schools, compared to 7,469 male teachers in the common schools and 71 in the high schools. The balance shifted during the Civil War—in 1863, there were 3.8 percent more female teachers than male. By 1865, the number of qualified women teachers had quadrupled. In 1960, women teachers continued to outnumber men teachers in the elementary grades 33,803 to 5,762, while in high schools men teachers outnumbered women teachers 12,492 to 8,640.[44]

Men's salaries also outpaced those of women in education. Society believed that women did not need the same salary because they were not supporting a family. The average salary of a male teacher in the common schools in 1865 was $36.25 per month, while female teachers received on average $21.55 per month. In the high schools, male teachers received on average $73.31 per month, while female teachers received only $41.97. This difference would continue throughout the twentieth century. Part of the pay problem was indeed the expectation, if not requirement, that female teachers must be single. Ohio had no specific law regarding the employment of married female teachers, but many local communities did. A 1930 survey found that 56 percent of Ohio communities had explicit rules concerning the employment of married women. Seventy-four percent did not employ married women at all, and 66 percent refused to allow a teacher who married to continue working, many not even allowing her to complete the school year.[45]

As in higher education, a few women teachers were able to move into administrative positions, such as Betsey Mix Cowles, discussed earlier. S. E. Haight became the first principal of Piqua High School's Female Department in 1856, and Mary E. Hall became the first female principal of Piqua High School in 1879. Hall served in that capacity until 1905. Margaret K. Feldner was appointed principal of the junior and senior high schools in Ravenna in 1917, serving for nine years. Ann Cutler Coburn became headmistress of Hathaway Brown School in 1930 and served as president of the National Association of Principals of Schools for Girls. She was also a trustee of Lake Erie College.

Education of young children also became a concern of female

educators in Ohio. Early in the 1830s, Betsey and Cornelia Cowles conducted several infant schools in the Austinburg area. These infant schools were forerunners of kindergarten education and focused on the involvement of the student. Teachers in infant schools used rhyming songs to teach multiplication tables, and visual aids and models to teach about the solar system and geography. In 1879, St. Ursula's Academy in Toledo opened the first kindergarten in the city. At about the same time, Molana Harris helped bring free kindergartens to the Akron schools. The Cincinnati Kindergarten Association was formed in 1894, with the purpose of organizing and supervising kindergartens and operating a training school for teachers. During 1902–3, the association sponsored twenty-five kindergartens, all of which were supported by donations from concerned citizens. The training school provided a two-year course of study, leading to a diploma.[46] Around this same time, Mary Law had established the Law Kindergarten Training School in Toledo. In the twentieth century, many of these ideas concerning early childhood education would be formalized in the training provided by state normal schools and colleges of education. Throughout the twentieth century, women continued to be concerned with the education of young children as they introduced the ideas of Maria Montessori and worked to bring Head Start preschool programs to various communities in the 1970s.

The public, in time, accepted women as educators of their children, particularly young children. But another role traditionally performed by women—that of healer and nurse—would not be so willingly accepted outside the home. Women's desire to receive formal training as medical doctors grew throughout the latter half of the nineteenth century. Several medical schools in the state admitted women during the 1850s, including the Cleveland Medical College, Cleveland Homeopathic College, Cincinnati Eclectic College of Medicine, and the Physio Medical College of Cincinnati.

At a faculty meeting at the Cleveland Medical College on February 12, 1850, Professor Kirtland moved "that respectable ladies who were fitting for the practice of medicine be admitted to attend all the lectures of the school on the same footing as gentlemen." Two women, Eliza Brown of Cleveland and Mrs. Nancy E. Clark of Sharon, Pennsylvania, were admitted in 1850. Clark graduated March 2, 1852, moved to Boston, and opened a dispensary for women and children. In February 1851, the faculty voted to end the admission of women but reversed themselves on October 6, 1853. Two more women, Mary Frame Thomas and Emily Blackwell, were admitted then. During the 1850s, the Cleveland Medical College was the only school of "good standing" in the country to admit women. In 1856, four women received medical degrees from Western Reserve, including Dr. Elisabeth Grisell and Dr. Marie Elizabeth Zakrzewska. Zakrzewska then joined the faculty of the New England Female Medical College in Boston. The primary reason many of these women left the state to practice was that the Ohio Medical Association did not admit women until 1875.

Between 1879 and 1885 only three women graduated from Western Reserve Medical College, and between 1912 and 1919 no women students were enrolled. The medical school at Wooster University admitted women students from 1872 until 1896, when it became a department of Ohio Wesleyan University. Ohio Wesleyan continued to admit women, but this changed in 1910, when it consolidated with Western Reserve University. Finally on January 8, 1919, the medical faculty of Western Reserve University approved the admittance of women under the same conditions as men. Between 1843 and 1930, 90 women graduated from regular medical schools in Cleveland. In 1950, Western Reserve Medical School enrolled 31 women, and in 1980 it admitted 199. These numbers continue to grow.[47]

Women had more of an opportunity to obtain a medical education if they enrolled at a homeopathic facility. The Eclectic Medical Institute of Cincinnati was established in 1845 and began admitting women in 1849. The first woman graduate was Dr. Caroline Brown in 1853. Between 1853 and 1859, 32 women graduated from the institute, but then no more graduated until 1874 because the institute stopped the admittance of women. From 1874 to 1900, 79

women graduated, and from 1901 to 1926, 20 women graduated—
a total of 131 by the time the institute closed in 1926. In 1850, the
Western College of Homeopathic Medicine (Cleveland Homeopathic Medical College) opened in Cleveland and admitted three
women to its first session. Dr. Helen Cook was the first female
graduate in 1852, and by the end of the decade eleven women had
graduated. Women were barred from attending the college in the
late 1860s, so Dr. Myra King Merrick and C. O. Seaman opened the
Cleveland Homeopathic Hospital College for Women on December 28, 1867. Dr. Merrick became the first female medical teacher
in the West. Six women enrolled for the first session. In 1871 the
two institutions merged, and by 1875 there were six women graduates out of twenty-nine. Between 1850 and 1914, 260 graduated
from homeopathic institutions in Cleveland. During this time, the
women's General Hospital was established in Cleveland and was
the only hospital in the city founded entirely by women. General
Hospital began as a homeopathic dispensary and grew into the
third largest maternity hospital in Cleveland by 1929. It closed in
1984 due to financial difficulties.[48]

Admittance to a nursing school was a more acceptable way for
women to be involved in the medical profession, but it would take
the work of some very dedicated professionals to bring about this
acceptance. Cleveland had numerous nursing schools. The first
was a homeopathic facility, the Cleveland Training School for
Nurses, which opened in 1884. A few of the nursing schools had religious affiliations. Cleveland City Hospital opened its nursing
school in 1897, and in 1898 Lakeside Hospital, in conjunction with
the Western Reserve University Medical School, opened the first
collegiate nursing program. The first professional school of nursing in Cincinnati, the Cincinnati Training School, opened in 1889
with Annie Murray Hunt as its first superintendent. It was affiliated with Cincinnati Hospital. The Sisters of the Holy Cross
opened a training school for nurses in 1903 in Columbus.[49]

The most difficult professional education for women to obtain
was in the legal field. The Western Reserve University School of

Law did not admit women until 1918, although Cleveland Law School, which was affiliated with Baldwin Wallace College, did admit women earlier. In 1930 Western Reserve admitted three women, and by 1980 234 were admitted. As the end of the twentieth century approached, women were gaining the ability to obtain a graduate and professional education. But their rate of education was still not equal to that of men. In 1990, 50 percent of the undergraduates enrolled in Ohio's public universities were women; 53 percent of those enrolled in master's programs were women; and 43 percent of those pursuing doctorates were women. However, law, business, and dental schools were still predominantly male.[50]

Women's concerns for education and intellectual development were not limited to establishing, attending, or teaching school. They also were aware of the power of the written word. In early years, they organized literary societies to challenge themselves intellectually and, in conjunction with those societies, established the first private lending libraries, then free public libraries. Besides ensuring the preservation of ideas through these institutions, they also committed their ideas to the written word.

The elite of Cincinnati formed the Semi-Colon Club early in the nineteenth century to discuss essays, poetry, and current events. This group contained both men and women, and the evening was the social event of the month, ending with food and dancing. The women in Tallmadge formed a literary society in 1815, which included both married and single women. In 1834, Betsey Mix Cowles and several other young women from Austinburg formed the Young Ladies Society for Intellectual Improvement. The group met every two weeks to discuss a particular topic, and each member was responsible for discussing the assigned theme. The "Young Ladies Association of Oberlin Collegiate Institute for the Promotion of Literature and Religion" was organized in July 21, 1835. This development began the traditional connection between women's groups and literary societies that would continue into the late nineteenth century and would culminate in the woman's club movement.[51] Some of these societies also formed private lending libraries, which supported these groups. The Tallmadge Literary Society had a library in 1815. Establishing libraries was one of the primary activities of the woman's club movement in the late nineteenth and early twentieth centuries. As noted previously, many settlement houses had libraries that were supported financially by club women. The Lorain Sisterhood, a women's literary and charitable group, reorganized itself as a library committee in 1900. They raised $120 for the purchase of books, and the Wemodaughses family contributed eighty volumes.[52] Other groups and cities, such as the town of Lima, Ohio, received funds from Andrew Carnegie to help establish a public library. Carnegie gave $10,000 to establish a library, as long as the city was able to provide the building. Similar philanthropic endeavors by Carnegie helped to fund many other Ohio libraries.

Certainly with the lack of library facilities, the access to reading materials was limited for many women. To help address the problem, several women's magazines and journals were established that could be sent through the mail to women's homes on a periodic basis. One of the earliest secular magazines was the *Social Circle*, a monthly established in 1827 at Mt. Pleasant by Rebecca Bates. Beginning in January 1830, Joel T. Case of Cincinnati began editing the weekly *Ladies' Museum and Western Repository of Belle Lettres*, and in October 1831 it combined with the *Cincinnati Mirror and Ladies' Parterre*, edited by William Gallagher. However, the magazine ceased publication in 1836. The *Ladies Repository* (1841–76) published in Cincinnati was sponsored by the Methodist Church and had a circulation of 31,000 by 1857. It was not devoted to "household hints of various kinds with menus to tempt lagging appetites of the family," but rather "sought to stimulate and develop feminine interest in religious and intellectual matters."[53] Another Cincinnati publication was the *Western Monthly Magazine*, with contributors such as Mrs. Caroline Lee Hentz and Harriet Beecher. Calista Cummings of Akron published the *Home Journal* in 1836, and Maria M. Herrick of Ohio City published *Mothers and Young Ladies Guide* from 1837 to 1840.[54] One of the most popular secular magazines was *Moore's Western Ladies' Book,* published in Cincinnati for about eight years. Its motto was "the stability of our Republic and the Virtue of her Institutions is with the Ladies."[55] It contained fashion plates and music along with literary pieces. It also contained a column entitled "The Genius of Liberty," which provided information on women's rights written by Elizabeth Aldrich. *The Parlor Magazine* started its run in July 1853. The owner, Jethro Jackson, brought in Alice Cary as editor after six months, but the magazine was not a financial success. It merged with the *West American Review* in 1855, but soon died. *Demorest's Monthly Magazine, Happy Hours Magazine, Woods Household Magazine,* and *Oliver's Optics Magazine* provided diversions for many rural Ohio women.

A few women attempted to publish or edit reform journals in the mid-nineteenth century in Ohio. In 1849, Rebecca Sanford began editing *The True Kindred* from Akron. In 1850, she moved to Chagrin Falls where she merged it with her husband's paper *The Politician* to become *The True Kindred and Politician.* Elizabeth Aldrich was the editor of *The Genius of Liberty,* which advocated a broader sphere for women, including the right to vote. This publication did not last long and, as noted above, Aldrich continued her writings in *Moore's Western Ladies' Book.* Amelia Bloomer, a well-known advocate of women's rights and dress reform, moved her publication *The Lily* from New York to Mount Vernon, Ohio, early in 1854 and continued publishing from there for two years.[56] Ella Wentworth of Cincinnati attempted to show her support for women's rights through a different approach. She published the *Literary Journal* in Cincinnati in 1853, and all the writing and production were done by women.

A perusal of lists of Ohio women writers shows that the Buckeye State has produced thousands of published writers, each important individually and to the local community but not always well known in the larger literary world. Harriet Church Francis of Berea was a paid contributor to the *Methodist Ladies' Repository, Arthur's, Godey's Magazine,* and several newspapers. Jan Chapin was a frequent contributor to religious journals and, under the pen name "Lily Underwood," to the literary weeklies and magazines. The first Ohio woman to gain literary recognition was Julia L. Dumont (1794–1841), who wrote both verse and prose. Another popular early writer was Caroline Lee Hentz (1800–1854), who was known for the poem "Lamorah of the Western Wild." Two other early Ohio writers were Alice and Phoebe Cary. The Cary sisters were born near Cincinnati, Alice in 1820 and Phoebe in 1824. Alice was known for her poetry as well as several novels, while Phoebe wrote hymns and poetry; both were considered very talented by critics in the 1850s. Alice published her first book of stories, *Clovernook,* in 1851 and her first novel, *Hagar, a Story of Today,* in 1852. In 1849, a joint volume of Alice's and Phoebe's work was published, enhancing their reputations. Both moved to New York soon after.

Patriotic poetry was a mainstay of nineteenth-century American literature, particularly after the Civil War. The public had a need to honor and commemorate those who had died and to come to terms with the magnitude of the loss. In addition, the public had to deal with extensive changes in the social and economic systems due to industrialization and immigration. Patriotic poetry and songs were popular because they helped to define the values of America and Americans during this turbulent time. Kate Brownlee Sherwood of Toledo wrote what the public liked. Her books of verse *Camp Fire and Memorial Day Poems* and *Dreams of the Ages, A Poem of Columbus* were best-sellers. Mary E. Kail, a native of Washington City, was also noted for her patriotic songs and poems, in particular the song "Crown Our Heroes."[57]

Sarah Morgan Bryan Piatt was described as a "poet whose name shines in American literature like some great jewell[sic] of fire." Some critics characterized her writings as "quite inventive." However, while London critics praised her work, American critics were not so kind. Her *Complete Poems* in two volumes was published in 1894 by Longman, Green and Company in New York and London. Edith M. Thomas (1854–1925) was born in Chatham Center, Medina County, and educated at the Geneva Normal Institute. She gained a national reputation for her verses and novels, which reflected the culture of the Western Reserve. Her poems include "A New Year's Masque and Other Poems," "The Inverted Torch" (a memorial to her mother), "The Dancers," and "The Children of Christmas." She claimed to be influenced by the writings of Helen Hunt Jackson, the nineteenth-century author of many books, including *A Century of Dishonor: A Sketch of the United States Government's Dealing with Some of the Indian Tribes* and *Ramona, A Story*. Ohio's women continued to write poetry throughout the twentieth century, but few achieved the recognition of Rita Dove from Akron, who received the Pulitzer Prize in 1987 for her poems *Thomas and Beulah* (based on her grandparents' experiences as they migrated from the South to Akron), and Mary Oliver, who won the Pulitzer Prize in 1985 for her book *American Primitive*.

Other writers focused on producing novels. Metta Victoria Fuller (1831–1886) was a popular writer in her day. Her novel *The Senator's Son* (1853) attempted to expose the evils of alcohol and support the temperance movement. Due to its popularity, the publisher printed six editions, with 30,000 copies being sold in England. In 1856, Fuller married Orville J. Victor, a publisher from Sandusky, who inaugurated mass production of popular fiction. He published many of his wife's dime novels, including *Maum Guinea and Her Plantation Children*, *The Backwoods Bride*, and *Blunders of a Bashful Man*. She also published poetry under the pen name "Singing Sybil."[58] Another writer, though not born in Ohio, is claimed by the state because of her long residence. Harriet Beecher Stowe, the author of *Uncle Tom's Cabin*, lived in Cincinnati for many years before writing the novel that had such an impact on the minds and souls of countless Americans. Mary Hartwell Catherwood, born in Luray, Licking County, in 1847, was called "the first American woman novelist of any significance born west of the Appalachians" by critic Robert Price.[59] Catherwood's novels, particularly *Craque-O'Doom* (1881), realistically portrayed life in the west. She was best known for her historical romances, set during the time when France and England were fighting for con-

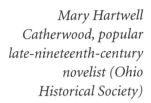

Mary Hartwell Catherwood, popular late-nineteenth-century novelist (Ohio Historical Society)

trol of the Ohio Valley. She also wrote a juvenile book, *Rocky Fork,* which portrayed a school in central Ohio during the 1860s. Mary Stanbery Watts was born in Delaware County in 1868 and educated at the Convent of the Sacred Heart in Cincinnati. She began her literary career by writing short stories, which appeared in *McClure's Magazine,* and critical essays for the *New York Times.* Her novels, *Nathan Burke, The Rise of Jennie Cushing,* and *The Fabric of the Room,* also reflected the reality of life in Ohio during the nineteenth century.

Another writer not born in Ohio but raised in a multiethnic neighborhood in Cleveland was Jo Sinclair (née Ruth Seid, 1913–1995). The neighborhood Sinclair grew up in provided the background for many of her novels. She worked with the Works Progress Administration during the Depression, was a freelance writer, and won the Harper Prize for her first novel, *Wasteland,* the story of a young man who struggles to accept his own ethnic identity. Her 1995 book *The Changeling* describes a Jewish neighborhood in Cleveland and how the people there deal with blacks moving into the neighborhood, an explosive topic for that time. In 1993, Sinclair published her memoirs, *The Seasons: Death and*

Transfiguration.[60] Another writer who drew on childhood experiences was Ruth McKenny from Akron. McKenny wrote the Broadway play *My Sister Eileen* and a dozen books, including *Industrial Valley,* which reflects experiences of the Great Depression in Akron. Helen Hoover Santmyer drew on her life experience in Xenia when writing the book *And Ladies of the Club,* which follows several generations from the Civil War to the 1930s. Another writer, Toni Morrison of Lorain, won a Pulitzer Prize in 1988 for *Beloved,* a novel based on her grandparents' experiences, and in 1993 she became the first African American woman to win the Nobel Prize for literature.[61]

One of America's favorite humorists was Erma Bombeck, who was born in Dayton in 1927. After Bombeck graduated from high school she worked for the *Dayton Journal-Herald* before attending the University of Dayton, where she graduated in 1942. She continued to write for the *Journal-Herald* until the birth of her first child in 1953. In 1964 Bombeck returned to writing and had a weekly humor column in the *Kettering-Oakwood Times.* She then began contributing a twice-weekly column entitled "At Wit's End" to the *Journal-Herald.* The column was syndicated and by 1968 more than two hundred newspapers carried it. She continued writing the newspaper column along with several books and magazine articles. She died in 1996.[62]

American children have grown up reading Ohio authors. Julia P. Ballard (1828–1849) wrote children's stories such as "The Hole in the Bag," "Gathered Lilies," "Left a Little," and "Little Gold Keys." Sarah Chauncey Woolsey (1845–1905) wrote under the name Susan Coolidge. She wrote history books for children, along with a series entitled "What Katy Did." Sarah K. Bolton was a prolific children's book author who came to Cleveland in 1866. She published several biographies, histories, and poems for children that were meant to teach them morals and values. She was careful to point out the achievements of women in her works. But certainly the most prolific of these early writers was Martha Finley (1828–1909), who was born in Chillicothe and used the name

Martha Farquahaison for some of her writings, including several Sunday school books. However, she is best known for her series "Elsie Dinsmore" and "Mildred." Between 1860 and 1890, she published forty-nine volumes. Many young girls also grew up with the adventures of detective Nancy Drew, created by Toledo native Carolyn Keene. Another award winner was Lois Lenski, an author and illustrator of children's books, born in 1893 in Clark County. Lenski received the Newbery Medal in 1946 for *Strawberry Girl.*

As we enter the twenty-first century, the list of Ohio women writers continues to grow. Access to education has led women into many more scholarly and literary pursuits. Access to professional education has begun to open the doors in law, medicine, and dentistry. But the door is not yet standing wide open. Women, with their male allies, are still battling throughout the state for higher quality school systems, a more equitable way of funding education, and affordable college education.

Conclusion

WOMEN MIGRATED TO Ohio with expectations, much like those of their male counterparts, of starting a new life whereby they and their families could prosper. Many settlers expected to do this by replicating the societal structures and institutions from their former homes and by transplanting the values of their former homes to their new communities. The responsibility for keeping these values alive typically fell to women as the educators of good citizens ("republican motherhood") and as the keepers of morality.

For those with wealth and social position, this proved easier to do than for those who were just barely scraping by. The demands of their new environment led many women to be more concerned with the daily needs of their family than with transplanting the culture and values of another time and place. In addition to the secular and religious training of their children, women were also responsible for their usual domestic duties. But by undertaking the directive to oversee the education of their children, women began to open the door of opportunity. These new opportunities would continue to grow as Ohio achieved statehood and continued to expand as Ohio developed into a vital industrial player in the national and world economies.

However, rural women of Ohio often needed to focus their attention on helping male family members establish farms or businesses. This did not exempt them from providing for their children's education, but it limited the time and type of involvement they had with their children's education. Much of this education for children and women was, therefore, of a practical nature. This practical education for women crossed gender boundaries, and by necessity women found themselves doing jobs usually reserved for men, such as plowing. In this way, rural women, like their counterparts in the growing towns and cities, also helped to expand the role of women.

Many women who came to the Ohio frontier complained of the isolation and the breakdown of the social network that had given them needed support in their previous situations. In time, the establishment of educational and religious institutions throughout the state helped to re-establish this social network, thus providing for the sharing of ideas—ideas that would eventually begin to challenge society's expectations of women and other minorities. But these institutions were not always progressive; sometimes, churches and schools were the main forces attempting to maintain the status quo during times of change.

Women throughout Ohio established religious groups, such as the Oberlin Moral Reform Association, which promoted certain values and provided women an opportunity for social interaction. Benevolent societies, moral reform societies, and missionary aid societies abounded in Ohio. Each sought to better its members, as well as to uplift those who were either materially or morally less fortunate.

These groups perpetuated the cultural norms of white middle-class Americans, while at the same time expanding the role of women into the public sphere. But they did so in a way that coincided with the expectations of women as the morals keepers of the family and the community. Ohio's women led national movements such as abolition, temperance, and women's rights—all causes rooted in the notion that there are definite rights to which all people in a society are entitled.

The strong presence of Quakers in Ohio had a significant impact on the leadership roles that women from Ohio assumed in these causes. Quaker women did not have to endure the religious discrimination that forced many women into an inferior position. The Quakers believed in the religious equality of women and allowed them to participate directly in the governance of the community. Quaker women preached in mixed meetings and controlled their own gatherings, thus gaining skills that other women didn't have access to. And Quakers were committed to social justice, so they used the skills they acquired by running their own meetings to work for causes such as abolition, temperance, and women's rights. The networks they established through the Quaker meetings gave them access to a large number of supportive women. Other women, committed to the same causes, perhaps for different reasons, found the Quaker women an able source of leadership and, in time, role models for the development of their own leadership skills. Participating in the abolition, temperance, and women's rights movements served a twofold purpose. It gave women the opportunity to devote themselves to the betterment of society by promoting Christian, middle-class values, while also bettering the economic circumstances of blacks, children, and other women.

Fighting the battles to end slavery, drunkenness, and women's lack of legal recognition took women outside of the home and into the public sphere—a sphere formerly seen as the exclusive purview of men. Ohio's women spoke in public forums, presented petitions to the state legislature, and even ventured into saloons, all in the name of Christian and patriotic duty. Those experiences, along with greater access to higher education, opened a new world to some women—a world of new ideas, questions, contradictions, and activism. It became apparent to many that in order for women to continue in their role as morals keepers, they had to have the right to vote. One of the first gains in that battle allowed women to participate in school board elections as voters and candidates.

From that point forward, Ohio's women continued to pursue elective office, though they were most successful on the local level. Women served as city council members, school board members, county clerks, and municipal court judges dealing with domestic issues. During the 1970s, women began to move into other political arenas, but only in recent years have Ohio women been attaining positions in the state executive or winning federal appointments. Besides cleaning up the political arena, women's role as morals keepers took them into the workplace, where their attempts at reform were imbued with white, middle-class values. By the end of the nineteenth century, the majority of women employed in Ohio's factories and sweatshops or as domestic workers were immigrants with different cultural, ethnic, and religious backgrounds than those women who were committed to helping them. Middle-class women, who were members of the Women's Trade Union League, the women's club movement, or part of the settlement house movement, committed themselves to Americanizing the immigrant workers. Settlement houses in Cleveland, Columbus, Toledo, and Cincinnati held classes in English, vocational training, parenting skills, and social activities, all aimed at making the transition to (white, middle-class) American culture easier. A few settlement workers did recognize the importance of each group's ethnic identity, such as Karamu House in Cleveland, but for most it was a well-meaning exercise in inculcating their own values concerning women's roles, the care of children, and use of alcohol. However, the efforts of these groups provided better working and living conditions for many through statewide protective labor legislation, women's cooperatives in major cities, and the recognition (even if it didn't always work) of what could be done if women joined forces.

The challenge of inclusion is still one that faces Ohio's women. Organizations such as WomenSpace and 9 to 5 worked to bring women together to address similar concerns. Women across the state are leaders in initiatives to bring citizens together to address issues dealing with race. During the past two hundred years, women of Ohio have had the opportunity to develop networking and problem-solving skills that will help them tackle the problems of the twenty-first century. Women are aware of the barriers that race and class can impose on community building and problem solving. Ohio's women have a rich history they can call upon to give them insights into overcoming these barriers as they continue to address issues such as access to health services, domestic abuse, salary equity, family care issues, and educational opportunities.

The history of Ohio's women parallels the movements of U.S. women's history. This parallelism does not, however, detract from the unique character of Ohio's women, their accomplishments, and the roles they have played in the development of the state. Every woman who lived in Ohio is a part of the state's history, and each has a story to tell. The woman who shot a wolf to protect her family, the woman who traded with Native Americans, the women who helped establish churches and schools, the women who worked in the fields and factories, the women who founded museums and orchestras, the women who joined together to form workers' unions—each of these stories has added to the rich tapestry of Ohio's history, and without each and every one of them, the tapestry would be incomplete. Whether the accomplishments of each were small or large, publicized or given no attention, each was invaluable to the story. Ohio's history is a record of the voices of its women—a story unique and everlasting.

Notes

Chapter One

1. Emily Foster, ed., *The Ohio Frontier: An Anthology of Early Writings* (Lexington: University Press of Kentucky, 1996), 61.

2. Emilius O. Randall and Daniel J. Ryan, *History of Ohio: The Rise and Progress of an American State* (New York: Century History Company, 1912), 2:8.

3. Beverley W. Bond, Jr., *The Foundations of Ohio* (Columbus: Ohio State Archaeological and Historical Society, 1941), 2:395–96.

4. Margaret Van Horn Dwight, *A Journey to Ohio in 1810* (Lincoln: University of Nebraska Press, 1991), 46.

5. Mrs. Gertrude Van Rensselaer Wickham, ed., *Memorial to the Pioneer Women of the Western Reserve*, 5 vols. (Cleveland: Woman's Department of the Cleveland Centennial Commission, 1896, 1897, 1924), 4:719; 1:160.

6. John Mack Faragher, *Women and Men on the Overland Trail* (New Haven, Conn.: Yale University Press, 1979), 170–72.

7. Andrew R. L. Cayton, *The Frontier Republic: Ideology and Politics in the Ohio Country, 1780–1825* (Kent, Ohio: Kent State University Press, 1986), 21.

8. Hermina Sugar, "The Role of Women in the Settlement of the Western Reserve, 1796–1815," *Ohio State Archaeological and Historical Quarterly* 46 (1937): 53. Mildred Covey Fry, "Women on the Ohio Frontier: The Marietta Area," *Ohio History* 90 (winter 1981): 70.

9. Sugar, "Role of Women," 53.

10. Wickham, *Memorial*, 4:299.

11. Ibid., 1:176. Henry Howe, *Historical Collections of Ohio in Two Volumes: An Encyclopedia of the State* (Cincinnati: C. J. Krehbiel and Company, Printers and Binders, 1907), 1:324.

12. Faragher, *Women and Men on the Overland Trail*, 119.

13. Wickham, *Memorial*, 1:98; 2:236. Imogen Davenport Trolander, ed., *Women of Greene County* (Xenia, Ohio: Women's History Project of Greene County, Inc., 1994), 85.

14. Wickham, *Memorial*, 2:224.

15. Fry, "Women on the Ohio Frontier," 69. Charles Theodore Greve,

Centennial History of Cincinnati and Representative Citizens (Chicago: Biographical Publishing Co., 1904), 1:490.

16. Wickham, *Memorial,* 1:79, 115.

17. Ibid., 1:8, 102, 105.

18. Ibid., 4:683, 666.

19. Ibid., 3:426.

20. Fry, "Women on the Ohio Frontier," 61. James McBride, *Pioneer Biography: Sketches of the Lives of Some of the Early Settlers of Butler County, Ohio* (Cincinnati: Robert Clarke and Co., 1871), 2:159.

21. Foster, *Ohio Frontier,* 164.

22. Ibid., 61.

23. Trolander, *Women of Greene County,* 90.

24. Wickham. *Memorial,* 1:112, 71.

25. Ibid., 2:283.

26. Ibid., 3:476.

27. Foster, *Ohio Frontier,* 599. Wickham, *Memorial,* 3:464, 521. S. P. Hildreth, M.D., *Biographical and Historical Memoirs of the Early Pioneer Settlers of Ohio* (Cincinnati: H. W. Derby and Company Publishers, 1852), 320, 323.

28. Wickham, *Memorial,* 3:414, 396.

29. Ibid., 4:667.

30. Ibid., 4:587; 3:526.

31. Ibid., 1:17.

32. Ibid., 1:33, 106.

33. Ibid., 2:807; 1:22; 5:866; 4:637; 3:458.

34. Ibid., 4:786.

35. Ibid., 2:277, 366.

36. Ibid., 3:404. Howe, *Historical Collections,* 554.

37. Wickham, *Memorial,* 3:542; 5:947; 4:637.

38. Ibid., 4:670, 794.

39. Ibid., 2:262; 4:603; 3:384; 4:618.

40. Luke B. Knapke, ed., *Liwwat Boke 1807–1882 Pioneer: The Story of an Immigrant Pioneer Woman and Her Husband Who Settled in Western Ohio, as Told in Her Own Writings and Drawings* (Minster, Ohio: Minster Historical Society, 1987), 89. Wickham, *Memorial,* 1:95.

41. Wickham, *Memorial,* 5:958; 2:288.

42. Ibid., 1:2; 2:374.

43. Ibid., 2:356; 1:171.

44. Ann Natalie Hansen, *Westward the Winds: Being Some of the Main Currents of Life in Ohio, 1788–1873* (Columbus: At the Sign of the Cock, 1974), 73–76. Bond, *Foundations of Ohio,* 1:280.

45. Hansen, *Westward the Winds*, 14.

46. George W. Knepper, *Ohio and Its People*, 2d ed. (Kent, Ohio: Kent State University Press, 1997), 121, 122.

47. Wickham, *Memorial*, 2:266.

48. Knapke, *Liwwat Boke*, 115

49. Wickham, *Memorial*, 3:444.

50. Ibid., 3:118.

51. Ibid., 3:456.

Chapter Two

1. Wickham, *Memorial*, 2:340, 345.

2. Ibid., 3:396, 414.

3. Ibid., 1:35; 4:775; 2:356. Amy H. Clifford, "Feminism in Ohio, 1848–1851" (M.A. thesis, Kent State University, 1972), 356.

4. Hunt, *History of Salem*, 23, 26, 27.

5. Clifford, "Feminism in Ohio," 12, 235. Mrs. W. A. Ingham, *Women of Cleveland and Their Work, Philanthropic, Educational, Literary, Medical, and Artistic* (Cleveland: W. A. Ingham, 1893), 319.

6. Wickham, *Memorial*, 3:521. Ingham, *Women of Cleveland*, 315. George D. Hunt, *History of Salem and Its Immediate Vicinity* (Salem, Ohio: published privately, 1898), 150. Wickham, *Memorial*, 4:599.

7. Philip D. Jordan, *Ohio Comes of Age* (Columbus: Ohio State Archaeological and Historical Society, 1943), 5:234.

8. Hansen, *Westward the Winds*, 148.

9. Clifford, *Feminism in Ohio*, 232.

10. Marian J. Morton, *Women in Cleveland: An Illustrated History* (Bloomington: Indiana University Press, 1995), 16. Ingham, *Women of Cleveland*, 407.

11. Morton, *Women in Cleveland*, 52.

12. Nancy Elizabeth Bertaux, "Women's Work, Men's Work: Occupational Segregation by Sex in Nineteenth-Century Cincinnati, Ohio" (Ph.D. diss., University of Michigan, 1987), 77, 95.

13. Lois Scharf, "A Woman's View of Cleveland's Labor Force: Two Case Studies," in *The Birth of Modern Cleveland, 1865–1930*, ed. Thomas F. Campbell and Edward M. Miggins (London: Associated University Presses, 1988), 172.

14. James C. Oda, *Hustle and Bustle, 1861–1920: A History of the Women in Piqua, Ohio* (Piqua, Ohio: Piqua Historical Society, 1988), 7, 4.

15. Knepper, *Ohio and Its People*, 304. Morton, *Women in Cleveland*, 43.

16. Ingham, *Women of Cleveland*, 417.

17. Oda, *Hustle and Bustle*, 7. Knepper, *Ohio and Its People*, 304.

18. Jordan, *Ohio Comes of Age,* 234.

19. Morton, *Women in Cleveland,* 44.

20. *Cincinnati Enquirer,* April 13, 1890.

21. Scharf, "Woman's View of Cleveland's Labor Force," 175.

22. Morton, *Women in Cleveland,* 47, 48.

23. Ingham, *Women of Cleveland,* 415.

24. Scharf, "Woman's View of Cleveland's Labor Force," 177, 179. Morton, *Women in Cleveland,* 49.

25. Hoyt Landon Warner, *Progressivism in Ohio, 1897–1917* (Columbus: Ohio State University Press, 1964), 403.

26. Ingham, *Women of Cleveland,* 142, 412.

27. Morton, "From Saving Souls to Saving Cities," in Campbell and Miggins, *Birth of Modern Cleveland,* 334.

28. Jordan, *Ohio Comes of Age,* 234.

29. Bertaux, "Women's Work, Men's Work," 84.

30. Oda, *Hustle and Bustle,* 5.

31. Edward M. Miggins and Mary Morgenthaler, "The Ethnic Mosaic: The Settlement of Cleveland by the New Immigrants and Migrants," in Campbell and Miggins, *Birth of Modern Cleveland,* 113.

32. Genevieve Sackett, *Legal Status of Women in Ohio* (Columbus: n.p., [1911?]). Louise Ogan Biggs, *A Brief History of Vinton County* (Columbus: Herr Printing, 1950), 170–77.

33. Wickham, *Memorial,* 5:831. Linda Lowe Fry and Cheryl Mack Urban, *Politics and the Women of Summit County* (Akron, Ohio: Women's History Project of the Akron Area, Inc., 1992), 18. *Ohio Women of Achievement* (Columbus: Martha Kinney Cooper Ohioana Library Association, 1951), 3, 4. William A. Duff, *History of North Central Ohio: Embracing Richland, Ashland, Wayne, Medina, Lorain, Huron, and Knox Counties* (Indianapolis: Historical Publishing Company, 1931), 1:244.

34. *Ohio Women of Achievement,* 3. *The Columbus Club Women,* Centennial Number, September 1912, 22.

35. Fry and Urban, *Politics and the Women of Summit County,* 32. *Ohio Women of Achievement,* 7.

36. *Ohio Women of Achievement,* 3. Eleanor Iler Shapior, *Wadsworth Heritage* (Wadsworth, Ohio: Wadsworth News-Banner, 1964), 169. Knepper, *Ohio and Its People,* 353.

37. Oda, *Hustle and Bustle,* 5.

38. *A Portrait and Biographical Record of Allen and Van Wert Counties, Ohio* (Chicago: A. W. Bowen and Company, 1896), 599.

39. Randolph Chandler Downes, *History of Lake Shore Ohio, Volume III,*

Family and Personal History (New York: Lewis Historical Publishing Company, 1952), 370.

40. Ruth Kane, *The Better Halves: The Story of Massillon's Women* (Massillon, Ohio: privately published, 1989), 66.

41. Clara Longworth de Chambrun, *Cincinnati: Story of the Queen City* (New York: Charles Scribner's Sons, 1939), 129–30.

42. Hunt, *History of Salem*, 150. Oda, *Hustle and Bustle*, 12. Fry and Urban, *Politics and the Women of Summit County*, 17. Duff, *History of North Central Ohio*, 3:1202–3. Kane, *Better Halves*, 59.

43. Morton, *Women in Cleveland*, 50. Bertaux, "Women's Work, Men's Work," 84.

44. Duff, *History of North Central Ohio*, 3:1398. Oda, *Hustle and Bustle*, 12.

45. Morton, *Women in Cleveland*, 178. Downes, *History of Lake Shore Ohio*, 235.

46. Scharf, "Woman's View of Cleveland's Labor Force," 186. Morton, *Women in Cleveland*, 179–80.

47. Oda, *Hustle and Bustle*, 4. Morton, *Women in Cleveland*, 50. Miggins and Morgenthaler, "Ethnic Mosaic," 133.

48. Duff, *History of North Central Ohio*, 3:675. Downes, *History of Lake Shore Ohio*, 384. Andrea Tuttle Kornbluh, *Lighting the Way . . . The Woman's City Club of Cincinnati, 1915–1965* (Cincinnati: Young and Klein, Inc., 1986), 91.

49. The Ohio Federation of Business and Professional Women's Clubs, *Pride in the Past; Promise for the Future: A History* (Columbus: Ohio Federation of Business and Professional Women's Clubs, 1970), 51, 76.

50. Knepper, *Ohio and Its People*, 382.

51. Annette Mann, "Women Workers in Factories: A Study of Working Conditions in 275 Industrial Establishments in Cincinnati and Adjoining Towns" (1918). Reprinted in *Working Girls of Cincinnati* (New York: Arno Press, 1974), 1.

52. Ibid., 10, 16.

53. Ibid., 39.

54. Frances Ivins Rich, "Wage-Earning Girls in Cincinnati: The Wages, Employment, Housing, Food, Recreation, and Education of a Sample Group" (1927). Reprinted in *Working Girls of Cincinnati* (New York: Arno Press, 1974), 7, 13, 21.

55. Ibid., 56.

56. Frances R. Whitney, "What Girls Live On and How: A Study of the Expenditures of a Sample Group of Girls Employed in Cincinnati in 1929" (1930). Reprinted in *Working Girls of Cincinnati* (New York: Arno Press, 1974), 41.

57. Morton, *Women in Cleveland*, 44, 52.

58. Sheila Rowbotham, *A Century of Women: The History of Women in Britain and the United States* (New York: Viking, 1997), 157. Sara M. Evans, *Born for Liberty: A History of Women in American.* 2d ed. (New York: Free Press, 1991), 192.

59. Ibid., 191.

60. Alexander D. Gaither, "Negro Women Employed in Domestic Service in Columbus, Ohio" (M.A. thesis, Ohio State University, 1938), 29, 49.

61. *Ohio Women of Achievement,* 6. Earl R. Hoover, *Cradle of Greatness: National and World Achievements of Ohio's Western Reserve* (Cleveland: New Cleveland Campaign, 1979), 85. Bell, *Ohio Women,* 5.

62. Downes, *History of Lake Shore Ohio,* 275. Oda, *Hustle and Bustle,* 19–22.

63. Lois Scharf, "Employment of Married Women in Ohio, 1920–1940," in *Women in Ohio History,* ed. Marta Whitlock (Columbus: Ohio Historical Society, 1976), 23.

64. Scharf, "Employment of Married Women in Ohio," 23–25. Ohio Federation of Business and Professional Women's Clubs, *Pride in the Past,* 35.

65. Morton, *Women in Cleveland,* 192, 196.

66. Ibid., 199, 201.

67. Steve Love and David Giffels, *Wheels of Fortune: The Story of Rubber in Akron* (Akron, Ohio: University of Akron Press, 1999), 121–23, 125.

68. Fry and Urban, *Politics and the Women of Summit County,* 57.

69. Morton, *Women in Cleveland,* 201. Love and Giffels, *Wheels of Fortune,* 121–22.

70. Morton, *Women in Cleveland,* 201–2.

71. Love and Giffels, *Wheels of Fortune,* 124.

72. Morton, *Women in Cleveland,* 208.

73. Ohio Federation of Business and Professional Women's Clubs, *Pride in the Past,* 37. Bell, *Ohio Women,* 5.

74. Shapior, *Wadsworth Heritage,* 391. Ohio Governor's Committee on the Status of Women, *Women in the Wonderful World of Ohio,* (Columbus: n.p., April 13, 1967), 46, *Webster's Dictionary of American Women* (New York: Smithmark Publishers, 1996) 644.

75. *Ohio Women Entrepreneurs Directory* (Columbus: U.S. Small Business Administration, 1984), 11.

76. Morton, *Women in Cleveland,* 211.

77. Ohio International Women's Year Coordinating Committee, *The Worlds of Ohio Women: Report of the Ohio Meeting for Observance of International Women's Year* (Columbus: n.p., June 11–12, 1977), 122. Bell, *Ohio Women,* 36.

78. Morton, *Women in Cleveland,* 117, 225, 119, 229.

79. Ohio Federation of Business and Professional Women's Clubs, *Pride in the Past,* 38.

80. *Women in the Wonderful World of Ohio,* 18, 21, 40.

81. Governor's Task Force on Women in State Government, *Report* (Columbus: n.p., 1978).

82. Morton, *Women in Cleveland,* 231.

Chapter Three

1. Clifford, *Feminism in Ohio,* 61.

2. Carl M. Becker, *The Village: A History of Germantown, Ohio, 1804–1976* (Germantown: Historical Society of Germantown, 1981), 43.

3. Robert W. Audretsch, comp. and ed., *The Salem, Ohio 1850 Women's Rights Convention Proceedings* (Salem: Salem Area Bicentennial Committee and Salem Public Library, 1976), 17–20.

4. Ibid., 26–28.

5. Ibid., 23–25.

6. Diane Van Skiver Gagel, "Ohio Women Unite: The Salem Convention of 1850," in *Women in Ohio History,* ed. Marta Whitlock (Columbus: Ohio Historical Society, 1976), 6.

7. Clifford, *Feminism in Ohio,* 146.

8. Linda L. Geary, *Balanced in the Wind: A Biography of Betsey Mix Cowles* (London: Associated University Presses, 1989), 79. Clifford, *Feminism in Ohio,* 160.

9. Caroline Severance, *Memorial on Behalf of Woman's Rights in Respect to Property and the Exercise of the Elective Franchise* (Columbus: n.p., [1854?]).

10. Clifford, *Feminism in Ohio,* 199.

11. Florence E. Allen and Mary Welles, *The Ohio Woman Suffrage Movement: "A Certain Unalienable Right": What Ohio Women Did to Secure It* (Columbus: Committee for the Preservation of Ohio Woman Suffrage Records, 1952), 21.

12. Clifford, *Feminism in Ohio,* 228.

13. Allen and Welles, *Ohio Woman Suffrage Movement,* 33.

14. Eileen Regina Rausch, "Let Ohio Women Vote: The Years to Victory, 1900–1920" (Ph.D. diss., University of Notre Dame, 1984), 32.

15. Ibid., 31.

16. Ibid., 43, 50.

17. Allen and Welles, *Ohio Woman Suffrage Movement,* 38, 39.

18. Rausch, "Let Ohio Women Vote," 75, 76.

19. Ibid., 122, 142.

20. Ibid., 77.

21. Ibid., 78, 124, 140.

22. Ibid., 124.

23. Ibid., 67.

24. Ibid., 133–34.

25. Ibid., 148, 152.

26. Ibid., 184–85.

27. Ibid., 214.

28. Ibid., 223.

29. Ibid., 168–69.

30. Ibid., 210–11.

31. Ibid., 254, 292.

32. Ibid., 293–94.

33. Ibid., 295–96.

34. Ibid., 297.

35. Evans, *Born for Liberty*, 188.

36. Morton, *Women in Cleveland*, 181.

37. Marian J. Morton, "From Saving Souls to Saving Cities: Women and Reform in Cleveland," in *The Birth of Modern Cleveland, 1865–1930*, ed. Thomas F. Campbell and Edward M. Miggins (London: Associated University Presses, 1988), 341–42.

38. Evans, *Born for Liberty*, 190–91.

39. William A. Duff, *History of North Central Ohio* (Indianapolis: Historical Publishing Co., 1931), 3:1606.

40. Evans, *Born for Liberty*, 151.

41. Morton, *Women in Cleveland*, 197.

42. Kornbluh, *Lighting the Way*, 2.

43. Ibid., 30–31.

44. Ibid., 31.

45. Ibid., 32.

46. Kane, *Better Halves*, 136–37. Fry and Urban, *Politics and the Women of Summit County*, 75.

47. Kornbluh, *Lighting the Way*, 2.

48. Fry and Urban, *Politics and the Women of Summit County*, 85, 84. *Ohio Women of Achievement* (Columbus: Martha Kinney Cooper Ohioana Library Association, 1951), 9.

49. Edward M. Miggins and Mary Morgenthaler, "The Ethnic Mosaic: The Settlement of Cleveland by the New Immigrants and Migrants," in Campbell and Miggins, *Birth of Modern Cleveland*, 135.

50. Kornbluh, *Lighting the Way*, 37, 38–39.

51. Fry and Urban, *Politics and the Women of Summit County*, 30–31. Morton, "From Saving Souls," 341. Morton, *Women in Cleveland*, 213.

52. Sherry S. Bell, ed., *Ohio Women*. 4th ed. (Columbus: Ohio Bureau of Employment Services, Women's Services Division, 1981), 5. Knepper, *Ohio and*

Its People, 352. Morton, *Women in Cleveland,* 216. Fry and Urban, *Politics and the Women of Summit County,* 44–45.

53. Fry and Urban, *Politics and the Women of Summit County,* 17.

54. *Ohio Women of Achievement,* 6.

55. Bell, *Ohio Women,* 5. Fry and Urban, *Politics and the Women of Summit County,* 31–32, 35–36.

56. Bell, *Ohio Women,* 5. Knepper, *Ohio and Its People,* 408.

57. Morton, *Women in Cleveland,* 184.

58. Fry and Urban, *Politics and the Women of Summit County,* 63. Bell, *Ohio Women,* 5. David W. Bowman, *Pathways of Progress: A Short History of Ohio* (New York: American Book Co., 1951), 413.

59. *Ohio Women of Achievement,* 9. Bowman, *Pathways of Progress,* 412.

60. *Ohio Women of Achievement,* 6. Clyde Hissong, *Ohio Lives: The Buckeye State Biographical Record* (Hopkinsville, Kentucky: Historical Record Association, 1968), 353. Fry and Urban, *Politics and the Women of Summit County,* 47–48. Morton, *Women in Cleveland,* 213. Bell, *Ohio Women,* 5.

61. Kane, *Better Halves,* 159. Morton, *Women in Cleveland,* 186, 216. *Ohio Women of Achievement,* 8. Hissong, *Ohio Lives,* 73.

62. Fry and Urban, *Politics and the Women of Summit County,* 48, 73.

63. Bell, *Ohio Women,* 5.

Chapter Four

1. Evans, *Born for Liberty,* 72–73.

2. Ibid., 74.

3. Francis P. Weisenburger, *The Passing of the Frontier, 1825–1850,* vol. 3 of *The History of the State of Ohio,* ed. Carl Wittke (Columbus: Ohio State Archeological and Historical Society, 1941), 366.

4. Geary, *Balanced in the Wind,* 31–33.

5. Ibid., 54–58.

6. Ibid., 59–60.

7. George D. Hunt, *History of Salem and Its Immediate Vicinity* (Salem, Ohio: privately published, 1898), 144.

8. Kathleen Moser, "J. Elizabeth Jones: The Forgotten Activist" (Honors thesis, Kent State University, 1996), 5.

9. Wickham, *Memorial,* 2:306.

10. Henry Louis Taylor, Jr., *Race and the City: Work, Community, and Protest in Cincinnati, 1820–1970* (Urbana: University of Illinois Press, 1993), 77, 79.

11. Ibid., 80.

12. Leeann Whites, "The Civil War as a Crisis in Gender," in *Divided Houses:*

Gender and the Civil War, ed. Catherine Clinton and Nina Silber (New York: Oxford University Press, 1992), 3.

13. Wickham, *Memorial,* 4:661.

14. Ingham, *Women of Cleveland,* 111.

15. Clifford, *Feminism in Ohio,* 184.

16. Eugene H. Roseboom, *The Civil War Era, 1850–1873* (Columbus: Ohio State Archaeological and Historical Society, 1944), 4:224.

17. Paul S. Boyer, *Urban Masses and Moral Order in America, 1820–1920* (Cambridge: Harvard University Press, 1978), 124–25.

18. Ruth Bordin, "The Temperance Crusade as a Feminist Movement," in *Major Problems in American Women's History,* ed. Mary Beth Norton (Lexington, Mass.: D. C. Heath and Company, 1989), 217.

19. Ruth Bordin, "'A Baptism of Power and Liberty:' The Women's Crusade of 1873–1874" *Ohio History* 87 (autumn 1978): 397.

20. Hansen, *Westward the Winds,* 138.

21. Eliza Stewart, *Memories of the Crusade,* 2d ed. (Columbus: William G. Hubbard and Company, 1889), 133; *Ohio Women of Achievement,* 8.

22. Stewart, *Memories,* 133.

23. Oda, *Hustle and Bustle,* 15, 16.

24. Jordan, *Ohio Comes of Age,* 5:35.

25. Stewart, *Memories,* 12.

26. Ingham, *Women of Cleveland,* 171, 472.

27. David D. Van Tassel and John J. Grabowski, eds., *The Encyclopedia of Cleveland History* (Bloomington: Indiana University Press, 1996), 824–25; Knepper, *Ohio and Its People,* 277.

28. Morton, "From Saving Souls," 328.

29. William T. Utter, *The Frontier State, 1803–1825,* vol. 2 of *The History of the State of Ohio,* ed. Carl Wittke (Columbus: Ohio State Archaeological and Historical Society, 1942), 385.

30. Robert Samuel Fletcher, *A History of Oberlin College* (Oberlin, Ohio: Oberlin College, 1943), 1:301.

31. Ibid., 1:310.

32. Wickham, *Memorial,* 5:830. Clifford, *Feminism in Ohio,* 55.

33. Fletcher, *History of Oberlin College,* 1:312.

34. Howe, *Historical Collections of Ohio,* 515. Ingham, *Women of Cleveland,* 106.

35. Ingham, *Women of Cleveland,* 140.

36. Luke Feck, *Yesterday's Cincinnati* (Miami, Fla.: E. A. Seeman Publishing, 1976), 76; Greve, *Centennial History of Cincinnati,* 1032.

37. Ingham, *Women of Cleveland,* 149. Morton, "From Saving Souls," 326. Ingham, *Women of Cleveland,* 471.

38. Morton, *Women in Cleveland,* 18.

39. Ibid.

40. De Chambrun, *Cincinnati: Story of the Queen City,* 107.

41. Kane, *Better Halves,* 14–15.

42. *Manual of the Columbus Female Benevolent Society with Annual Reports of 1877* (Columbus: Ohio State Journal Steam Printing Establishment, 1878). Ingham, *Women of Cleveland,* 114, 116.

43. Oda, *Hustle and Bustle,* 14. Emily Apt Geer, "Lucy Webb Hayes: A Governor's Wife a Century Ago," in *Women in Ohio History,* ed. Marta Whitlock (Columbus: Ohio Historical Society, 1976), 10.

44. Hansen, *Westward the Winds,* 143. Howe, *Historical Collections,* 558. William A. Duff, *History of North Central Ohio,* 2:581. Roseboom, *Civil War Era,* 247.

45. Wickham, *Memorial,* 1:35; 5:858.

46. Howe, *Historical Collections,* 190. Ingham, *Women of Cleveland,* 125. Morton, *Women in Cleveland,* 22. Roseboom, *Civil War Era,* 442. Greve, *Centennial History of Cincinnati,* 844.

47. Knepper, *Ohio and Its People,* 234, 246.

48. *Ohio Women of Achievement,* 8. Fry and Urban, *Politics and the Women of Summit County,* 15.

49. Kane, *Better Halves,* 52–54.

50. Boyer, *Urban Masses,* 146–47.

51. Evans, *Born for Liberty,* 139–40.

52. Greve, *Centennial History of Cincinnati,* 1028. Kornbluh, *Lighting the Way,* 2.

53. Oda, *Hustle and Bustle,* 13. Elaine S. Anderson, "Pauline Steinem, Dynamic Immigrant," in *Women in Ohio History,* ed. Marta Whitlock (Columbus: Ohio Historical Society, 1976), 14. Morton, *Women in Cleveland,* 159. Rausch, "Let Ohio Women Vote," 21.

54. Shapior, *Wadsworth Heritage,* 338.

55. Morton, *Women in Cleveland,* 33.

56. Kornbluh, *Lighting the Way,* 1. Oda, *Hustle and Bustle,* 13. Becker, *Village,* 33.

57. Evans, *Born for Liberty,* 146, 149.

58. Ibid., 149–50.

59. Ruth Young White, ed., *We Too Built Columbus* (Columbus: Stoneman Press, 1936), 138–42.

60. Harry F. Lupold and Gladys Haddad, *Ohio's Western Reserve: A Regional*

Reader (Kent, Ohio: Kent State University Press, 1988), 202. Fry and Urban, *Politics and the Women of Summit County,* 14. Kornbluh, *Lighting the Way,* 10. Ruth Neely, ed., *Women of Ohio: A Record of Their Achievements in the History of the State* (Columbus: S. J. Clarke Publishing Co., n.d.), 2:5.

61. Morton, *Women in Cleveland,* 29. Kane, *Better Halves,* 162.

62. Hunt, *History of Salem,* 184–185. White, *We Too Built Columbus,* 151. Duff, *History of North Central Ohio,* 1:419.

63. Morton, *Women in Cleveland,* 38, 39, 34–35. Knepper, *Ohio and Its People,* 318. Edward M. Miggins, "A City of 'Uplifting Influences': From 'Sweet Charity' to Modern Social Welfare and Philanthropy," in *The Birth of Modern Cleveland,* ed. Thomas F. Campbell and Edward M. Miggins (London: Associated University Presses, 1988), 147.

64. Morton, *Women in Cleveland,* 35, 37. Miggins and Morgenthaler, "Ethnic Mosaic," 131, 132.

65. Elisabeth Lasch-Quinn, *Black Neighbors: Race and the Limits of Reform in the American Settlement House Movement, 1890–1945* (Chapel Hill: University of North Carolina Press, 1993), 29.

66. Rich, "Wage-Earning Girls in Cincinnati," 28–30. White, *We Too Built Columbus,* 145.

67. Greve, *Centennial History of Cincinnati,* 1033. Neely, *Women of Ohio,* 431.

68. Morton, "From Saving Souls," 326.

69. Morton, *Women in Cleveland,* 183–84.

70. Duff, *History of North Central Ohio,* 2:565. Kane, *Better Halves,* 54.

71. Morton, *Women in Cleveland,* 177–78.

72. *Emeritae: Women Leaders of the University of Cincinnati* (Cincinnati: Center for Women's Studies, University of Cincinnati, [1985?]).

73. Morton, *Women in Cleveland,* 182, 183. Kornbluh, *Lighting the Way,* 89.

74. Kornbluh, *Lighting the Way,* 91.

75. Knepper, *Ohio and Its People,* 368–69.

76. Mrs. Ben B. Nelson, *The Cincinnati Woman's Club Historical Sketch of the Last Thirty-nine Years in Honor of the Sixty-fourth Anniversary of the Founding of the Club* (Cincinnati: n.p., 1958), 27. White, *We Too Built Columbus,* 174.

77. Morton, *Women in Cleveland,* 196–97.

78. Kane, *Better Halves,* 158. Morton, *Women in Cleveland,* 199.

79. Nelson, *Cincinnati Woman's Club,* 30.

80. Morton, *Women in Cleveland,* 199.

81. Kornbluh, *Lighting the Way,* 79.

82. Ibid., 82.

83. Morton, *Women in Cleveland,* 218. White, *We Too Built Columbus,* 183–84.

84. Morton, *Women in Cleveland,* 215–17.

85. Ibid., 218.

86. Ibid., 225.

87. Ibid., 221, 224.

Chapter Five

1. *The Ladies, God Bless 'Em—The Women's Art Movement in Cincinnati in the Nineteenth Century* (Cincinnati: Cincinnati Art Museum, 1976), 7.

2. De Chambrun, *Cincinnati: Story of the Queen City*, 935.

3. Margaret Lynch, "The Growth of Cleveland as a Cultural Center," in *The Birth of Modern Cleveland*, ed. Thomas F. Campbell and Edward M. Miggins (London: Associated University Presses, 1988), 219.

4. Morton, *Women in Cleveland*, 167.

5. *Emeritae.*

6. Barbara Haskell, *The American Century: Art and Culture 1900–1950* (New York: W. W. Norton and Company, 1999), 36–37.

7. Ibid., 162.

8. *The Ladies, God Bless 'Em*, 7.

9. Ibid., 17.

10. Mary Louise McLaughlin, *China Painting: A Practical Manual for the Use of Amateurs in the Decoration of Hard Porcelain* (Cincinnati: R. Clarke, 1892 [c. 1889]); Mary Louise McLaughlin, *Pottery Decoration under the Glaze* (Cincinnati: R. Clarke, 1880).

11. *The Ladies, God Bless 'Em*, 19.

12. Morton, *Women in Cleveland*, 194.

13. Foster, *Ohio Frontier*, 167–68.

14. Morton, *Women in Cleveland*, 170; Lasch-Quinn, *Black Neighbors*, 29–32.

15. *Ohio Women: Their Portraits and Paintings* (Columbus: Ohio State Historical Society, 1956). Ohio International Women's Year Coordinating Committee, *Worlds of Ohio Women*, 19.

16. Emilius O. Randall and Daniel J. Ryan, *History of Ohio: The Rise and Progress of an American State* (New York: The Century History Co., 1912), 3:83.

17. Morton, *Women in Cleveland*, 194.

18. Kane, *Better Halves*, 98.

19. *Webster's Dictionary of American Women*, 1.

20. Hansen, *Westward the Winds*, 118.

21. Greve, *Centennial History of Cincinnati*, 922–23.

22. VanTassel and Grabowski, *Encyclopedia*, 723.

23. Morton, *Women in Cleveland*, 166.

24. Kane, *Better Halves*, 99–102.

25. Florence Galida, *Fascinating History of the City of Campbell* (State College, Penn.: Jostens American Yearbook Company, 1976), 164.

26. Wickham, *Memorial*, 3:383.

27. Bowman, *Pathways of Progress*, 463.

28. *Ohio Women of Achievement*, 6.

29. *Webster's Dictionary of American Women*, 52. Jennifer S. Uglow, ed., *The Continuum Dictionary of Women's Biography* (New York: Continuum, 1989), 140.

30. Kane, *Better Halves*, 86–92.

31. Uglow, *Continuum Dictionary of Women's Biography*, 151–52.

32. De Chambrun, *Cincinnati: Story of the Queen City*, 128.

33. Ohio International Women's Year Coordinating Committee, *Worlds of Ohio Women*, 121.

Chapter Six

1. Evans, *Born for Liberty*, 57, 95. For a discussion of these concepts see Linda Kerber, *Women of the Republic: Intellect and Ideology in Revolutionary America* (Chapel Hill: University of North Carolina Press, 1980); and Barbara Welter, "The Cult of True Womanhood: 1800–1860," in *Dimity Connections: The American Women in the Nineteenth Century* (Athens: Ohio University Press, 1976), 21–41.

2. Evans, *Born for Liberty*, 65, 73, 74,

3. Ingham, *Women of Cleveland*, 15. White, *We Too Built Columbus*, 118.

4. Ingham, *Women of Cleveland*, 53, 70. Virginia E. McCormick, ed., *Farm Wife: A Self Portrait, 1886–1896* (Ames: Iowa State University Press, 1990), 185.

5. Lois D. Ginzberg, "Women in an Evangelical Community: Oberlin 1838–1850," *Ohio History* 89 (winter 1980): 78–88.

6. Fletcher, *A History of Oberlin College*, 2:514.

7. John Barnard, *From Evangelicalism to Progressivism at Oberlin College, 1866–1917* (Columbus: Ohio State University Press, 1969), 30.

8. Wickham, *Memorial*, 5:983; 4:672. *Ohio Women of Achievement*, 8. Kane, *Better Halves*, 142. *Dictionary of American Women*, 509.

9. Howe, *Historical Collections of Ohio*, 1:324. Neely, *Women of Ohio*, 438.

10. Neely, *Women of Ohio*, 429. Morton, *Women of Cleveland*, 67.

11. Knapke, *Liwwat Boke*, 81–83.

12. Ingham, *Women of Cleveland*, 485.

13. J. P. MacLean, *Shakers of Ohio: Fugitive Papers Concerning the Shakers of Ohio, with Unpublished Manuscripts* (Philadelphia: Porcupine Press, 1975), 152; Ruby Rohrlich and Elaine Hoffman Baruch, eds., *Women in Search of Utopias: Mavericks and Mythmakers* (New York: Schocken Books, 1984), 58.

14. Wickham, *Memorial,* 1:98. Morton, *Women in Cleveland,* 18. Howe, *Historical Collections of Ohio,* 1:254.

15. *A Portrait and Biographical Record of Allan and Van Wert Counties, Ohio* (Chicago: A. W. Bowen and Co., 1896), 425.

16. Howe, *Historical Collections of Ohio,* 1:414; Albert Douglas, "Ohio's Only Witchcraft Case," *Ohio Archaeological and Historical Quarterly* 33 (1924): 205–14.

17. Kenneth W. Godfrey, Audrey M. Godfrey, and Jill Mulvay Derr, *Women's Voices: An Untold History of the Latter-Day Saints 1830–1900* (Salt Lake City: Deseret Books, 1982), 67.

18. Orton G. Rust, *History of West Central Ohio* (Indianapolis: Historical Publishing, 1934), 463. Morton, *Women in Cleveland,* 17. Randolph Chandler Downes, *History of Lake Shore Ohio,* vol. 3, *Family and Personal History* (New York: Lewis Historical Publishing, 1952), 512–13. White, *We Too Built Columbus,* 186–98.

19. Leslie L. Liedel, "Indomitable Nuns and a Determined Bishop: Property Rights, Religious Women, and Diocesan Power in Nineteenth Century Cleveland" (Ph.D. diss., Kent State University, 1998), 2.

20. Weisenburger, *Passing of the Frontier,* 125.

21. Rust, *History of West Central Ohio,* 471.

22. Ibid., 477.

23. De Chambrun, *Cincinnati: Story of the Queen City,* 545. Utter, *Frontier State,* 174.

24. Ingham, *Women of Cleveland,* 324, 327.

25. Morton, *Women in Cleveland,* 59.

26. Ibid., 13.

27. Clifford, *Feminism in Ohio,* 19.

28. Greve, *Centennial History of Cincinnati,* 890.

29. Lupold and Haddad, *Ohio's Western Reserve,* 110. Geary, *Balanced in the Wind,* 37.

30. Bowman, *Pathways of Progress,* 189–97.

31. Clifford, *Feminism in Ohio,* 230. Roseboom, *Civil War Era,* 191.

32. Morton, *Women in Cleveland,* 56.

33. Fletcher, *History of Oberlin,* 2:120.

34. Ibid., 2:644.

35. Neely, *Women of Ohio,* 1:155.

36. W. A. Joiner, ed. *A Half Century of Freedom of the Negro in Ohio* (Wilberforce, Ohio: Wilberforce University, n.d.), 60.

37. White, *We Too Built Columbus,* 94, 96.

38. *Ohio Pioneer Women,* Spring Meeting of the Ohioana Library Association —Betsey Mills Club (Marietta, Ohio: n.p., May 21, 1949).

39. *A Portrait and Biographical Record of Allan and Van Wert Counties, Ohio*, 282.

40. Geary, *Balanced in the Wind*, 86–89.

41. Kane, *Better Halves*, 113–17.

42. *Emeritae*. White, *We Too Built Columbus*, 375.

43. Kane, *Better Halves*, 140. White, *We Too Built Columbus*, 372.

44. Clifford, *Feminism in Ohio*, 24–25. Roseboom, *Civil War Era*, 184. Scharf, "Employment of Married Women in Ohio," 21.

45. Roseboom, *Civil War Era*, 184. Scharf, "Employment of Married Women in Ohio," 21.

46. De Chambrun, *Cincinnati: Story of the Queen City*, 1029.

47. Frederick C. Waite, "The Medical Education of Women in Cleveland, 1850–1930," *Western Reserve University Bulletin* 16, September 15, 1930: 7, 19.

48. Ibid., 22–23.

49. Morton, *Women in Cleveland*, 61. White, *We Too Built Columbus*, 195.

50. Morton, *Women in Cleveland*, 210.

51. Hansen, *Westward the Winds*, 116. Wickham, *Memorial*, 1:126–27. Geary, *Balanced in the Wind*, 24.

52. Duff, *History of North Central Ohio*, 1:431.

53. Weisenburger, *Passing of the Frontier*, 189, 154.

54. Ibid, 189. Knepper, *Ohio and Its People*, 200. Ingham, *Women of Cleveland*, 256.

55. Greve, *Centennial History of Cincinnati*, 1:801.

56. Hansen, *Westward the Winds*, 147.

57. Wickham, *Memorial*, 4:718; 3:359. Mrs. James R. Hopley, "The Part Taken by Women in the History and Development of Ohio," in *Ohio Centennial Anniversary Celebration, Complete Proceedings*, ed. E. O. Randall (Columbus: Ohio State Archaeological and Historical Society, 1903), 611.

58. Duff, *History of North Central Ohio*, 1:545. Roseboom, *Civil War Era*, 158.

59. Knepper, *Ohio and Its People*, 49.

60. Morton, *Women in Cleveland*, 211.

61. Knepper, *Ohio and Its People*, 423.

62. *Webster's Dictionary of American Women*, 62–63.

Selected Bibliography

Abbott, Virginia Clark. *The History of Woman Suffrage and the League of Women Voters in Cuyahoga County, 1911–1945*. Cleveland, 1949. Consumer League of Ohio Records, Western Reserve Historical Society, MS 1000, Reel 2, Folder 10.

Allen, Florence E., and Mary Welles. *The Ohio Woman Suffrage Movement: "A Certain Unalienable Right": What Ohio Women Did to Secure It*. Columbus: Committee for the Preservation of Ohio Woman Suffrage Records, 1952.

Anderson, Elaine S. "Pauline Steinem, Dynamic Immigrant." In *Women in Ohio History*, ed. Marta Whitlock, 4–8. Columbus: Ohio Historical Society, 1976.

Audretsch, Robert W., comp. and ed. *The Salem, Ohio 1850 Women's Rights Convention Proceedings*. Salem, Ohio: Salem Area Bicentennial Committee and Salem Public Library, 1976.

Bacher, Jacqueline Lois Miller. *Life on the Ohio Frontier: A Collection of Letters from Mary Lott to Deacon John Phillips, 1826–1846*. Baltimore, Md.: Gateway Press, 1994.

Barlow, William, and David O. Powell. "Homeopathy and Sexual Equality: The Controversy over Coeducation at Cincinnati's Pulte Medical College." *Ohio History* 90 (spring 1981): 101–13.

Barnard, John. *From Evangelicalism to Progressivism at Oberlin College, 1866–1917*. Columbus: Ohio State University Press, 1969.

Bartlow, E. O., ed. *Vocational Survey: Girls' and Women's Occupations*. Toledo, Ohio: n.p., 1938.

Becker, Carl M. *The Village: A History of Germantown, Ohio, 1804–1976*. Germantown, Ohio: Historical Society of Germantown, 1981.

Bell, Sherry, ed. *Ohio Women*. 4th ed. Columbus: Ohio Bureau of Employment Services, Women's Services Division, 1981.

Bertaux, Nancy Elizabeth. "Women's Work, Men's Work: Occupational Segregation by Sex in Nineteenth-Century Cincinnati, Ohio." Ph.D. diss., University of Michigan, 1987.

Biggs, Louise Ogan. *A Brief History of Vinton County*. Columbus: Herr Printing, 1950.

Bond, Beverley W., Jr. *The Foundations of Ohio*, 2 vols. Columbus: Ohio State Archaeological and Historical Society, 1941.

Bordin, Ruth. "The Baptism of Power and Liberty: The Woman's Crusade of 1873." *Ohio History* 87 (autumn 1978): 393–404.

————. *Woman and Temperance: The Quest for Power and Liberty, 1873–1900.* Philadelphia: Temple University Press, 1981.

Bowman, David W. *Pathways of Progress: A Short History of Ohio.* New York: American Book Co., 1951.

Boyer, Paul. *Urban Masses and the Moral Order in America, 1820–1920.* Cambridge: Harvard University Press, 1978.

Brown, Martha McClellan. Papers. Wright State University Special Collections, Dayton, Ohio.

Cangi, Ellen Corwin. "Patrons and Proteges: Cincinnati's First Generation of Women Doctors, 1875–1910." *Cincinnati Historical Society Bulletin* 37 (summer 1979): 89–114.

Casement, Frances Jennings. Papers. Ohio Historical Society, Collection 510, Columbus.

Cayton, Andrew R. L. *The Frontier Republic: Ideology and Politics in The Ohio Country, 1780–1825.* Kent, Ohio: Kent State University Press, 1986.

Centennial Manual of the Columbus Female Benevolent Society, 1835–1935. Columbus: n.p., reprint 1965.

Cincinnati Women: Jewels in the Crown. Cincinnati: Cincinnati Creative Consortium, 1988.

Clifford, Amy H. "Feminism in Ohio, 1848–1851." M.A. thesis, Kent State University, 1972.

Clinton, Catherine, and Nina Silber, eds. *Divided Houses: Gender and the Civil War.* New York: Oxford University Press, 1992.

Collins, William R. *Ohio: The Buckeye State.* 2d ed. Englewood Cliffs, N.J.: Prentice Hall, 1962.

The Columbus Club Women. Centennial Number, September 1912.

The Columbus Female Benevolent Society, 1901–1911: A Summary. Columbus: Ohio Historical Society, 1912.

Cowles, Betsey Mix. Papers. American History Research Center, Kent State University, Kent, Ohio.

De Chambrun, Clara Longworth. *Cincinnati: Story of the Queen City.* New York: Charles Scribner's Sons, 1939.

Downes, Randolph Chandler. *History of Lake Shore Ohio.* Vol. 3, *Family and Personal History.* New York: Lewis Historical Publishing Co., 1952.

Duff, William A. *History of North Central Ohio: Embracing Richland, Ashland, Wayne, Medina, Lorain, Huron and Knox Counties.* 3 vols. Indianapolis: Historical Publishing Co., 1931.

Dwight, Margaret Van Horn. *A Journey to Ohio in 1810.* Lincoln: University of Nebraska Press, 1991.

Emeritae: Women Leaders of the University of Cincinnati. Cincinnati: Center for Women's Studies, University of Cincinnati, [1985?].

Endress, Kathleen L. "The Power of Tradition, The Potential for Change: The Women of Cleveland, 1850–1890." Ph.D. diss., Kent State University, 1986.

Evans, Sara M. *Born for Liberty: A History of Women in America.* 2d ed. New York: Free Press, 1991.

Faragher, John Mack. *Women and Men on the Overland Trail.* New Haven, Conn.: Yale University Press, 1979.

Feck, Luke. *Yesterday's Cincinnati.* Miami, Fla.: E. A. Seemann Publishing, 1976.

Filler, Louis, ed. *An Ohio Schoolmistress: The Memoirs of Irene Hardy.* Kent, Ohio: Kent State University Press, 1980.

Fletcher, Robert Samuel. *A History of Oberlin College: From Its Foundation through the Civil War.* 2 vols. Oberlin, Ohio: Oberlin College, 1943.

Foster, Emily, ed. *The Ohio Frontier: An Anthology of Early Writings.* Lexington: University Press of Kentucky, 1996.

Frost, John. *Pioneer Mothers of the West or Daring and Heroic Deeds of American Women.* Boston: Lee and Shepard, 1869.

Fry, Linda Lowe, and Cheryl Mack Urban. *Politics and the Women of Summit County.* Akron, Ohio: Women's History Project of the Akron Area, Inc., 1992.

Fry, Mildred Covey. "Women on the Ohio Frontier: The Marietta Area." *Ohio History* 90 (winter 1981): 55–73.

Gabel, John B., ed. "Medical Education in the 1890s: An Ohio Woman's Memories." *Ohio History* 87 (winter 1978): 53–66.

Gagel, Diane Van Skiver. "Ohio Women Unite: The Salem Convention of 1850." In *Women in Ohio History,* ed. Marta Whitlock, 4–8. Columbus: Ohio Historical Society, 1976.

Gaither, Alexander D. "Negro Women Employed in Domestic Service in Columbus, Ohio." M.A. thesis, Ohio State University, 1938.

Galida, Florence. *Fascinating History of the City of Campbell.* State College, Penn.: Jostens American Yearbooks Co., 1976.

Geary, Linda L. *Balanced in the Wind: A Biography of Betsey Mix Cowles.* London, England: Associated University Presses, 1989.

Geer, Emily Apt. *First Lady: The Life of Lucy Webb Hayes.* Kent, Ohio: Kent State University Press, 1984.

———. "Lucy Webb Hayes: A Governor's Wife a Century Ago." In *Women in Ohio History,* ed. Marta Whitlock, 8–12. Columbus: Ohio Historical Society, 1976.

Godfrey, Kenneth W., Audrey M. Godfrey, and Jill Mulvay Derr. *Women's Voices: An Untold History of the Latter-Day Saints, 1830–1900.* Salt Lake City, Utah: Deseret Book Company, 1982.

Governor's Task Force on Women in State Government. *Report.* Columbus: n.p., 1978.

Greve, Charles Theodore. *Centennial History of Cincinnati and Representative Citizens.* 2 vols. Chicago: Biographical Publishing Co., 1904.

Haas, Frances. *The Greater Federation of Women's Clubs/Ohio Federation of Women's Clubs.* Vol. 4, *1974–1994.* Columbus: n.p., 1995.

Hansen, Ann Natalie. *Westward the Winds: Being Some of the Main Currents of Life in Ohio, 1788–1873.* Columbus: At The Sign of the Cock, 1974.

Hauser, Elizabeth. "The Woman Suffrage Movement in Ohio." *Ohio Magazine* 4 (February 1908): 83–92.

Havighurst, Walter. *Ohio: A Bicentennial History.* New York: W. W. Norton and Company, 1976.

Hickok, Charles Thomas. *The Negro in Ohio, 1802–1870.* Reprint, New York: AMS Press, 1975.

Hildreth, S. P. *Biographical and Historical Memoirs of the Early Pioneer Settlers of Ohio, with Narratives of Incidents and Occurrences in 1775.* Cincinnati: H. W. Derby and Co., Publishers, 1852.

Hissong, Clyde. *Ohio Lives: The Buckeye State Biographical Record.* Hopkinsville, Ky.: Historical Record Association, 1968.

A History: The Ohio Federation of Business and Professional Women's Clubs. Columbus: Ohio Federation of Business and Professional Women's Clubs, 1970.

History of the Ohio Federation of Women's Clubs. Vol. 3, *1954–1974.* Columbus: Ohio Federation of Women's Clubs, 1975.

Hoover, Earl R. *Cradle of Greatness: National and World Achievements of Ohio's Western Reserve.* Cleveland: New Cleveland Campaign, 1979.

Hopley, Mrs. James R. "The Part Taken by Women in the History and Development of Ohio." In *Ohio Centennial Anniversary Celebration, Complete Proceedings,* ed. E. O. Randall. Columbus: Ohio State Archaeological and Historical Society, 1903.

Howe, Barbara J. "Uniting the Useful and Beautiful: The Arts in Cincinnati." *Old Northwest* 4 (December 1978): 319–36.

Howe, Henry. *Historical Collections of Ohio in Two Volumes: An Encyclopedia of the State.* Centennial Edition, vol. 1. Cincinnati: C. J. Krehbiel and Company, 1907.

Howells, William Cooper. *Recollections of Life in Ohio, from 1813 to 1840.* Cincinnati: The Robert Clarke Company, 1895.

Hull, Robert. *Mad Marshall Country—The Grit and Spirit of Mid-Ohioans.* Bay Village, Ohio: Bob Hull Books and Features, 1981.

Hunt, George D. *History of Salem and Its Immediate Vicinity.* Salem, Ohio: privately published, 1898.

Ifkovic, Edward. "The Ethnic Imagination: Cleveland's Immigrant Writers." In *The Birth of Modern Cleveland, 1865–1930*, ed. Thomas F. Campbell and Edward M. Miggins, 270–89. London, England: Associated University Presses, 1988.

Ingham, Mrs. W. A. *Women of Cleveland and Their Work, Philanthropic, Educational, Literary, Medical, and Artistic.* Cleveland: W. A. Ingham, 1893.

Joiner, W. A., ed. *A Half Century of Freedom of the Negro in Ohio.* Wilberforce, Ohio: Wilberforce University, n.d.

Jordan, Philip D. *Ohio Comes of Age.* Vol. 5 of *The History of the State of Ohio,* ed. Carl Frederick Wittke. Columbus: Ohio State Archaeological and Historical Society, 1943.

Joyce, Rosemary O. *A Woman's Place: The Life History of a Rural Ohio Grandmother.* Columbus: Ohio State University Press, 1983.

Kane, Ruth. *The Better Halves: The Story of Massillon's Women.* Massillon, Ohio: privately published, 1989.

Knapke, Luke B., ed. *Liwwat Boke 1807–1882 Pioneer: The Story of an Immigrant Pioneer Woman and Her Husband Who Settled in Western Ohio, as Told in Her Own Writings and Drawings.* Minster, Ohio: Minster Historical Society, 1987.

Knepper, George W. *Ohio and Its People.* 2d ed. Kent, Ohio: Kent State University Press, 1997.

Kornbluh, Andrea Tuttle. *Lighting the Way . . . The Woman's City Club of Cincinnati, 1915–1965.* Cincinnati: Young and Klein, 1986.

Kusmer, Kenneth L. *A Ghetto Takes Shape: Black Cleveland 1870–1930.* Urbana: University of Illinois Press, 1976.

The Ladies, God Bless 'Em—The Women's Art Movement in Cincinnati in the Nineteenth Century. Cincinnati: Cincinnati Art Museum, 1976.

Lasch-Quinn, Elisabeth. *Black Neighbors; Race and the Limits of Reform in the American Settlement House Movement, 1890–1945.* Chapel Hill: University of North Carolina Press, 1993.

Lasser, Carol, and Merrill, Marlene, eds. *Soul Mates: The Oberlin Correspondence of Lucy Stone and Antoinette Brown, 1846–1850.* Oberlin, Ohio: Oberlin College, 1983.

Laughlin, Kathleen A. "Sisterhood Inc. The Status of Women Commission Movement and the Rise of Feminist Coalition Politics in Ohio, 1964–1974." *Ohio History* 109 (winter/spring 1999): 39–60.

Laws, Annie, ed. *History of the Ohio Federation of Women's Clubs, 1894–1924.* Cincinnati: Ebbert and Richardson, 1924.

Lewis, Alexander Leonard, ed. *Greater Cincinnati and Its People: A History.* New York: Lewis Historical Publishing Co., 1927.

Lewis, Dottie L., ed. *Women in Cincinnati: Century of Achievement, 1870–1970.* Cincinnati: University of Cincinnati, [1984?].

Liedel, Leslie L. "Indomitable Nuns and a Determined Bishop: Property Rights, Woman Religious, and Diocesan Power in Nineteenth Century Cleveland." Ph.D. diss., Kent State University, 1998.

Love, Steve, and Giffels, David. *Wheels of Fortune: The Story of Rubber in Akron*. Akron, Ohio: University of Akron Press, 1999.

Lupold, Harry F., and Haddad, Gladys. *Ohio's Western Reserve: A Regional Reader*. Kent, Ohio: Kent State University Press, 1988.

Lynch, Margaret. "The Growth of Cleveland as a Cultural Center." In *The Birth of Modern Cleveland, 1865–1930*, ed. Thomas F. Campbell and Edward M. Miggins, 200–230. London, England: Associated University Presses, 1988.

MacLean, J. P. *Shakers of Ohio: Fugitive Papers Concerning the Shakers of Ohio, with Unpublished Manuscripts*. Philadelphia: Porcupine Press, 1975.

Mann, Annette. "Women Workers in Factories: A Study of Working Conditions in 275 Industrial Establishments in Cincinnati and Adjoining Towns" (1918). Reprinted in *Working Girls of Cincinnati*. New York: Arno Press, 1974.

Manual of the Columbus Female Benevolent Society with Annual Reports of 1877. Columbus: Ohio State Journal Steam Printing Establishment, 1878.

McBride, James. *Pioneer Biography: Sketches of the Lives of Some of the Early Settlers of Butler County, Ohio*. 2 vols. Cincinnati: Robert Clarke and Co., 1869–71.

McCormick, Virginia E., ed. *Farm Wife: A Self Portrait, 1886–1896*. Ames: Iowa State University Press, 1990.

McCormick, Virginia, and Robert W. McCormick. *New Englanders on the Ohio Frontier: The Migration and Settlement of Worthington, Ohio*. Kent, Ohio: Kent State University Press, 1998.

McLaughlin, Mary Louise. *China Painting: A Practical Manual for the Use of Amateurs in the Decoration of Hard Porcelain*. Cincinnati: R. Clarke, 1892.

———. *Pottery Decoration under the Glaze*. Cincinnati: R. Clarke, 1880.

Miggins, Edward M. "Becoming an American: Americanization and the Reform of the Cleveland Public Schools." In *The Birth of Modern Cleveland, 1865–1930*, ed. Thomas F. Campbell and Edward M. Miggins, 345–73. London, England: Associated University Presses, 1988.

———. "A City of 'Uplifting Influences': From 'Sweet Charity' to Modern Social Welfare and Philanthropy." In *The Birth of Modern Cleveland, 1865–1930*, ed. Thomas F. Campbell and Edward M. Miggins, 141–71. London, England: Associated University Presses, 1988.

Miggins, Edward M., and Mary Morgenthaler. "The Ethnic Mosaic: The Settlement of Cleveland by the New Immigrants and Migrants." In *The Birth of Modern Cleveland, 1865–1930*, ed. Thomas F. Campbell and Edward M. Miggins, 104–40. London, England: Associated University Presses, 1988.

Mihok, Janet A. "Women in the Leadership Role, Past and Present, in the Public Schools of Northeastern Ohio." In *Women in Ohio History,* ed. Marta Whitlock, 26–31. Columbus: Ohio Historical Society, 1976.

Morton, Marian J. "From Saving Souls to Saving Cities: Women and Reform in Cleveland." In *The Birth of Modern Cleveland, 1865–1930,* ed. Thomas F. Campbell and Edward M. Miggins, 325–44. London, England: Associated University Presses, 1988.

———. *Women in Cleveland: An Illustrated History.* Bloomington: Indiana University Press, 1995.

Neely, Ruth, ed. *Women of Ohio: A Record of Their Achievements in the History of the State.* 4 vols. Columbus: S. J. Clarke Publishing Co., n.d.

Nelson, Mrs. Ben B. *The Cincinnati Woman's Club Historical Sketch of the Last Thirty-nine Years in Honor of the Sixty-fourth Anniversary of the Founding of the Club.* N.p., 1958.

Oda, James C. *Hustle and Bustle, 1861–1920: A History of Women in Piqua, Ohio.* Piqua, Ohio: Piqua Historical Society, 1988.

Ohio Federation of Business and Professional Women's Clubs. *Pride in the Past; Promise for the Future, 1920–1970: A History.* Columbus: Ohio Federation of Business and Professional Women's Clubs, 1970.

Ohio Federation of Negro Women's Clubs. Newsletter 1910, Central State University, Wilberforce, Ohio.

Ohio Governor's Committee on the Status of Women. *Women in the Wonderful World of Ohio.* Columbus: n.p., April 3, 1967.

Ohio International Women's Year Coordinating Committee. *The Worlds of Ohio Women: Report of the Ohio Meeting for Observance of International Women's Year.* Columbus: The Committee, 1977.

Ohio Pioneer Women. Spring Meeting of the Ohioana Library Association—Betsey Mills Club. Marietta, Ohio; n.p., May 21, 1949.

Ohio Woman Suffrage Association. *Yearbooks.* Warren, Ohio: n.p., 1903–4; 1912–20.

Ohio Women Entrepreneurs Directory. Columbus: U.S. Small Business Administration, 1984.

Ohio Women of Achievement. Columbus: Martha Kinney Cooper Ohioana Library Association, 1951.

Ohio Women: Their Portraits and Paintings. Columbus: Ohio State Historical Society, 1956.

A Portrait and Biographical Record of Allen and Van Wert Counties, Ohio. Chicago: A. W. Bowen and Co., 1896.

Randall, Emilius O., and Daniel J. Ryan. *History of Ohio: The Rise and Progress of an American State.* 5 vols. New York: Century History Company, 1912.

Rausch, Eileen Regina. "Let Ohio Women Vote: The Years to Victory, 1900–1920." Ph.D. diss., University of Notre Dame, 1984.

Rerick, Rowland H. *State Centennial History of Ohio.* 2 vols. Madison, Wisc.: Northwestern Historical Association, 1902.

Rich, Frances Ivins. "Wage-Earning Girls in Cincinnati: The Wages, Employment, Housing, Food, Recreation and Education of a Sample Group" (1927). Reprinted in *Working Girls of Cincinnati.* New York: Arno Press, 1974.

Rohrlich, Ruby, and Elaine Hoffman Baruch, eds. *Women in Search of Utopia: Mavericks and Mythmakers.* New York: Schocken Books, 1984.

Roseboom, Eugene H. *The Civil War Era, 1850–1873.* Vol. 4 of *The History of the State of Ohio,* ed. Carl Wittke. Columbus: Ohio State Archaeological and Historical Society, 1944.

Roseboom, Eugene H., and Francis P. Weisenburger. *A History of Ohio.* Columbus: Ohio Historical Society, 1967.

Rowbotham, Sheila. *A Century of Women: The History of Women in Britain and the United States.* New York: Viking, 1997.

Rust, Orton G. *History of West Central Ohio.* Vol. 2. Indianapolis: Historical Publishing Co., 1934.

Sackett, Genevieve. *Legal Status of Women in Ohio* [1911?], (pamphlet). Ohio Historical Society, Box 595.

Scharf, Lois. "Employment of Married Women in Ohio, 1920–1940." In *Women in Ohio History,* ed. Marta Whitlock, 19–26. Columbus: Ohio Historical Society, 1976.

———. "A Woman's View of Cleveland's Labor Force: Two Case Studies." In *The Birth of Modern Cleveland, 1865–1930,* ed. Thomas F. Campbell and Edward M. Miggins, 172–94. London, England: Associated University Presses, 1988.

Severance, Caroline. *Memorial on Behalf of Woman's Rights in Respect to Property and the Exercise of the Elective Franchise.* Columbus: n.p., [1854?].

Shapior, Eleanor Iler. *Wadsworth Heritage.* Wadsworth, Ohio: Wadsworth News-Banner, 1964.

Sherr, Lynn, and Jurate Kazickas. *The American Woman's Gazetteer.* New York: Bantam Books, 1976.

Silberstein, Iola Hessler. *Cincinnati Then and Now.* Cincinnati: League of Women Voters, 1982.

Stanton, Elizabeth Cady, Susan B. Anthony, Matilda Joslyn Gage, and Ida Husted Harper. *A History of Woman Suffrage.* 6 vols. Vols. 1–3, Rochester, N.Y.: Charles Mann, 1881–89; vol. 4, Indianapolis: Mollenbeck Press, 1902; vols. 5–6, New York: J. J. Little and Ives Co., 1922.

Stanton, Mary Marjorie. "The Woman Suffrage Movement in Ohio prior to 1910." M.A. thesis, Ohio State University, 1947.

Stewart, Eliza. *Memories of the Crusade: A Thrilling Account of the Great Uprising of the Women of Ohio in 1873, Against the Liquor Crime.* 2d ed. Columbus: William G. Hubbard and Company, 1889.

Sugar, Hermina. "The Role of Women in the Settlement of the Western Reserve, 1796–1815." *Ohio State Archaeological and Historical Quarterly* 46 (1937): 51–67.

Taylor, Henry Louis. *Race and the City: Work, Community and Protest in Cincinnati, 1820–1970.* Urbana: University of Illinois Press, 1993.

Trolander, Imogen Davenport, ed. *Women of Greene County.* Xenia, Ohio: Women's History Project of Greene County, 1994.

Tuve, Jeanette E. *First Lady of the Law, Florence Ellenwood Allen.* Lanham, Md.: University Press of American, 1984.

Uglow, Jennifer S., ed. *The Continuum Dictionary of Women's Biography.* New York: Continuum, 1989.

Upton, Harriet Taylor. *History of the Western Reserve.* Vol. 1. Chicago: Lewis Publishing Co., 1910.

———. *Random Recollections of Harriet Taylor Upton.* Columbus: Martha Kinney Cooper Ohioana Library Association, [1955?],

Utter, William T. *The Frontier State, 1803–1825.* Vol. 2 of *The History of the State of Ohio,* ed. Carl Wittke. Columbus: Ohio State Archaeological and Historical Society, 1942.

Van Raaphorst, Donna I. "I Won't Give Up, I Can't Give Up, I'll Never Give Up: The Motto of Geraldine Roberts, Founder of the Domestic Workers of America." In *Women in Ohio History,* ed. Marta Whitlock, 31–38. Columbus: Ohio Historical Society, 1976.

Van Tassel, David D., and John J. Grabowski, eds. *Cleveland: A Tradition of Reform.* Kent, Ohio: Kent State University Press, 1980.

———. *The Encyclopedia of Cleveland History.* 2d ed. Bloomington: Indiana University Press, 1996.

Vitz, Robert C. *The Queen and the Arts: Cultural Life in Nineteenth-Century Cincinnati.* Kent, Ohio: Kent State University Press, 1989.

Waite, Frederick C. "The Medical Education of Women in Cleveland, 1850–1930." *Western Reserve University Bulletin* 16 (September 15, 1930): 7–23.

Warner, Hoyt Landon. *Progressivism in Ohio, 1897–1917.* Columbus: Ohio State University Press, 1964.

Webster's Dictionary of American Women. New York: Smithmark Publishers, 1996.

Weisenburger, Francis P. *The Passing of the Frontier, 1825–1850.* Vol. 3 of *The History of the State of Ohio,* ed. Carl Wittke. Columbus: Ohio State Archaeological and Historical Society, 1941.

Welker, Martin. *Farm Life in Central Ohio Sixty Years Ago.* Cleveland: Western Reserve Historical Society, 1895.

Werner, Ronald R., and Carol A. Beal. "The Sixth City: Cleveland in Three Stages of Urbanization." In *The Birth of Modern Cleveland, 1865–1930,* ed. Thomas F. Campbell and Edward M. Miggins, 24–53. London, England: Associated University Presses, 1988.

White, Ruth Young, ed. *We Too Built Columbus.* Columbus, Ohio: Stoneman Press, 1936.

Whitney, Frances R. "What Girls Live On and How: A Study of the Expenditures of a Sample Group of Girls Employed in Cincinnati in 1929" (1930). Reprinted in *Working Girls of Cincinnati.* New York: Arno Press, 1974.

Wickham, Mrs. Gertrude Van Rensselaer, ed. *Memorial to the Pioneer Women of the Western Reserve.* 5 vols. Cleveland: The Woman's Department of the Cleveland Centennial Commission, 1896, 1897, 1924.

Witten, Sally Sue. *Lakeside's Women of Distinction.* Lakeside, Ohio: privately published, n.d.

Wittke, Carl. *The First Fifty Years: The Cleveland Museum of Art, 1916 to 1966.* Cleveland: Cleveland Museum of Art, 1966.

Index